Winning the Minds

Travels Through the Terrorist Recruiting Grounds
of Yemen, Pakistan, and the Somali border

Francisco Martin-Rayo

CITA
PRESS

CITA Press
New York

ISBN-10: 0615653448
EAN-13: 9780615653440
Library of Congress Control Number: 2012941769
CITA Press, Johns Creek, GA

This book is dedicated to the refugee and IDP children I met throughout my journey, who taught me the value of life and true happiness. I will never be able to repay your kindness and openness, but I hope that the ideas in this book can make a small difference in your difficult lives. You are truly extraordinary.

Acknowledgments

This project, from inception to publication, would not have been possible without the invaluable assistance of dozens of people around the world, from those who helped me gain entry to the various refugee camps, to those who actually edited and published the book. Most importantly, this book could not have been written without the cooperation of dozens of teachers and thousands of students in the refugee and IDP camps who opened their hearts (and homes in many cases) to me over the trip, helping me understand the failings of our policy in the region. The names below are by no means exhaustive, and at times purposefully omit individuals' names for their safety, but I have tried my best to remember all of them.

First and foremost, I would like to thank my mother, who tirelessly read (and re-read) the various first drafts and helped shape the initial narrative. My father and Claudia provided encouragement and a home in which I was able to regroup my thoughts after the trip. Hanna

Trudo was an indefatigable source of support before and after the trip; while I was in Peshawar her wit and good humor provided much light in a difficult place. Stacia Decker did a great job with line by line edits. Rob, sorry it's not on a bike, but thank you again for being a great friend and for inspiring me to write this.

I will never be able to thank my friend Abboud, his mother Sima, and the rest of the Kattan clan enough for the hospitality they showed me over those few months. Sima, thank you so much for your care, concern, and for creating a home away from home. Abboud, you are my brother. Thank you again for everything.

The Belfer Center at the Harvard Kennedy School and the many teachers and colleagues there were a tremendous source of support, both financially and academically, throughout this project. Meghan O'Sullivan, a friend and mentor, provided critical insight to the conclusion and made valuable and significant edits. Greg Harris did a wonderful job editing the introduction to this book and helping me structure the narrative so that it flowed more seamlessly. Ben Smith, an impressive professor of Arabic in his own right, provided key comments to the paragraphs on Arabic and Islam. Eric Rosenbach fought hard for me within the Belfer Center, and I can honestly say that without his support, funding for this trip would never have occurred. David Mansfield, the world's foremost expert on the opium trade in Afghanistan, taught me everything I know about the subject and provided wonderful edits to various sections in the book. With his experiences and sage advice, Rolf Mowatt-Larssen did his best to instruct me on how to stay safe. Julie Boatright

Wilson helped me prepare and expedite my application through IRB. Though not at Harvard at the time, I would be remiss not to thank the late Richard Holbrooke for inspiring me to a life of public service through his extraordinary book, "To End a War." Graham Allison, Jacqueline Bhabha, Nick Burns and Joe Nye were all wonderful teachers and have forever shaped the way I look at the world.

I cannot thank enough the various staff of the United Nations High Commissioner for Refugees, who are heroes every day, and who were always friendly, welcoming and far more helpful than I could have ever hoped for. A special thanks in Pakistan to Akbar Nasir Khan, his friend Asmatullah Shah, Fazal Rabbi, Dr. Mehran, Blakeman Allen, and Nasir Sahibzada, who made the visit to Pakistan both possible and productive, and who showed me great hospitality while I was there. In Sana'a, I cannot thank Rayman, Hazim, and Fadhl al-Eryani enough, who helped me maneuver the labyrinth that is the Yemeni bureaucracy and took me into their homes. In Aden, a big thank you to Hadil, who guided me through Kharaz and invited me to my first Yemeni wedding. In Dadaab, a thank you to Randi Gramshaug and Damien McSweeney, who made access and transport possible.

Finally, from a literary perspective I owe a debt of gratitude to: Anthony Bourdain, who encouraged me to try all kinds of food on my travels, parasites be damned; Bill Bryson, whose humor kept me company on the trip and inspired me to write a better book; Paulo Coelho, whose book "The Alchemist" has provided much comfort in the search for happiness; and finally, Salman Rushdie, whose brilliant prologue in "Midnight's Children" taught me that writing is not a romantic activity best performed in a dark bar with a glass of scotch and a cigarette, waiting for inspiration, but is instead a lonely, extraordinarily difficult and ultimately highly rewarding activity that can only be accomplished by sitting at a desk every day for hours on end putting words to paper, with a glass of water by your side.

The Beginning

"The camps are breeding grounds for terrorists."
—Blakeman Allen,
Founder of the Pakistani Educational Project

Introduction

The Yemeni intelligence officer was yelling at me now, his moustache bristling with rage as he showered me with flecks of spit. "Enta muhim ma'a il jehuddi? Enta muhim?!" I tried to translate his words in my head, the fear paralyzing my brain as I begged for a translator. This only seemed to infuriate him even more, as up until this point we had been speaking in Arabic. Muhim... Important. Jehuddi... Jewish. He was asking me if I was important with the Jews. He thought I was Jewish. Another spate of insults and spit followed, and all I caught was Yisrael. He was implying I was a spy for Israel. I gasped as the significance of this accusation hit me. The Yemeni intelligence officers thought they had caught an Israeli spy. If I couldn't convince him otherwise, I would soon find myself handcuffed naked to a chair while they tortured me for information I didn't have.

How had I ended up here? Less than a year ago I was sitting on the 46th floor of a building in midtown Manhattan, part of the indistinguishable group of young college grads working in finance, and now I was seconds away from disappearing into a Yemeni prison. What turn of events, what decisions, had led me to this moment?

* * *

Why would a seemingly happy and successful young man with no suicidal tendencies choose to travel to Yemen, Pakistan, and the Somali border (the 15th, 10th and 1st most failed states in the world) to study al-Qaeda, the Taliban, and al-Shabaab?

In order to answer that question, I must take you back to a typical Thursday night in New York City over a year and a half ago. I remember dancing that night at one of the generic clubs in the Meatpacking district, one of the many that catered to the hordes of finance guys dumb enough to pay thousands of dollars for a minuscule table, an ice bucket, and two bottles of Grey Goose vodka. I was trying to drink my boredom away, again, thankful for the dark lights that made us look prettier and the loud music that made us sound smarter and more interesting. But it wasn't working tonight. Deep down, no matter how many watered down vodka sodas I bought, I knew that I wasn't interesting – not even to myself. I envied people who were truly passionate about what they did, their eyes lighting up at the thought of their jobs, their enthusiasm infectious. I pictured myself twenty years from now, balder, fatter, and unhappier, and I knew that something had to change.

Up until that point, the most professionally courageous act of my life had been starting a technology company coming out of college, an endeavor that had fallen flat on its face within a month of graduation and had left me broke and risk averse.

In movies, this is the moment when the main character gets that determined look in his eyes and twenty minutes later is incredibly successful at changing his life: from investment banker to schoolteacher; from housewife to successful businesswoman; from bad dad to great dad. But in real life it takes more than twenty minutes to change your life. How do you even know what the right change to make is? Paulo Coelho, in his book *The Alchemist*, writes, "Everyone, when they are young, knows what their destiny is. At that point in their lives, everything is clear and everything is possible." I was still young, only twenty-four, but nothing was clear and I had no idea what my "destiny" was supposed to be. Mind you, Coelho also thinks that, "To realize one's destiny is a person's only real obligation. And, when you want something, all of the universe conspires in helping you to achieve it." However over-the-top that sentence sounds, something did happen that helped point me in the right direction. I started reading a book.

Amazon.com, during a search I did on negotiations and foreign policy recommended to me Richard Holbrooke's extraordinary book *To End a War*, about his successful negotiation of the Dayton Peace Accords. The book was more engaging than anything I had read in years, and I happily read it and re-read it, highlighting whole paragraphs and writing extensive notes in almost all the margins – things I hadn't done since I was required to write book reports in college. I had always found foreign policy interesting, but I had no idea it could be this exciting. I had never even considered working outside of the private sector, but it was clear now that whatever change I made in my life would have to involve solving our problems abroad. To drive the point home, I read a quote by then-candidate Barack Obama, "Focusing your life solely on making a buck shows a certain poverty of ambition. It asks too little of yourself. ... Because it's only when you hitch your wagon to something larger than yourself that you realize your true potential."

The first step became an application to a Masters in Public Policy at Harvard. Once at Harvard, I immersed myself in anything that had to do with international affairs, taking courses on Iraq, Afghanistan, and Counterterrorism, learning Arabic, and attending as many lunches and lectures with guest speakers as I could fit into my schedule. I worked hard to make up for my lack of experience in foreign policy, especially when so many of my peers had served, both as civilians and in the military, in the places I had only read about in the paper.

But I was shocked to find that even the most respected foreign policy minds relied heavily on reading the *Washington Post* and *The New York Times*, without any independent verification or personal knowledge of the situation. A number of the wonks who came to talk to us about policy in trouble spots had never even been there. If the reporters were wrong, then we had no idea what we were talking about. And what if they were wrong? What if these reporters, most of whom spent less than forty-eight hours cooped up in the safety of green zones heavily manned by the military and in armored vehicles, in fact had no idea what they were talking about? Given our reliance on second- and third-party accounts of the on-the-ground situation, the opinion of the person who has actually set foot in the country being discussed almost always carries the most weight.

I became more and more interested in counterterrorism, which over the past few years has become one of the driving forces of our foreign policy, and began studying terrorist recruitment. I read articles that reported on Hezbollah recruitment in Lebanese refugee camps, a subject that had been heavily studied and given significant coverage. But what about other refugee populations? The *Washington Post* had published an article about Somali refugees in Yemen being recruited by al-Qaeda and *U.S. News and World Report* had published a piece in 2009 on Afghan refugees near Peshawar, Pakistan, joining the Taliban in droves. Why weren't more people studying this?

I then met a senior counterterrorism official in the Obama administration who was visiting the University, and mentioned to him the articles I had read about terrorist recruitment in refugee camps. He admitted, off the record, that he knew very little about this new threat and that neither his office nor the State Department was doing a good job of researching it. To me, these words were nothing short of an invitation. I had to go and see for myself what the situation was really like. Relying on reporters, who in this case had never been to the refugee camps, was unacceptable. Dexter Gate, one of the portals to Harvard Yard famously proclaims the following words, etched in stone across the top, "Depart to serve thy country and thy kind." Depart indeed!

I decided to travel to the three countries that I thought were most important to our foreign policy, had refugee populations that were actively being recruited by terrorists, and that we knew the least about. Thus, I began to make plans to travel to Dadaab, the largest refugee camp in the world, located on the Kenyan-Somali border; to Kharaz, a small Somali encampment in Yemen on the Gulf of Aden; and to Peshawar, a city in Pakistan that hosts many Afghan refugee camps and is known for its virulent anti-Americanism and thriving pro-Taliban population.

* * *

Paul Theroux keenly notes, "Say you're leaving for a dangerous place. Your friends [will] call sympathetically as though you've caught a serious illness." As word of my summer plans got out, I began to receive a series of condolences. A colleague of mine who had spent last summer working in Pakistan (cooped up in the safety of Islamabad), shouted to me upon learning of my plans to go to Peshawar, "You'll get shot! You'll never survive Peshawar! Seriously, I hope you have your affairs in order because you're not coming back." Even Harvard rejected my application for funding, the faculty Board of Directors stating, "We're just not comfortable letting you go to Yemen. It's too dangerous."

In their defense, the State Department's unclassified travel advisory stated, at the time of the trip:

"The U.S. Embassy in Sana'a, Yemen closed on January 3 and 4, 2010, in response to ongoing threats by Al-Qaeda in the Arabian Peninsula (AQAP) to attack American interests in Yemen. Following the attempted attack aboard Northwest Airlines flight 253 on December 25, 2009, Al-Qaeda in the Arabian Peninsula (AQAP) publicly claimed responsibility for the incident and stated that it was in response to what they described as American interference in Yemen. In the same statement, the group made threats against Westerners working in embassies and elsewhere, characterizing them as 'unbelievers' and 'crusaders.' On the morning of September 17, 2008, armed terrorists attacked the U.S. Embassy in Sana'a, Yemen."

The situation didn't look much better in Pakistan:

"The presence of Al-Qaida, Taliban elements, and indigenous militant sectarian groups poses a potential danger to U.S. citizens throughout Pakistan... Terrorists and their sympathizers regularly attack civilian, government, and foreign targets, particularly in the Khyber Pakhtunkhwa (KPk) province. On April 5, 2010, a complex attack on the U.S. Consulate in Peshawar was carried out, with several Pakistani security and military personnel killed or wounded. The October 2009 attack on the World Food Program headquarters resulted in the serious injury of a U.S. citizen. On November 12, 2008, a U.S. citizen contractor and his driver in Peshawar were shot and killed in their car."

Or even Kenya:

"In July 2009, three NGO workers were kidnapped and taken into Somalia by suspected members of a terrorist group that operates out of Somalia. In November 2008, armed groups based in Somalia crossed into Kenya near the town of El Wak and kidnapped two Westerners. Somali-based armed groups have on occasion crossed into Kenya to stage attacks or to commit crimes."

Despite the news coming out of these countries and the wishes of virtually every person who cared for me, I became more determined than ever to travel to these most dangerous places. I cajoled and pleaded my way through visas and access to places that even within these countries were considered hazardous. Without the initial funding or support from the University, I bought my tickets anyway and showed the Faculty Director my credit card receipt. The message was clear: *I'm going to study terrorist recruitment in refugee camps. You can decide to help me or not, but we both know that this trip will be safer with your support than without it.* I finally received permission, and the related funding, from the faculty Board of Directors, cleared only once I was in Amman, Jordan, and on my way to the Somali border.

In the end, this trip did change me, both intellectually and emotionally, in more ways than I will ever be able to understand. After meeting Somalis who had undergone and seen more horror than I could comfortably write about, meeting Pakistani teachers whose arms were shriveled by Taliban bombs, and eating with Yemenis who lived under the threat of al-Qaeda attacks, a civil war, and a notorious intelligence service, I came back even more convinced in the innate goodness of human beings. Most important, I learned the key difference between those individuals who choose to join terrorist organizations and those who don't, an insight that stunned academics and policy makers back home. But I'm getting ahead of myself. Let's start at the beginning.

Tabha and Mercedes

Amman, Jordan

I found myself at Logan Airport in Boston, trying to fight off feelings of nausea, dizziness, and watery eyes—all byproducts of too many cucumber gimlets imbibed during a farewell dinner party the night before. I had never embarked on a trip abroad with a purpose that could not be summarized with the word "beach" or "museum." This was my first "non-fun" trip, and yet I looked more like a tourist than on any tourist trip I'd ever taken, with my large camera bobbing around my neck. It had taken me months to get to this point, and I still hadn't been able to finalize permission to travel to Dadaab, the Somali refugee camp in Kenya, or even to secure a visa to Yemen. Frankly, I was starting to believe that the real reason more people didn't take these trips was not because of the dangers involved but rather because of the almost insurmountable bureaucratic hurdles. At this point I was unconcerned with the dangers that awaited me, unwilling to believe anything could go wrong—the very same reason why children take risks, even when aware of the potential consequences.

I was flying first to Amman, where I would be based between visits to the refugee camps. The gate was teeming with children, some wailing loudly, quieting only to gasp for air before giving an encore performance. Their mothers looked away and tried to disassociate themselves from the embarrassing spectacle. Almost all of the women were wearing *abayas*, loose black robes that cover a person from head to toe and are common in Muslim countries, and I had already become self-conscious about looking at them directly for fear of being disrespectful. My eyes nonetheless still wandered and inadvertently came to rest on a Jordanian woman who, although wearing a *hijab* (the headscarf worn by Muslim women that conceals the neck and hair and may sometimes have a veil), was also wearing a chest-hugging black T-shirt that accentuated a perfect upper body. Taking in this contradiction, I began to realize that the flight was not just taking me to a different country, but to a different world.

According to a conversation I overheard between two flight attendants, forty-five children would be on the plane, setting the stage for a painful eleven-hour ride. (In fact, I would end up sitting in front of three of the forty-five children, one of whose mothers unceremoniously dropped him into the chair from over two feet high. He immediately began crying, setting off other babies in the cabin.) There was an additional security check once we had presented our tickets, with two X-ray machines right outside the entrance to the little bridge that takes you to the plane, all overseen by a large, black female supervisor who screamed at passengers while calling them each "darling." As I passed through she complimented my camera, asking me if it was a new model (no idea) and telling me, "Yep, I get along with Canons. Good stuff." The camera was a heavy, bulky contraption that I was forced to carry around my neck, both for lack of originality and an inability to come up with a better solution. Who knew that before the trip was over the camera would be stolen and almost land me in a Yemeni jail?

* * *

Amman, Jordan, is a city built on seven hills and was originally founded in 7000 BC. It has over two million inhabitants today. There are pictures of King Abdullah everywhere: in plazas, inside hair salons, on buildings (both official and private), and taxi cabs, with his visage alternating between the angry piercing blue eyes that I imagine denote royalty and a tight though friendly smile with an ill-formed goatee. When he took the throne after his father's death, a surprise to almost everyone who thought his uncle would take over, he spoke halting Arabic and was ridiculed for being such a foreigner. He has since burnished his image and now appears relatively well liked, although a first-rate intelligence service known for its harsh questioning methods makes it difficult for the average commoner to say otherwise.

The city is extremely safe, thanks in large part to the military personnel on nearly every corner of the city worth guarding, all happily equipped with sub-machine guns. The roads and buildings are generally modern, and on the drive from the airport to West Amman the barren hills are peppered with large, at times grotesque, Jordanian versions of McMansions, all of which overlook the main highway and lack gardens. A discernible difference can be seen between the rich—who live in large gated houses, drive Mercedes and Porsches, host pool parties full of bikini-clad women, and are generally non-religious—and the rest of the population, which wears hejabs, prays more often, and has become poorer over the past ten years. Some of the rich lament this dichotomy, afraid that the current social structure is unsustainable and will lead to great upheaval within the next twenty years. Overall, the city is not particularly pretty or notable, but it is extremely friendly toward tourists—with most taxi drivers understanding basic sentences in English and all road signs written in both Arabic and English (as is usually the case in former British colonies).

After arriving in Amman, I practiced the few sentences I knew fluently in Arabic on taxi drivers—receiving either long and, to me, unintelligible responses or fervent pleas to address them in English and stop butchering their language. It became obvious that my year of studying Arabic at school was useless here, where the words and pronunciation were markedly different from *fusHa*. Here the language of choice was the famous 'aamiya, essentially colloquial spoken Arabic, which changes from country to country, sometimes even city to city, and makes communication within the Middle East that much harder. "You mean there are different types of Arabic?" you ask. Kind of. The Quran was revealed to the Prophet Muhammad around 611 AD, after which Islam

was founded and expanded under the Prophet's leadership. The Quran was initially memorized by his many
followers, and only written many years after its revelation.
The Arabic of the Quran is now referred to as Classical
Arabic. Over the last millennium and a half, written
Arabic has evolved uniformly across all Arabic speaking
countries (think of old English versus grammatically
correct English today), and is commonly referred to as
Modern Standard Arabic. Spoken Arabic, as might be
expected, has not evolved uniformly across all Arabic
speaking countries, with significantly different accents
and words forming part of the everyday lexicon. This is
what is commonly referred to as *'aamiya*, or colloquial
Arabic. For example, people in Morocco use different
vocabulary for some words and have a different accent
than Yemenis, who in turn have a different vocabulary
and different accent than Egyptians. But all three of
them write Arabic the same way.

My first two days in Jordan I felt exhausted all day
and was unable to sleep for more than ninety minutes at
a time, always hoping that the luminescent dial on the
bedside table would point closer to 7 instead of 3 AM. On
the bright side, though, I woke up at three that second
morning and was able to listen to the *adhan*, the prayer
call, at 3:45. I could hear the ghostly recorded voice of
the *muezzin*, the person who leads the call for prayer,
chanting, *"La ilaha illa Allah"* (There is no God but
Allah), against the silence of a city at rest. Looking out
the window, I saw lights on in some of the surrounding
apartments as people prostrated in the comfort of their
homes and on individual prayer mats.

Muslims are expected to pray five times a day, during the *fajr* (before sunrise), *zuhr* (literally, after the sun begins to decline from its zenith), *asr* (mid-afternoon), *maghrib* (just after sunset), and *isha* (night). Each of the five daily prayers consists of saying the *al-Fatihah* (which is composed of the seven verses of the first chapter of the Quran) two to four times and then adding a memorized verse or chapter from the Quran. Although the prayer movements may vary between cultures and types of Islam (Shiism versus Suniism, for example), all Muslims pray toward Mecca (as the Prophet did during his lifetime). In spite of the differences in the *adhan*, as Shiite and Sunni *muezzins* will chant different verses, by and large the call starts with the famous *Allahu Akbar* (God is the greatest) and ends with *La ilaha illa Allah*. The most famous muezzin today is Ali Ahmed Mulla, who has been working at the al-Haram mosque in Mecca, Saudi Arabia, for over thirty years.

I heard the prayer call again that day on my way to the Jordanian Ministry of Health. Despite my attempts to find individuals praying, though, I could not find anyone in the streets or shops of Amman acting differently during that time. I was going to the Ministry to get a health certificate—the latest requirement by the Yemeni Embassy in my quest for a visa, a process that would take six months and almost force me to cancel the entire trip. (I promise to tell you all about the difficulties related to getting a Yemeni visa later on.)

The building that I went to for my government-issued blood test was simultaneously whitewashed and dirty on all four floors. I paid a receptionist who was sitting outside, protected from the mass of immigrants by a metal grate, 20 Jordanian Dinars ($28) and then traveled up four flights of stairs to a room sparsely populated with men waiting to have blood drawn. I prayed the needle used on me was sterilized (it came with a green plastic covering, which was some comfort), and the actual procedure was notable only in how painless it was—no better example of the value of repetition on the nurse's part, who I imagine averaged over a hundred pricks per day, five days a week, or approximately twenty-five thousand repetitions a year. This was definitely the woman you wanted to pick when getting blood drawn. The room adjacent to ours was packed with approximately thirty foreign women, almost all beautiful, none with a *hijab*, twenty of whom were Spanish, and three of whom smiled at me when I popped my head in and gawked at this unexpected splendor in the otherwise bleak surroundings. I asked the Spanish women what they were doing here, and they excitedly replied that they were going to live in Amman for the next few months and work in various agencies and the Embassy.

Buy why were all these foreigners in a government building getting their blood drawn? The purpose of this particular building, seemingly dedicated to extracting the blood of *ajnabis* (foreigners), is linked to Jordan's requirement that all individuals wishing to reside or work in Jordan be clear of serious communicable diseases. The system is charmingly democratic in nature, and it is not uncommon to see a woman from the Philippines, the country that exports the most maids to Jordan, waiting in front of the rich expat who hired her. Assuming they are both women, they will have their blood drawn by the same nurse in succession.

* * *

Because I had a few days before I was set to leave for the first refugee camp, I had time to be a tourist in Jordan for a bit. My last sightseeing trip would inadvertently bring me in contact with the first of many extraordinary children I would meet on this journey, children who would teach me how important education and opportunity really are. Children who would help me understand how the United States can win hearts and minds.

I spent my last day before leaving Amman visiting Petra, a short three and a half hour drive from Amman. Petra is considered a UNESCO World Heritage Site, and was founded around 600 BC as the capital of the Nabataean tribe. What makes the site extraordinary are the hundreds of tombs, big and small, both intricately designed and barely decorated, carved into the surroundings—essentially an ancient city carved into the pink rock.

I arrived in Petra at 9 AM, having booked my trip through a travel agency, only to discover a tourist's two routine nightmares: I had severely overpaid for the most basic tour, and I was stuck with an obese, smelly, and unfriendly guide who gave only the barest of explanations. Prior to starting the tour he told me, "Your package comes with a guide. But it *does not* include tips to the guide. Do you understand?" I laughed, but his narrowed eyes and quivering jowls made sure I knew he was serious. I spent the next ten minutes convincing him that I had no interest in riding a donkey during my trip, both because I feared I would look ridiculous and out of pity for the decrepit and malnourished animal with patches of hair missing, exposing a gaunt, yellowish skin. The last thing the poor beast needed was to carry my additional 200lbs. The road on the way to the sites was expectedly full of vendors selling trinkets in multiple languages, with one young man accosting me to ask if I would like to buy a pretty necklace for my wife.

"No, thank you," I quickly replied.

"Then how about for your secretary, sir?"

At this point the guide, who seemed unaccustomed to making this trip without torturing a donkey with his weight, had asked me five times if I wasn't tired or needed a rest. He eventually collapsed on a boulder in the shade, breathing and perspiring heavily, and asked if we could sit down for a bit. Seemingly embarrassed by his behavior, he beckoned over an old Bedouin man, whose face was etched with deep wrinkles filled with dust and a smile with few teeth held steady by brown gums. The guide explained to me that this man was a grave robber who would go visit the hundreds of unexplored tombs in Petra (even today, it is estimated that only 35 percent of the entire site has been discovered, with hundreds of tombs left sealed) in search of gold and old coins. He now showed me two of those ancient coins, covered in caked sand, and offered to sell them to me for 20JDs (Jordanian Dinars, $28 USD). Although I assumed that both coins were fakes and that the Bedouin put on this performance for every unsuspecting tourist, I immediately accepted, excited at owning something that looked so old and unwilling to negotiate a lower price with a man who was clearly unaware of where his next meal might come from. Little did I realize then that this carefree attitude toward artifacts would get me in serious trouble with Yemen's scary intelligence service. "Make sure you hide those coins. Don't let any of the policemen here see you with them, or immigration, because they will confiscate them and you'll be in real trouble," the guide helpfully advised. If only I'd paid more attention to this warning.

We ambled onward, the guide increasingly cranky and less effective as he lagged behind, until we finally reached the "center" of Petra and he exhaled. "This is as far as I take you," he rejoiced. I saw that virtually all of the other guides kept going. "Are you sure you don't want me to negotiate a camel ride for you? It will be much more expensive if you try and negotiate it on your own." I declined his assistance, gave him a tip that was unsatisfactory enough for him to almost complain before seeing my annoyance, and we parted ways.

Though the main road through Petra takes you to see two of the three major sites (the Treasury and the center of town), hundreds of caves and adorned tombs still wait in the hills that surround the gorge. Excited to be free again I decided to go off-piste and explore some of the out of the way caves, all while idiotically wearing boat shoes. After going up and down some rocky hills, I was soon lost. I spent the remaining three hours climbing up and down more steep boulders, only to find myself stranded again and again on a precipice looking downward. During this time I met a Belgian student, riding a donkey with dexterity over the ruins, who directed me toward the famous Lost Soldier Tomb, and farther away from my starting point. I ended up resting inside one of the cool tombs for a bit after climbing down from the Path of Sacrifice, and then finally made it to the top of a precipice that overlooked a group of French tourists. As I began a seriously precarious descent, a voice floated up, shouting, *"Non! Non! A gauche!"* (No, no, to the left!) The French guide looked horrified as he pointed me toward another, much safer, descent and whispered, "Stupid American tourist." I finally made it down, tired and scratched up, but otherwise happy to be back on the easy path. I realized I had still not seen the Monastery, and the famous End of the World view some gracious tourists from Washington had insisted I see. Much farther from where I had started three hours earlier, I began trekking back up the mountain.

The Monastery was, as are all major structures in Petra, breathtaking. Even more so was the promised view of the End of the World. It was a flat granite slab that jutted out six feet into nothingness, surrounded by a deep abyss where three mountains meet and nothing but green and sand for as long as the eye could see. I said a brief prayer, elated and at peace, feeling as though I were sitting on air. There was not a single tourist around. As I walked back from the view to the Monastery, exhausted, hungry, and dehydrated, a little girl manning a jewelry stand called out to me in a perfect British accent. She was wearing a black sweater and black jeans, and had dirty black hair, bare feet adorned by chipped black nail polish, and a beautiful dirt-streaked face. Her name was Tabha she informed me, and I was soon so charmed by this eleven-year-old who spoke perfect English that I purchased bracelets and necklaces I didn't need and knew my mother would never wear. I mistakenly pulled out two 100JD notes ($280 USD), rather than two 10JDs and gave them to her. She laughed, took my wallet out of my hands, replaced the hundreds, and took out exact change. I thanked her profusely, as it was all the Jordanian money I had left and I would have been in serious trouble had she taken it, but she refused any reward for her honesty.

As I walked away, she called out to me, "Hey! Mister! Do you want a picture with the Monastery?"

A typical tourist, I was loath to part with my expensive Canon (the one the lady at airport security had gotten along with so well), but I couldn't refuse the offer and reluctantly gave Tabha my camera.

"Back up. Go farther. Farther." she commanded, and I realized every step took me farther from a little girl who could easily outrun me. I had in vain tried to explain how the complicated camera operated, but she had brushed me aside. Before I knew it, she had figured out the controls and put on the self-timer (which I had yet to figure out), placed the camera on a rock, and run over to be in the picture with me.

We raced over to look at the picture and she started scrolling through all of my images, even deleting some she didn't like, and inquiring whether I had any pictures of my family. I explained that I didn't have any on the

camera but that I carried two pictures of my grandmothers in my wallet if she wanted to see them.

After showing the photographs to her I told her I
had to leave, as I was already an hour late for my ride
back and still had 850 steps to climb down. Before I
could excuse myself, however, she took out a wad of
bills—around 130JDs ($182 USD, we counted them to-
gether)—and asked me if I could buy her something
to eat and drink, and bring it back up. She explained
that she couldn't leave her stand unmanned. I accepted
the mission, grateful the store on the mountaintop was
only 100 steps down, not the full 850, but rejected her
offer to pay for the food. (She tried six times to shove
the money in my hands.)

"No problem, Tabha, what do you want?"

"I want two Cokes, two bags of peanuts, two chocolate
bars, two bottles of water, one large chips, and the milk
with the chocolate inside."

"Chocolate milk?"

"Yes!"

"Ok, let me go get it."

"Wait! Repeat it to me so I know you have my order
right."

After she was satisfied that I had memorized her order,
she again tried to give me a 20JD note, which I happily
refused. One hundred steps up and down, and 22JDs
later (it sure pays to have a store on a mountaintop), I
returned to Tabha with the goods.

"I'm really sorry, Tabha, but they didn't have any bags
of peanuts so I bought you four chocolate bars instead
of two."

She pursed her lips at this news and inspected the food I had brought back.

"No, no, no. I don't like this or this." She was pointing at the Snickers and Mars bars. "Go exchange them for Almond Joy and Twix."

I laughed at the sheer brazenness of this amazing little girl, who had now made me an hour and a half late, and went to exchange her chocolate bars.

I was very sad to leave Tabha atop the mountain, brilliant and charming as she was. She seemed happy, but I had no idea what her life at home was really like, and even in the best of circumstances her talents were going to waste here, selling trinkets to tourists. How many more opportunities would she have access to if, for example, she had been born in Atlanta, the city where I grew up? If Tabha, with her intelligence and great personality, was dirty and barefoot atop a tourist path, how much worse were the lives of refugee children who didn't even have the benefit of being in their own country? How many more children like her, or in a more precarious position than her, would I meet in the camps of Kenya, Pakistan, and Yemen? Children whose lives would be entirely different if only they had access to the same opportunities I had been given in the United States.

I began the 850-step descent, only to find myself exhausted and two hours behind schedule when I reached the bottom with two miles left to go. The hour-long trek back loomed ever heavier in the horizon, but I again dismissed the idea of riding the decrepit donkeys.

"Ride back in a Mercedes! Ride Mercedes!" shouted a young Jordanian man walking past me.

Mercedes? The allure of air-conditioned luxury and a faster means of travel convinced me to ask the young man how much the ride back would cost.

"Only 10JDs! But we can only take you to the Treasury," which was about halfway.

As I contemplated the offer, almost certain I was going to shell out the $14 for the ride, he pointed to the camels in the corner. "So, you ride Mercedes or Ferrari?"

I stared dumbfounded at the animals.

"You named the camel Mercedes?"

"Yes, yes! Both camels very fast, like Mercedes and Ferrari!"

I laughed and wearily agreed to ride Mercedes, the fatter one of the two. I had finally succumbed to the temptation all Western tourists face when visiting the Middle East and found myself a camel to ride on. Out of respect for the small shred of dignity I retained after caving to my banal desires, I asked him not to take a picture of me. I lumbered up onto Mercedes' hump, almost falling face forward as she stood up. (Camels stand up and lie down two legs at a time, so that at any point during this exercise their backs point to a 45 or 135 degree angle, which leads to some uproarious tourist tipping and great pictures of middle-aged riders clinging on for dear life.)

I made the mistake of asking the guide to go as fast as possible, and he obliged by smacking his camel with a white plastic-coated cable—which in turn pulled poor Mercedes by the snout, who in turn pulled Ferrari behind her, in a comical three-camel caravan. The uneven rhythm of their semi-gallop soon had me banging my manhood ferociously against the saddle, and with no stirrups to put my feet in, there wasn't much to do except hope for no permanent damage. Small rickety carriages made of rusted metal pipes, covered in pretty but dusty shawls, zoomed by, being pulled by horses and driven by men wearing Arafat-style headgear (commonly known as a *keffiyeh*). In spite of their experience, the drivers still held on fiercely as the contraptions jumped up to a foot in the air and came crashing down as they made their ways along the rocky path.

The thump thump of my manhood against the saddle and the pain I came to associate with the sound had become too much to bear. I frantically looked around for a solution and curiously found that my guide was sitting cross-legged upon his camel (no doubt named Porsche), with the hump of the saddle between his legs. I tentatively attempted to imitate him, and after almost losing my camera and sliding off my German-named but Jordanian-born vehicle, I succeeded.

Cross-legged! Who would have imagined this was the right way to ride a camel? My lower body now moved in perfect unison with the camel's gait, and I felt like a true rock star—until Mercedes stooped downward and I again almost slid off, head first.

Exhausted, sweaty, and dizzy from lack of food, I limped over to my fuming driver, whose scorn at having to wait an additional two and a half hours was only matched by the serious chafing of my thighs. I got into the backseat, adorned with floor mats that said "Good Luck," and asked him to drive me to get a shawarma, please. Pretty please. I wish there were a better story to my first shawarma in the Middle East, the sandwich-like wrap of shaved meat, vegetables, and toppings associated with the region, but the truth was it was a bit dry, and made even less authentic (in my mind) by the radio blaring Mariah Carey's "I Can't Live" in the background.

Welcome to the Middle East.

Focus on the 2.5%

Dadaab

(Somalia-Kenya border)

A few days later I found myself sitting on a Turkish Airlines flight from Istanbul to Nairobi. As I noticed the small screen in front of me, I felt fear for the first time since I had begun to plan this trip. The cities we were flying over were highlighted: Addis Ababa, known to me only for our military cooperation and embedded CIA agents; Mogadishu, home to the floundering government of Sharif Ahmed, which was embroiled in a violent civil war; and finally, Khartoum, seat of some of the most damned genocidal leaders in history. I was flying to a lawless part of Kenya, to a place where I didn't understand the language and had no one to turn to in times of trouble.

The danger of being all alone in a very foreign country finally dawned on me. Dadaab seemed a lot scarier and foreign than before, and the thought of occupying a cheap and lonely guesthouse in Peshawar, Pakistan, a few weeks from now seemed outright foolish. My mother's advice reverberated in my head: "Remember, if you don't like it, you can always come home early. Just get on a plane back home." At the time she'd said it, her advice seemed unnecessarily paranoid, even silly, nothing more than the words of a concerned parent who had never traveled to a dangerous place. Now the words were reassuring. The work of covert CIA agents no longer seemed Matt Damon-esque, full of rippling muscles and "man as weapon" imagery, but rather lonely and frightening.

* * *

I arrived in Nairobi at two in the morning on the sparsely populated flight and spent the night at the Sarova Stanley hotel. The hotel, according to various ads around the lobby and bar areas, has been around since 1902, sixty-one years longer than Kenya itself, and has hosted a series of consequential old white guys: most significantly, Teddy Roosevelt on one of his safaris. Included in my room rate was the service of someone arriving at my chamber around seven o'clock in the evening to close the curtains. Ostensibly this was part of normal turn-down service, but it was done in large part for security purposes, since the hotel is located in downtown Nairobi and you don't want strangers looking into your room.

I took a taxi to Wilson Airport at five o'clock the next morning, hoping I would be able to secure a spot on the twice-weekly (on Mondays and Wednesdays) flight from Nairobi to Dadaab. The previous day had been Kenyan Independence Day, which meant that everything in the city was closed, including the offices of the United Nations Refugee Agency (the UNHCR), where I was supposed to purchase my plane ticket on the UN transport. When

I arrived at the terminal, which also hosted propeller planes that flew to Mount Kilimanjaro and other romantic safari destinations, I was surprised by how much nicer than the main airport it was. Signs announcing free wi-fi and a blow-up of a menu that boasted club sandwiches dominated the landscape, and I began to negotiate with the attendant to allow me on the plane in spite of my absence from the flight registrar. The flight was fully booked, but his supervisor said if I were very lucky and someone was a no-show, I could take their place. Otherwise, I would wait until next Monday, which would force me to return that Wednesday in order to make my Pakistan flight before my Pakistani visa expired.

At one of the tables in the gate I met John, an Australian finance officer who had joined the World Food Program (WFP) in Kuwait after the first invasion of Iraq, and Mark, a Scottish cop who manned security for WFP. They happily boasted to me about their respective wives (Finnish and Ethiopian), and Mark summarily dismissed any concerns I had about traveling by car to Dadaab (in case I missed a spot on that day's flight). He confidently informed me that I would make it there in eight to fifteen hours, depending on whether the roads were flooded. Of course, he added, I would have to hire a security escort, effectively a train of police cars, to which John laughed, "Not much the police can do against criminals, though!"

"True, but you've got to get them if you don't want to be extorted by them on your way!" countered Mark.

They both had a good laugh.

I saved myself the trouble with criminals and corrupt cops by making it onto the plane and managed to sit next to John. He immediately entertained me with the story of his friend's son, who holds a German passport but speaks no German, is of mixed race with a Ugandan mother, was born in Iran, and has spent most of his life in Afghanistan. The punch line was how difficult it was for this poor guy to get through immigration. I brought up the subject of terrorist recruitment in the camps, and John mentioned that Somali refugees were recruited and trained not only by al-Shabaab (the members of which were in many cases of the same tribe) but also by the Kenyan army—although the army had not yet felt comfortable enough with the Somali recruits to send them into Somalia.

Harakat al-Shabaab al-Mujahideen, commonly referred to as Al-Shabaab, is a radical guerilla group that controls large swaths of land in central and southern Somalia and a large part of the capital, Mogadishu. Al-Shabaab espouses an extremist interpretation of Islam, publicly flogging people who listen to music (it has banned radio stations), dance, or, most recently, watch or play soccer (during the World Cup, no less). In October 2008, not for the first or last time, its members stoned to death a thirteen-year-old girl accused of adultery. The UN later stated that she had in fact been raped.

In February 2010 the group officially declared its alliance with al-Qaeda, and in July 2010 it carried out its first terrorist attack outside Somalia: dual bomb blasts in Kampala, the Ugandan capital, killing dozens of civilians who were watching the World Cup final. This was done in retaliation for Uganda supplying troops to an African Union peacekeeping force in Somalia. To make matters worse, al-Shabaab murdered forty-two relief workers between 2008 and 2009, and has declared war on the UN and other NGOs sheltering, feeding, and clothing Somalis. Given these attacks, virtually no international organization has a presence in Somalia today. No one is really sure how many fighters comprise al-Shabaab—estimates range from 5,000 to 15,000—or when exactly it was founded. What is certain is that the majority of Somalia is now under its control, and that if this trend continues, al-Qaeda will have its first country in the next two years.

* * *

The plane was a surprisingly comfortable propeller aircraft with leather seats and a helpful brochure explaining why the United Nations had needed to rent planes for this journey. An hour later we landed at a single-runway airstrip. Waiting for us were a few white, older Toyota 4Runners emblazoned with the names of the respective organizations that owned them: WFP, UNHCR, Save the Children, and so forth. Like any newbie, I stood next to John, the only person I knew in the group. John now looked radiantly colonial in a brown felt hat, aviator sunglasses, khakis, and a WFP vest with endless pouches. (He had informed me he hoped to redesign the vest, patent the design, and live off the royalties of the new perfect vest.) I was sufficiently unconvincing in my attempt to exude self-confidence that a man approached me and confidently said, "You're Francisco." I blamed my amateur look on my camera, which I had started to carry around with the strap wrapped around my left hand, like a child afraid of losing an expensive new toy.

When Randi Gramshaug, my contact in Dadaab, had informed me that someone from external relations would be waiting for me, I had secretly imagined myself arriving inside an air conditioned building (there were none) to a smiling Kenyan man holding up a sign that said "Welcome, Francisco." Instead, Damien McSweeney, the man who had approached me, was short, very Irish, and balding with gray hair and a beard. He extended a ham of a hand attached to a forearm tattooed with large barbed wire that extended from his elbow to his wrist. "Stop hanging out with the WFP guys," he growled. "You're coming with me."

Damien had the gruff manner of someone who understands you are a temporary visitor who is unlikely to contribute much but, with luck, will stay out of the way. I would discover later he was also funny, extremely helpful, and great company to share a beer with. Attached to the front bumper of the Toyota 4Runner Damien drove was a five-foot-long antenna that shook vigorously as we drove up and down the hilly road and was used to communicate by radio across long distances. The short ride to the compound took us through a path paved with red sand, peppered with deep undulations from the April and May floods–an off-roader's dream if only the truck hadn't been going so slowly up the mini-hills. The road was flanked by small groups of people walking leisurely and small huts made of several pieces of tin that had been nailed together. The poverty was obvious and depressing, but no different from the now-common photographs of poor African villages that have desensitized Westerners. We entered the compound through a chain-link fence and were let into a narrow, unpaved road framed on the right by a security barrier and on the left by multiple signs announcing the various NGO offices and residences. After a sharp left-hand turn past another two manned checkpoints, we arrived at the UN headquarters.

Dadaab is a refugee camp in the northeastern part of Kenya, fifty miles away from the Somali border. It was set up by the UNHCR over eighteen years ago to accommodate the flood of Somali refugees fleeing the violence back home. It is difficult to try and understand the tragedy that has befallen Somalia, but knowing the country's most recent history helps. In 1941, the "administration" of Somalia passed from Italian hands to Great Britain. Northern Somalia remained a protectorate while Southern Somalia became a trusteeship—different names, same colonialism. In 1960 the union of the two regions formed the Somali Republic, and on July 20, 1961, the country's new constitution was ratified through a popular referendum. Things began to turn ugly in 1969 with the assassination of Somali President Abdirashid Ali Shermarke and the establishment of a military dictatorship under Muhammad Siad Barre. Barre ruled in a totalitarian fashion until 1991, a twenty-two year period marked by a war with Ethiopia, an invasion by twenty-two thousand Cuban troops supported by the Soviet Union, and a growing relationship with the US government. (We funded this dictatorship as a counterweight to Soviet influence in the region.)

1991 was an important year for Somalia, as a coalition of clans, backed by Ethiopia, ousted President Barre. In May of that year the former British protectorate in the north declared its independence as Somaliland, which, to this day, the international community has not recognized as a country. Although the coalition voted in Ali Mahdi Muhammad as the interim president, this choice was rejected by some of the organizations within the coalition and the current civil war broke out. Al-Shabaab's tactic of attacking humanitarian workers is unfortunately not new to the region, as General Muhammad Farrah Aidid, the commander of the United Somali Congress, attacked the United Nations Mission in Somalia (Operation Restore Hope) in 1993, killing a thousand civilians, eighty Pakistani troops, and finally, nineteen American soldiers in the Battle of Mogadishu. This is the famous "Black Hawk Down" episode.

Since then, the United States has by and large given up on stabilizing Somalia, which has suffered from a host of bloodthirsty warlords over the years. In 2006, the United States encouraged the Ethiopian Army (with funds, arms, and training) to invade Somalia, in part at the request of the Somali Transitional Federal Government. Ethiopian and TFG troops battled militias operating under the Islamic Court Union, an Islamist umbrella organization, and in late December retook Mogadishu. Around this time al-Shabaab, formerly an organization within the Islamic Court Union, split from the umbrella group and became independent. Ethiopia did not remove its troops from Somalia until January 2009, in large part because of a vicious insurgency campaign against its presence there. The Ethiopian Army's reputation for killing and raping civilians increased local support for al-Shabaab dramatically during this period. In addition, US support for Ethiopia's actions in Somalia fueled the migration of Somali-Americans from the United States to Somalia, many to join al-Shabaab, and increased radicalization in the Somali-American community.

Our current strategy relies on funding and arming the Transitional Federal Government of Somalia, an organization that currently controls less than half of the capital and is widely seen as inept. Most of the troops that we train and send to Somalia to prop up the Transitional Government are not in fact Somalis, but instead fighters from Uganda and Burundi, and act under the umbrella of the African Union. If the current trend continues, al-Shabaab is likely to retain control over most of the country and take over Mogadishu in its entirety after the AU forces leave.

* * *

The UN compound in Dadaab is a collection of small concrete buildings, pretty white stones set in the red sand to delineate paths, and a surprising amount of vegetation and mostly harmless wild animals that roam the grounds. The cafeteria, affectionately known as The Mess, is inside an octagonal concrete building with a blue roof that resembles a very large hut. It has eight tables covered with red checkered tablecloths, each surrounded by eight metal chairs upholstered in a royal blue fabric. Small fans in every corner of the room do little to cool the 100°+ weather or scare away the few dozen African-sized black wasps that always manage to get inside. It was here that I was supposed to meet Randi, with whom I had been emailing these past few months to arrange my visit, and who had vouched for me, over the phone, this morning at the airport.

I decided to drop off my luggage first at room G-3, the place I would call home for the next ten days. The room was sparsely furnished with a small bed, a stand-alone wooden closet (which I promptly closed after finding two geckos, a lizard, and various gigantic grasshoppers inside), a small, white plastic table (the kind you find at Target) with only a few ants running on it, and lo!—its own bathroom! This was a very welcome surprise, even after discovering that there wasn't any water pressure in the shower and that I could never get the toilet to flush down what I'd eaten that day. Best of all, the toilet and shower were so close to each other that you could sit down and do your business while taking a shower, just in case you wanted to be really efficient with your time. Most important, the room was also blessed with its own air-conditioner and a mosquito net. Uneven sticks of wood had been nailed to the four corners of an otherwise normal bunk, specifically for the purpose of holding up the net. All of this was mine for the princely sum of $15.18 a night.

In spite of the additional amenities offered in the room, I felt lonely and unwelcome in these surroundings those first few days. I realized how spoiled I really was. I hadn't even spent a few hours in the room and already I was longing for the comforts of real bathrooms and beds in which you didn't have to worry about wasps the size of golf balls. I later asked a colleague, as valiantly as I could muster, just how dangerous these little fuckers were, to which he answered, "Only if you provoke them. But if you do manage to piss them off—OUCH." Maybe I wasn't cut out for this trip, I thought, maybe I wasn't courageous enough. I speculated on the types of people who choose to live in these conditions, far away from their families (the UN does not allow families to live together in Dadaab) and the comforts of home, perfectly fulfilled by the fact that they are making the world a better place and helping those most in need.

I locked the door to my room and headed over to The Mess to meet Randi. Randi Gramshaug turned out to be a Norwegian woman with neither blonde hair nor blue eyes. She was permanently leaving Dadaab today, only to start a new post in Sudan in three weeks. (She was thrilled.) I noticed she wasn't wearing a wedding band and immediately thought, "Of course! Who wants to marry someone who's thrilled to go to Sudan?" and chided myself for being such a dick. Randi, like all UN personnel I would meet on this trip, was friendly, kind, and extremely helpful. She handed me a copy of the schedule she had arranged for me over the next ten days, which already seemed much longer than I had imagined they could be, and we spoke for a bit about her life and why she had come to Dadaab. Apparently the job in Sudan with UNICEF had been her first choice, but UNICEF had taken so long to get back to her that she had taken the offer in Dadaab with UNHCR instead, and was leaving after only six months.

The United Nations High Commissioner for Refugees was founded in December 1949, although there had previously been two organizations under the United Nations that had dealt with the issue of refugees (the United Nations Relief and Rehabilitation Administration and the International Relief Organization). Although the mandate for the UNHCR was only intended to last three years, after the Convention relating to the Status of Refugees was signed in 1951, member states realized the scope of the global refugee problem and extended its mandate permanently. The agency is responsible for leading and coordinating international action to protect refugees, as well as to safeguard the rights and well-being of refugees. Its mandate has been expanded over the years to include protecting other "persons of concern," which includes internally displaced persons. Today, it acts primarily as a coordinator in the field for the multiple non-governmental organizations that have been set up to help refugees, rather than attempt to provide all the services themselves. Within the United Nations, it is considered one of the most prestigious agencies to work for. Dadaab was initially set up as a temporary base for Somalis and was meant to accommodate only 90,000 refugees, 30,000 per sub-camp. Instead there were over 300,000 inhabitants, making Dadaab the largest refugee camp in the world.

The UN has also recently begun building an "extension" to host the influx of new refugees now fleeing al-Shabaab's violence and extremism. The difference between building a new refugee camp and "extending" the existing one is purely political. Kenya, like almost all countries doomed to host refugees, refuses to admit that better, more durable camp infrastructure needs to be built to accommodate the refugee population. Its government fears that better facilities would anger the local population and legitimize the presence of Somali refugees—by, in effect, accepting that the refugees are in fact there to stay.

As Damien wrote to me before I arrived, "In essence, the Dadaab operation has two de facto operations running side by side—the long-term protracted refugee population on the one hand and the emergency operation on the other—both of which offer a mountain of challenges: health, sanitation, protection, water, shelter, and education but to name but a few. Due to the presence of al-Shabaab in the area, the UN mission is operating at phase three security (curfew from 6 until 6 in a secure UN compound, no free movement in the camps without a police escort, etc) as there is a threat to humanitarian workers, so special permission from the Department of Refugee Affairs is needed before you can come to Dadaab."

Like most countries that host refugees, Kenya has decided to send these poor people to the most miserable part of the country, where they would disturb the fewest locals and take up as few natural resources as possible (particularly water and pasture). Dadaab is an exceedingly hot (80 degrees in the winter, 110 degrees in the summer), barren patch of land that few Kenyans inhabit due to its hostility, its arid climate, and its abundance of deadly wild animals. Refugees are sometimes eaten by lions or poisoned by red spitting cobras or scorpions, or simply perish in the middle of the desert from the sheer heat. On top of that, the heat guarantees that all the insects in the area are at least twice the size of the largest ones you have seen on the Discovery Channel, and have the ability to infiltrate living quarters in the hundreds. It is, for lack of a more original phrase, a living hell.

The Kenyan government has established an "encampment" policy for Somali refugees, which means that refugees are not allowed to leave the camp without official permission, much less to look for jobs or use public services. What this means in reality is that Somali refugees are forced to bribe their way around the country, face constant extortion from police, and work exclusively in unregulated jobs.

This encampment practice is common in countries with refugee populations. By fervently refusing citizenship and access (to schools, professional opportunities, and healthcare) to refugees, these countries further alienate this population and force it to rely on non-governmental organizations almost exclusively for its survival.

* * *

My next meeting that day was with a genial Kenyan gentleman who represented CARE in the camp and explained to me the various educational programs CARE ran there. CARE is a humanitarian organization that was founded in 1945 with the original mission of caring for the survivors of World War II. Today, in over seventy countries, it runs programs that target education, women's rights, health and sanitation, and myriad other issues.

In spite of his boasts of high enrollment rates in primary schools (over 80 percent!), I soon began to see major cracks in the system. Although children were required to take year-end final examinations, they weren't required to be held back a year if they failed the tests. Instead, teachers were encouraged to advance them, regardless of their performance. Under this system, students often passed through multiple grades and yet remained illiterate. The CARE representative informed me that the program didn't hold students back both because it was bad for a child's morale and also due to a lack of facilities. Classrooms were increasingly overcrowded. The average student to teacher ratio was 100 to 1; the student to textbook ratio was 7 to 1; and five children were required to sit at each desk, instead of the three for which it had been built. At the end of eighth grade all students were expected to present a final examination monitored by the Kenyan government. Depending on how they performed, they would either go on to secondary school or be demoted to a lower grade. Approximately 75 percent of all refugee students who took the exam failed. Some were demoted as far down as the third grade. Most students who failed the examinations did not return to school or attempt the examination again.

Although the CARE representative told me that the program kept children in school from 8 AM to 5 PM every day, the reality was that the classrooms operated in two shifts, with most children receiving only four hours of schooling per day. In total, over 42,000 pupils, the majority boys, were in primary school, being taught by 259 teachers – only 6 of whom had received any formal teacher training and were certified by the Kenyan government. The remaining 253 teachers were "incentive workers," refugees who had applied to be teachers and were given an additional 5,000 Kenyan Shillings (Ks) per month, about $63. I was invited to attend their teacher training seminar the upcoming Saturday.

The curriculum the CARE program follows is the same one followed by Kenyan public schools, a condition mandated by the Kenyan government in return for allowing the refugees to be educated. This is a fairly typical condition of host governments, though in certain cases this policy helps radicalize a young population. For example, Palestinian refugees in Syria are taught using national textbooks that define Israel as a "terrorist entity" and that, according to Syrian President Assad, "create immeasurable support for resistance in the battlefield." In the Somali case, however, the CARE representative charged that the situation in Somalia was so bad that there was no Somali curriculum to speak of, so education would have had to be based off of the Kenyan one anyway.

During lunch at The Mess I met three young women who worked for the US Department of Homeland Security (although they recoiled when I said that, preferring to be known as employees of US Citizenship and Immigration Services), who traveled around refugee camps processing refugees for resettlement in the United States. One of them proudly mentioned that they were considered the "tree-huggers" and "hippies" within DHS. They told me the United States accepts more refugees to be resettled within its borders per year than any other country in the world. The yearly quota is approximately 80,000, of which 35,000 spots had most recently been reserved for Iraqis. Svetlana, who was originally Russian but had moved to Washington with her parents many years ago, happily informed me that we did not prioritize refugee resettlement by education level (i.e., accepting more highly educated professionals over other refugees) or English language proficiency, and that the focus was primarily on domestic terrorism concerns. I asked her how we ensured that refugees were not terrorists, to which she laughed and responded, "Are you a terrorist?"

"No."

"Sounds good to me. Checkmark!"

According to the Department of Homeland Security's 2009 Annual Flow Report on Refugees and Asylees (great word), "The United States Refugee Admissions Program (USRAP) has a priority system for determining access to the program, including individuals referred by the United Nations High Commissioner for Refugees, a U.S. Embassy, or certain nongovernmental organizations (Priority One), groups of special humanitarian concern (Priority Two), and family reunification cases (Priority Three).

Once an individual has been referred to the USRAP, an Overseas Processing Entity, working on behalf of the U.S. Department of State, conducts pre-screening interviews and completes the required documents for submission to USCIS. Once all application materials have been submitted, a USCIS officer interviews the applicant and determines whether the applicant is eligible for refugee resettlement to the United States. Security checks must be completed before an application is approved. Individuals who are found eligible must satisfy health requirements and be assigned to a sponsor. A sponsor is a resettlement agency that is responsible for meeting the refugee at the airport, making housing arrangements, and preparing a resettlement plan. If an applicant is approved for resettlement, the International Organization for Migration (IOM) makes arrangements for his/her travel to the United States. After arrival, refugees may request documentation for travel outside."

In summary, it is a long, complicated, and exhausting process that typically ends with very scared refugees arriving in the United States. Many of these refugees do not have the necessary skills to succeed in America because they've spent the last ten years living in a camp. Those who do decide to leave their refugee camps and search for jobs elsewhere lose their place "in line" and are no longer considered for resettlement.

After lunch I visited the Youth Education Program offices, a vocational program run by CARE that teaches Kenyan and Somali drop-outs how to become carpenters, tailors, beauticians, and electricians, among other vocations. There are six hundred students in the program, and the organization requires that 50 percent of them be local Kenyans and that there be an equal distribution of men and women. Priority is given to women, traumatized refugees, and handicapped individuals. Unfortunately, this means that if you are a healthy, non-traumatized young male, you have virtually no chance of getting accepted into the program that reserves only 150 spots for male Somali refugees. This policy contributes to Dadaab's notorious "idle youth" problem, whereby thousands of healthy young men sit around under the shade of short acacia trees all day, shooting the shit and unable to seek out jobs because of the encampment policy. These bored youth are prime recruits for al-Qaeda and al-Shabaab.

At dinner I was regaled with stories of red spitting cobras, mongeese, a four-foot-long lizard with a bad temper that lived in the camp, and African bees chasing people to their deaths. It seemed the black wasps in The Mess were the least of my worries, and I secretly thanked the people with the hindsight to put the net around my bed.

I got lost on the way back to my room, terrified of stepping in a bush and pissing off some angry animal, and cursed myself for not bringing a flashlight. I had to turn around three times before finally getting the courage to put my room key in and turn the lock, as I was scared stiff of the six black wasps that had decided to camp out near the door handle.

Once indoors I spent five minutes in a cold sweat, heart pounding, battling against the wasps that had gotten inside. Me: 5 Wasps: 0. I felt silly once they were all dead, and remembered the words of my tormentor at dinner, an old Scot with bags under his eyes, a heavy paunch, and a hell of a cynical attitude toward refugee resettlement and the UNHCR as a whole. He had driven home his last point with flourish and said, "Remember, you're in the middle of nowhere in the African bush. You should hear the stories of all the refugees who die from animal attacks."

I had smartly responded that I had already encountered a large gecko in my room and survived, and that I couldn't imagine anything scarier. I was saved from his wise-ass rebuttal by a woman from Maine, who was part of the tree-hugging DHSers and helpfully stated, "Oh no, geckos are your friends! They eat insects! The only problem is that they make tiny screeching noises at night."

As I walked into my bathroom, planning to sit and read for a while, I presciently remembered my third grade science teacher's warning about black widow spiders waiting for unsuspecting campers in toilets. God bless that woman. I checked before placing my butt cheeks as a ready target, only to find a spider web inside the toilet, crowned by a translucent yellow spider smack in the middle. I shut the toilet, shut the bathroom door, put on some more bug spray, and resigned myself to sleeping inside the mosquito net, fully clothed. With the lights on.

I heard the geckos all night.

* * *

After a fitful night in which I finally dozed off post-midnight, I woke up around seven o'clock, decided against inaugurating my shower (I waited until I developed an unbearable stench before I finally decided to shampoo and fight off the insects naked), and headed to The Mess. I couldn't eat more than two slices of toast with margarine and some Nescafe, ignoring the mysterious soggy tortilla and the blocks of white maize at the buffet. Four local Kenyan workers and I set off in a five-car security convoy to the camps at 8 AM; I realized I was the only non-African in the troop heading to Ifo, a mere twenty minutes away. The road was made up of the same hilly red sand that led to our compound, but on the way I saw a significant number of people sitting under trees, on the sides of the road, and a few shepherds. To their credit, the goats and donkeys they were caring for looked relatively healthy. The car caravan stopped at a rusty navy blue gate and the driver honked three times. The unarmed security guard ran over to unlock the gate and swung it open to reveal a medium-sized courtyard surrounded by three squat concrete buildings. As the local workers exited the 4Runners and went about their business, the driver took off with a friendly wave. I was alone, lost, and couldn't see anyone waiting for me. I looked again at the copy of the schedule I was clutching in my hands, and walked over to one of the buildings to ask for directions. The local Kenyan worker I found was incredibly gracious and used his cell phone to call the principal of the school I was to visit. The principal quickly sent over a teacher, Duncan, to walk me over.

Duncan was one of six Kenyan government teachers who worked in Dadaab, and my guide for the day. As we were walking along the dusty road, he pointed out that the camps were self-segregated by nationality (Block G was Sudanese, for example), and sometimes within these blocks by clan. The UN provides new refugee families with the materials to build a home: mostly corrugated tin that oxidizes in the rain and is plastered with the red, white, and blue letters "USA." The perimeter wall enclosing these blocks from the outside world is made up of tightly packed dried branches with long thorns, a construct that typically reaches over six feet high.

I first visited the Friends School, aptly titled because it is the only school, out of the eight primary schools, that integrates Ethiopian, Somali, and Sudanese students. Like the camp blocks, the school buildings were surrounded by a mixture of thorny dried branches and the odd concrete wall, and I counted two rows of rooms, each row consisting of five to seven classrooms overcrowded with wooden desks. In the middle of the school compound sat a medium-sized white tent emblazoned with the UNICEF logo. Underneath four blackboards hung from trees and younger children congregated to learn the alphabet and fun songs.

I introduced myself to the headmaster, himself a Somali refugee, and explained that I was conducting research on educational programs in refugee camps and would visit Pakistan and Yemen after this trip. He smiled genially—all Kenyans and refugees I had met thus far had been friendly—and instructed a refugee teacher to be my other guide. We walked a few steps to the nearest classroom, where I met the math teacher for eighth grade (and fourth, fifth, sixth, and seventh grades), who was writing a velocity conversion problem on the board. The students, aged between fourteen and sixteen, were segregated by gender and almost all the girls wore the long headcovering that is common in Sudan and Somalia. The headcoverings were in the green school uniform color, part of the school uniforms provided by CARE. Except for the odd rebel who wore a tattered soccer jersey with a European player's name printed on the back, all the students wore the same uniform. Although the students did look poor and thin, they did not look unhealthy, scared, or even unhappy.

The teenagers were clearly curious about the odd stranger standing in the back of the room (the desks were already overcrowded and I refused to unseat a student, in spite of the teacher's pleas), but they were generally engaged in the problem solving. The thirty-five-minute lesson consisted primarily of the teacher repeating the problem in the book, and then assigning a couple practice problems for students to work on. Given the forty-seven students in class, he was unable to monitor the progress of the students or spend more than a minute with each student. After class finished, I introduced myself to the students, explained to them that I was hoping my work could improve their educational system, and asked them if they would be willing to respond to three questions.

The first question, "Who do you admire most and why?" was a bit difficult for the students to understand initially, for although they are taught in English (a remnant of the British Empire is that the Kenyan education curriculum is taught in English, except for Swahili class), they were unable to distinguish between "like" and "admire."

Language barriers are one of the most pressing problems for refugee students when they arrive in a new country, and are a significant hurdle to better integration. A young Somali refugee must learn Somali to communicate with her family, but in the classroom she is expected to speak English (a language most teachers have nowhere near mastered). She is then also required to take Swahili in school, in order to communicate with the Kenyan population. Swahili was a subject at which none of the students I met excelled and few practiced outside of class. As I would find time and time again, the tendency of ideas to be "lost in translation" is a huge problem for refugee students and teachers, and hampers brilliant students who would have excelled back home.

Once we got over this definitional obstacle, however, the students excitedly poured forth answers, including soccer players like Carlos Vieira and Fernando Torres, best friends, President Obama (who had a laundromat named after him in the camp), and King Martin Luther (they meant Martin Luther King, Jr.).

I asked them next what they wanted to be when they grew up. Doctors and professors quickly became the most popular future careers, both because they were needed in the students' home countries. A girl wanted to become a scientist because, she said, she loved astronomy and wanted to learn more about the solar system. A couple kids wanted to be politicians and the president of Somalia, and one wanted to be a singer, "Like James Brown!" he said. My favorite, however, was a student who said he wanted to be a rapper. When asked why, he responded simply by shaking his hands like a disc jockey and nodding his head.

I was surprised at the people these children admired and the professions to which they aspired. Where were the recruits al-Shabaab was famously targeting? Those who couldn't wait to cut off people's hands and feet and ban music on the radio? Obama? James Brown? A rapper? *These* were the students al-Shabaab expected to draw back home and help them turn Somalia back to the Dark Ages?

I took off to my next class, a second grade class, where I asked the same questions and received similar answers (although the children were much shyer and stuck to doctors, professors, and presidents). As part of the research, I gave them paper and crayons and asked them to draw whatever they wanted to. The girls all drew pretty flowers. The boys, farm animals from their textbooks (which they shared with seven other students). One boy drew a helicopter and a military vehicle. I did not ask him where he had seen them, as I did not want to resuscitate potential images of trauma, but awarded him first prize (a box of crayons) for the quality of his drawing.

As I walked back with Duncan to the CARE compound, a girl from the eighth grade class began walking next to me. She was tall for a girl and had chubby radiant cheeks and a happy face framed by a tightly worn green hijab. Her name was Kauthar. I asked her where she was from (Somalia) and commented on how healthy the donkeys and goats looked—mocking those at Petra, who looked even more pathetic in comparison.   As we saw large groups of young men idling underneath trees, I asked her what all the older boys who failed out of primary school did. I asked her if they could seek work, or, thinking back to the conversation with WFP John, if any of them went to fight with the Kenyan army. She quickly dismissed this notion, explaining that there were Kenyan-Somalis, those who grew up and lived close to the border and hence spoke a similar language and had similar customs, and Mogadishu-Somalis, those who grew up in Somalia. The Kenyan-Somalis did join the army, but the Mogadishu ones weren't allowed. (Although she was technically correct, I would later find out much more about this covert program.)

Kauthar had been born in the camp in 1994, after her mother fled the violence in Somalia in 1991 and came to Dadaab. She had two brothers, one of whom had suffered a "heart attack" of sorts, or a serious medical condition to do with his heart; he had been waiting to see a doctor for over a year. Her father's family had apparently not liked her mother very much, so he had divorced her and she remarried a man with whom she now had eight daughters. All thirteen family members now lived together in one small hut. Kauthar spoke English very well, had an aunt living in California with whom she wanted to go live, and wanted to become a doctor. Her mother had been waiting for re-settlement to the United States for close to twenty years.

As we were walking I pointed at the boys in the shade and asked her if these were the people who were typically recruited to go back to Somalia and fight (presumably by al-Shabaab). She nodded. She told me that the families of the boys who left to fight typically received $100 a month (about 8000Ks, or 60 percent more than what the refugee teachers, those lucky enough to finish primary and secondary school, were paid).

"Do they receive the money regularly?" I asked.

"Yes."

"Well, how do they get the money?"

"At the bank, of course!" she said, looking at me as though I were daft.

"The bank? What bank?"

"She means Western Union," interrupted Duncan, who was obviously not enjoying this line of questioning at all.

"No," Kauthar responded. "I mean the bank we have inside our camp. Near Bosnia."

"Bosnia?"

"Oh, that's what we call our marketplace in Ifo."

"Can you take me there? To see this bank?" I pleaded. Duncan's mouth dropped open at the suggestion that this stranger lead us right into the heart of the camp.

"Francisco, *I've* never been inside the residential part of the refugee camp!" Duncan stammered.

Remember, Duncan was a teacher with the Kenyan government; he had been posted to Dadaab for the past four months. He was not a Somali refugee. These employees, like the other Kenyans working for various NGOs, rarely venture inside the camps.

"I'm sure it'll be fine," I countered, dismissing his look of concern. And off we went.

* * *

Once we entered the camp and passed the dried-branch perimeter, the refugees' interest level in us was upgraded from a few odd looks to a full-blown entourage that followed us around. I had imagined that refugee camps were composed of neat rows of relatively clean white and green tents, and that the majority of people would be lounging about, waiting for their weekly handouts. I could not have been more wrong.

There were no tents to be seen for miles. Instead, twig and rusted metal houses seemed to have sprung up everywhere haphazardly, their builders using any and all materials available, including bottles, plastic tarps, and twine to keep parts of it together. The camp looked like a regular African slum, with trash strewn in great patches around the roads and makeshift alleys. There were, surprisingly, no children who looked seriously malnourished, and the roads were filled with healthy looking goats that happily ate the leaves off all the bushes they could find.

The camp was teeming with life: donkeys pulling crates of food stamped with USAid, children playing in the street, people walking with a purpose, and more businesses than I ever imagined. There were shanty, one-story hotels; restaurants; the famous Obama Laundromat; a beauty parlor; dozens of small shops that sold vegetables, fruits, candy, coconut milk, and a selection of other items whose brands I didn't recognize; cell phone credits (we saw a man riding his bicycle while playing music on his bright red phone's speakers); and even an internet café! Mind you, the internet café had only two old desktops.

Twenty minutes had passed since we had entered the camp perimeter, our entourage had dispersed, and Duncan and I were totally lost and confused amid the myriad small alleys we had turned into. I began once again to feel like the silly foreigner with my big camera and white skin, in the middle of a refugee population the UN had deemed dangerous enough to prohibit its workers from entering the camp. The UN had erected barbed wire and multiple checkpoints to protect its workers from these refugees, and here I was, the only foreigner for miles, at the mercy of a little girl who could take me to the al-Shabaab recruiters for a reward.

"How much longer to the bank?" I asked Kauthar.

"Another fifteen minutes. Up ahead."

If she had decided to take me to the elders or the al-Shabaab recruiters, which we both knew were in the camp, and accuse me of asking the wrong questions, nobody would ever find out what happened to us. Instead, we arrived at the bank—a small, dark, and cool wooden shack with a computer and a wooden barrier over it. Once I came in and sat down a small crowd made up mostly of children gathered around once again, dispersing only when an old man used a thin long twig to swat them and scold them away.

"Who are you?" He seemed very unhappy I was here.

I explained in both English and Arabic that I was doing research on education, had met Kauthar at school, and was curious about how they received money in the camp. "Which I thought was such a good business idea!" I added.

He cracked a smile, albeit a small one, and explained it was through a computer, to a bank account, and that people had to send their families' "address in the camp" and name beforehand. He mentioned transfers from the US, UK, and Dubai.

The whole business seemed very much based on trust, to be honest, but I imagined there would be serious social, and physical, repercussions if he was found cheating refugees out of their transfers. This was my first look at the celebrated hawala system that operates in large parts of Africa and the Middle East. The system is designed so that a person in the US can visit a hawala broker and give him the money and the recipient's information. The hawala broker then contacts the broker where the recipient lives, who will pay out the money minus a commission. The two hawala brokers settle their debts at a later date.

I thanked him for his explanation, accepted his instruction not to take any pictures, and took off.

On the much shorter way back—the camp is circular, and Kauthar had taken me the long way so I could get a tour (now she tells me!)—I asked her if the owner of the bank was the same owner of the internet café. (They both had the look of impatient people you don't want to mess around with.)

"No, these are the Managing Directors," she told me. "The owners don't live here in the camp, they live in Dubai."

* * *

The next eighth grade class I attended was also an integrated classroom with Ethiopians, Sudanese, and Somalis, and was even livelier than the first one. Students again told me how much they admired Obama. ("He's even left-handed. Like me!" one of them mentioned.) One girl stated that she wanted to be President of Somalia, and another one countered by saying she'd like to be President of America. Both the people the students admired and the professions to which they aspired were similar to the answers I heard in the previous class, except for one younger boy who mentioned he wanted to be like Shibrahim (a name I had to ask him to spell on the board), because he was a famous Imam who studied all religions and brought people together. I imagine the student was referring to Sheikh Ibrahim al-Mukhtar Ahmed Omer, the celebrated Grand Mufti of Eritrea for thirty years who was renowned as a brilliant scholar and tolerant ruler.

I asked the students if they had any questions for me and they immediately pounced on the offer, asking me who I supported in the World Cup, where I was from, what was I studying, and why I had come here. Finally, I was given a math problem I had to estimate the answer to in my head. They laughed throughout my twenty-minute Q&A session, delighted by some of my funny answers and what they saw as my quirky way of looking at the world. As the bell rang to signal the end of the school day (it was an actual bell somebody rang outdoors, as there is no electricity in the school), I thanked them, started to leave, and was surprised by a spontaneous standing ovation. My first ever. Awesome.

I was exhilarated on the ride back to the compound. My driver in the UN security convoy on the way back was an extremely amiable Kenyan called Musa, who had thirty-seven brothers and sisters. Upon learning I was an only child, he diplomatically inquired whether everything was okay with my father "down there." After a vehement negation on my part (somebody had to defend Dad's honor in the middle of the African bush), he told me he couldn't understand why my father would have chosen to have only one child, in spite of my assurances that I was a handful as a young boy. He asked me if I was married (no) or had any children (definitely no), at which point he proudly informed me that he was twenty-eight, that he already had six children, and that I should hurry up. He told me his father had become a very rich man over the years, as his sons sent him money from Dubai, the US, and the UK. "Last week, my sister told him that he had received some money from London. But since he has so many sons in London that send him money, he doesn't know which one of them sent it!" he laughed.

"How does he keep track of all of you?" I asked.

"Oh, that's easy. When I call him and tell him it's Musa, he always asks me who my mother is. Then he knows which one of his four wives I came from. That way he usually recognizes who he's talking to!"

Dinner that night was uneventful, punctuated only by the discovery that the compound had been breached by camel spiders, semi-mythical creatures that, I was told, use their venom to numb the faces of our sleeping troops in Iraq and proceed to feast on their cheeks, only for the poor soldiers to awake hollowed out. The spiders apparently also scream, Samurai-style, when they rush at you to attack. Although Wikipedia disagrees with these statements, especially the cheek-feasting and screaming attack, the article notes that there is no real research about the creature.

Obviously I slept with the lights on. Clothes on. Again.

* * *

I spent the next day visiting the sub-camp of Haga-dera, populated almost exclusively by Somali Muslims—almost all of whom attend, as children, 6 AM classes to memorize the Quran. I inquired with a number of graduates of this program what exactly they were taught as children during this class, and they all emphasized that it had little to do with teaching and more with rote memorization.

The students in these single nationality classrooms were a lot more subdued than their integrated peers yesterday, and the girls were a lot more hesitant to answer any of my questions. I initially thought that I was doing something wrong, maybe something different than the day before, but soon found out that the blank stares from the children weren't a sign of lack of interest. Rather, the students were unable to understand English as well as their peers from the day before. Since they were all Somalis, they could communicate with one another in Somali rather than spend more time learning and practicing English, a necessity had they wanted to interact with other nationalities.

Once they understood what I was asking them, their responses were less colorful, but certainly similar, to yesterday's classes. Students admired their parents, teachers, and Obama, and hoped to become doctors, professors, and pilots (a common dream among refugee children, because they associate the profession with the ability to fly out of their current situation). One of the youngest children in class mentioned he wanted to become a Grand Ayatollah. I asked him why, to which he responded, "Because he is a great philosopher."

Allow me a brief digression to explain why this statement was surprising. Islam was founded by the Prophet Muhammad, who lived from around 570-571 AD until June 8, 632. Upon his death, a disagreement arose between his many followers as to who should become the next Caliph, in effect the leader of Islam. The leaders of the city of Medina believed that the first Caliph should be chosen by the elders, in line with the custom of the time in which elders voted for the leader of their community, independent of the current ruling family. Ali, the Prophet's first cousin and son-in-law (he married the Prophet's daughter Fatima), and his followers believed the leadership of Islam should remain within the Prophet's family. The leaders of Medina ended up choosing Abu Bakr, one of the Prophet's advisors, as the first Caliph. Although Ali and his followers were disappointed, they accepted this decision for the sake of unity.

Only after the third Caliph was assassinated was Ali finally chosen as Caliph. His rule lasted a mere five years (from 656 AD to 661), and was characterized by significant internal strife as other groups disputed his leadership and waged wars against him, eventually assassinating him. Ali's death marked the beginning of the split between these two groups, and his followers thereafter became known as Shi'atu Ali, or "the faction of Ali." Those opposing this group became known as

Ahl as-Sunnah wa'l-Jama'ah (the People of the Tradition and the Community), commonly referred to as Sunnis. Ali's son, Husayn ibn Ali (literally, Husayn son of Ali), later led a rebellion against Yazid I, the then-Caliph of the Umayyad Dynasty. He was killed in October 680 by the Umayyads, beheaded, and left without burial for three days (a tremendous offense in Islam, where bodies are meant to be buried as quickly as possible). His death is remembered every year during the Shiite festival of Ashura, in which Shiites take to the streets wailing and screaming, some even self-mutilating, all in remembrance of Husayn. Today the vast majority of Muslims are Sunnis. Only 10 to 15 percent of the global Muslim population ascribes to Shiism, most of whom are concentrated in Iran and Iraq.

Given the historic and on-going animosity between Sunnis and Shiites, a Sunni would not typically admire a Grand Ayatollah because, in one of the differences between Sunni and Shi'a Islam, that distinction is only given to Shiite clerics. Since most Somalis are Sunnis, I was rather shocked by this boy's choice of hero.

* * *

Back in Dadaab, all the students I interviewed that day extolled the value of education, in part I'm sure to pander to my research and due to the presence of their teachers. Some of them really did seem to mean it, though, telling me how much they enjoyed debate, academic competitions between classrooms (the different camps face off academically in quizzes), and reading.

On my way back to the UN compound, I stopped by the office of the academic coordinator, who looks over all of the headmasters and their schools in each camp. We spoke for a while about the existing conditions in the camp, and he highlighted: the need to improve the educational systems for these children; the need for more resources (a common complaint across all refugee camps); the difficulty of teaching the curriculum in English, by teachers who were not native speakers, to children who were not native speakers (and the subsequent loss in translation); and finally, the lack of a cultural connection between the Kenyan curriculum and Somali culture.

Toward the end, just as I was leaving his office, he pulled me aside and said conspiratorially, "You want to know what the real problem is?"

I nodded.

"Teacher quality. We need better teachers, who are actually trained as teachers. If we had that, the lack of textbooks and desks wouldn't really matter. Good teachers would make all the difference."

In spite of all the research I had done about education in refugee camps prior to this trip, this was the most revealing and powerful comment I had heard thus far in the mission to increase the quality of education.

Good teachers can overcome.

Good teachers can keep your attention even when you're under a tree in the hot sun and the dust is blowing in your face. Even when you can only afford one textbook for every seven children and the desks are overflowing. The question was: How do we get better teachers to come here, fifty miles away from a raging civil war in Somalia?

* * *

On the way back Ahmed, the head teacher who had been kind enough to serve as my guide and escort that day, asked me if they performed female genital mutilation where I came from. I told him that it wasn't really a problem in the United States. He then asked me if it was a problem in other refugee camps I had visited. I responded that Dadaab was the first camp I had ever visited.

The World Health Organization identifies three types of Female Genital Mutilation, or FGM. Type 1 refers to the partial or total removal of the clitoris; Type 2 is the partial or total removal of the clitoris and the labia minora; and Type 3 refers to the narrowing of the vaginal orifice by removing or cutting the labia minora and majora, which in many cases results in the young girl's vagina resealing itself except for a small orifice from which to urinate. Most FGMs are done without proper anesthesia, and the procedure makes it extremely painful to urinate or have intercourse for millions of women a year. The State Department reports that 80 to 96 percent of all girls in Somalia undergo this barbaric procedure, with approximately 80 percent of the victims suffering from Type 3 mutilation – in effect, dooming them to a life of constant pain and debilitating infections.

Ahmed told me he was happy that through public awareness campaigns they had reduced the practice in the camp, but stated that about 50 percent of all girls in the camp were still mutilated.

"Who encourages the practice?" I asked.

"The female elders, of course."

I was stunned. I had always imagined that FGM was instigated by decrepit and insecure men who believed that women should feel no pleasure during sex. Men who viewed the clitoris, a perfect part of the female anatomy made exclusively for pleasure, as an affront to their archaic and chauvinistic principles. I was disappointed, and very saddened, to hear that in fact it was the girls' mothers and grandmothers who forced this tragedy upon their young girls, adamant about continuing a traumatic and unsafe tradition.

As we were talking about these poor girls, Ahmed took me past the animal market in the camp, where refugees traded camels, goats, and donkeys for cash. I was amazed, for the umpteenth time, at how much healthier the dozen camels looked here, in the refugee market, than in Petra. As I was excitedly about to take a picture of a particularly beautiful camel, a group of very angry traders and one wife hustled over and badgered me aggressively to put away the camera.

I quickly put my hands up, palms showing. "No worries guys, no need for anger, no worries, no pictures."

I explained to them, through Ahmed, how much healthier their camels were, especially one lustrous creature who easily reached ten feet high and had glistening, pearly white teeth.

The main trader laughed and told me that these were his "skinny" camels, and that he had sold Brilliant Smile, as I affectionately called him, a little while ago for 23,500Ks (about $300). I could also buy a goat for 3000Ks ($40), but if she were pregnant it would cost me 500Ks ($6) more.

I laughed, thanked him, and promised him that if I moved to Dadaab I would buy my camel from him and ride it every day from the compound to the camps and back.

He smiled widely and told me I could take a picture, but just as I raised my camera again his wife scrambled over screaming, "No pictures! No pictures!"

It was obvious who wore the pants in that relationship.

Ahmed explained to me that in their culture camels were the most venerated animals. Their milk was considered the cleanest because the animals only ate from the trees and not from the ground. Their meat was also a delicacy, but, most important, Ahmed added, "They are so beautiful to look at!" He said that, unlike for cows, traffic would stop for camels as passersby would simply admire the animal until it had crossed the road. Camels, in the animal hierarchy, were followed by goats and, finally, by cows – lowest on the totem pole.

In my second photographic faux pas of the day, I picked up my camera quickly as I saw two young men racing toward us on bicycles carrying large duffel bags. Because the bags were made of a cream-colored canvas, I stupidly associated them with the postal service, and I tried to take a picture of these rudimentary postal employees. They immediately accelerated as they saw me raise the lens and held up the bags to their heads, covering their faces. Ahmed laughed when I exclaimed how impressed I was that the camps had a mail system.

He explained to me that in fact these gentlemen had been transporting *qat*, a plant that increases energy, dumbs you down a bit, and produces anorexic side effects. I had just taken a picture of the camp's drug dealers.

Just as we were reaching Hagadera's main offices, an older gentlemen, in a tight-fitting shirt that accentuated a bulging potbelly and a face decorated by patches of white beard, stopped dead in his tracks when he noticed the color of my skin. He pointed at me and commanded, "Information!" He shouted something in Somali to Ahmed, who replied back, turned to me, and said, "We better go introduce ourselves to him." We shuffled over, with a newfound entourage in tow, and introduced ourselves. The man excitedly informed me he was an official Somali journalist. From his wallet, he pulled a laminated piece of paper with the header (in English) "Transitional Federal Government of Somalia."

"And what exactly are you reporting on here?" I asked, much braver now that he wasn't shouting at me and I realized he wasn't an angry camp elder or one of the Managing Directors Kauthar had mentioned.

He explained he was writing about the population at large here. Since I worked in educational research (as I told him and everyone else, since explaining to strangers that I was studying terrorist recruitment would have been suicidal), he wanted me to know how impressed he was with how much the population had changed since the refugees began to take advantage of the camp's educational systems. "They came here ignorant," he said disdainfully, "and now they are different people. Most of them do not want to go back to Somalia because of the education system they have here."

I disagreed with the Somali journalist's comment about resettlement, however, as my conversations had pointed otherwise, with the vast majority of children proclaiming they wanted to go back and help their country (as teachers, doctors, and presidents). Moreover, the fact that almost all of the teachers, the education officers, and a lot of the NGO workers were refugees had created a thriving civil society with valuable skills and training in best practices that was just itching to go back and help its country. Suddenly, rather than a problem of 275,000 people, Dadaab looked like the training ground for the future Somali bureaucracy. Rather than a burden, these refugees were an invisible untapped resource for the future of Somalia.

However, his comments about the Somali educational system had been verified by several of the educational coordinators in the camp, who all attested that in spite of the drawbacks of the Kenyan curriculum, there was no Somali educational curriculum to fall back on. If there was one message I had learned over the past few days—one that would be reaffirmed over the next two months in Yemen and Pakistan—it was the tremendous difference that a that a practical, non-religious education had had on these children. Even a malfunctioning, and at times incompetent, system like Dadaab's, with extraordinarily high failure rates, had made a life-changing difference in the lives of these children and the temperament of the society they lived in. Of the 200 to 300 al-Shabaab recruits that the teachers had unwillingly estimated for me, all of them were typically newcomers who were too old and too uneducated to join the school system, and were thus left idling in the camp.

"By the way, since you're a journalist, there are a number of journalists in the United States writing articles about al-Shabaab recruiting refugees from this camp to go fight back in Somalia. Is this true?" I asked.

He cocked his head sideways, surprised by the question.

"Yes, we have read the same articles! But we are never sure who is going over there. Also, understand that the border is so porous that a lot of them go fight in Somalia and then return to the camp."

At this point he thrust out his hand, abruptly ending the conversation (made uncomfortable, I imagine, by the now thirty-person crowd that had been listening to us).

* * *

We were back at the UN compound earlier than usual, as Fridays are half-days for schools and NGO workers. I noticed people seemed particularly morose at lunch.

Before I continue, I imagine you've been wondering what the food was like. Sorry to disappoint those of you who had imagined dark, watered-down curries with mystery meat and bland bread, but the food at the compound was actually quite good, if unvarying. Breakfast consisted of steamed sweet potatoes, hard boiled eggs, the soft Ethiopian pancake-like bread called *Injera*, hominy tightly packed into bland white cubes, and slices of bread you could toast (the cafeteria was equipped with both a toaster and a microwave) and lather with jelly (not too bad), peanut butter (awful), and margarine (pretty good). All of this could be washed down with a Nescafe cup of coffee, made with one and a half teaspoons of dehydrated coffee mix.

Lunch and dinner were virtually identical, and included lots of white basmati rice, the packed hominy cubes, a surprisingly delicious mix of steamed spinach with onion, a mild curry with either fatty beef or bony chicken, at times a mixture of green beans and carrots, and always a tasty salad of fresh cucumbers, tomatoes, and carrots. On special days we would get a fruitcup of orange, ripe banana, and mango, all displayed in buffet-style open stainless steel containers that didn't attract too many flies.

In terms of conversation and interaction at the table, breakfasts were positively hostile, with grunts and avoidance of eye contact the norm; lunches were more open but hurried, as workers rushed to get back; and evenings were always punctuated by a communal urge to linger. Like the dynamic in a high school cafeteria, seating arrangements at the tables, although informal, didn't change a lot, and were largely ethnically based. Local African workers were relegated to the side tables; the transient white workers occupied a center table farthest from the buffet; and the mainstay UN and NGO workers, the "hard-asses" who expected to be here for an average of two years, sat in the center table closest to the food and were generally unfriendly to the others. There were no Americans at this table, only Europeans and Australians.

That Friday the mood was more somber than ever. I naively asked people what their plans for the weekend were, a question derisively answered with snorts and chuckles around the table.

"Well, Francisco, there's nothing to do here on the weekends," one of the American workers helpfully answered.

"Absolutely true. Most people drink themselves into a stupor on Friday and Saturday nights so that they can spend the weekend days recovering in the comfort of their rooms," another woman added. "On that note," she continued, "we'll see you at Pumzika tonight."

The Pumzika Club, the crown jewel of Dadaab nightlife, was located in the most incongruous part of the compound: in a corner section that included a concrete tennis court with deep grooves etched on its surface from disrepair, a volleyball court on sand, and a concrete structure with a tin roof that housed some weights and the requisite treadmill and elliptical from the early 2000s.

Tying together the three structures was the Pumzika Club, an octagonal structure (just like the dining hall) with a concrete wall about two feet high. Eight columns held up a thatched roof that sloped upward to reach twenty feet at its highest point. Right in the middle of the roof was a static disco ball that had lost one too many mirrored squares to be of any use reflecting light. Below sat white plastic chairs and tables, and a large bar broken into three counters, all wallpapered in a Moroccan-style pattern. Although most of the club's furniture was made of plastic, the bar stools were wooden and lacquered, proudly made by the carpenters in the Youth Education Program I had visited a few days ago.

Behind the bar were three Ethiopian refugees who were happy to serve you Tuskers (a surprisingly refreshing Kenyan ale that wasn't too bad lukewarm), Smirnoff Ice, various flavors of Fanta, a few dozen individual-size bottles of Smirnoff vodka (that people would buy and drink in the privacy of their rooms), some cheap brandy, a bottle of Bailey's, Myer's Rum, and even boxed wine (by the excellent South African vintners of Overmeer, for red, and Drostdy-Hof, for white). The bar's specialty, and only dish, was bony fried chicken with fries, to which you could add sweet, watery ketchup or a tangy, gooey hot sauce.

The club was founded in 2002, built with UNHCR funds, and run by an Ethiopian refugee (hence the Ethiopian, rather than Somali, bartenders). Although I had been told of the existence of five "bars" in the compound, only three of them served any alcohol, and Boar's Hole and No Name were more like counters with plastic chairs. Pumzika boasted a sound system, including, near the makeshift dance floor, raised speakers that belted out early 80s and 90s hits – most of which reminded me (somewhat desperately) of my early high school days in Atlanta. About 20 percent of the songs were so scratched up that they had to be skipped over. A small television set mounted to the right of the bar got access to African network channels that showed African and reggae music videos, American TV shows like "America's Dance Team," and sports (mostly soccer and rugby).

This whole section of the compound smacked decisively of old British colonialism, a refuge within a secure compound where the patrons could revel separate from the populace. I must admit that after spending a day among the refugees in the sweltering heat, the beads of sweat making inroads into the thick layer of dirt on my skin, it was nice to get away – but that doesn't mean it wasn't elitist as hell.

I arrived that night around nine o'clock to find the same segregation that was present in the dining hall, with locals sitting in the dark, at the tables outside the octagon, and the Europeans and transient Americans seated on opposite sides of the dance floor, gathered around small plastic tables. I sat down with the Americans and ordered a Fanta, terrified of getting drunk and lost in a compound known for camel spiders and red cobras. (If you haven't done so already, please Google an image of camel spiders so you understand what I was up against.) After two hours of listening to funny insects-in-the-room-stories and anecdotes from home I excused myself, both because I was tired and because I had little else to say. My cardinal sin that night, I would later learn, was not getting shit-faced with the expats, the preferred coping mechanism for many stuck in a compound in a foreign country far away from the comforts of home and the families they weren't allowed to bring with them. Drunken, desperate sex was part of the equation at the compound, but it was an activity that was relatively unappetizing to the guy who was there temporarily and remained stone cold sober. Not that other members of the group didn't have a good time that night.

* * *

The next day I went back to Ifo to visit their teacher training program for new refugee teachers, led by Kenyan public school teachers. As usual, we left in the security convoy of 4Runners that snaked out of the compound to the sub-camps in the early mornings. Most vehicles carried a sticker on the front that stated "No Guns," but the first and last vehicles of the group carried weapons. I asked my driver if the security situation had deteriorated recently and if they had increased their security measures, but he said it had been this way for as long as he could remember.

The teacher training course was unexceptional, with the head teachers lecturing off of professional training books and the new teachers desperately trying to write down notes for the three-hour lecture on the two sheets of paper they had been given. As usual, the women were more attentive than the men, asked more questions, and, vis-à-vis the real percentage of female teachers, were over-represented in the semi-voluntary training sessions. My appearance at the school was marked by curious stares from children outdoors and an accumulation of younger students near the door, studying the stranger and quickly giggling and looking away whenever we made eye contact. To my enduring sadness, the principal dispersed the crowd with the usual threat implied by his waving of a long, thin branch. The threat was enough to disperse the crowd—this time.

At lunch I was invited to a barbeque that night with the locals, courtesy of a Nepalese friend I had made over the past few days who worked for UNHCR and who had broken out of the segregated groups and hung out with Kenyans. I accepted and went back to my room for a nap. On the way, I was shocked once again to see enormous crickets bounding four to six feet with each jump. I killed a praying mantis that had settled itself on my doorknob, and the carcass was quickly hurried away by hundreds of hungry ants. Little did I know that that night I would meet one of the people who knew the most, outside of the Somali refugees, about al-Shabaab and their recruiting tactics within the camp.

* * *

The BBQ was hosted by Fortunato, a local Kenyan work-er who was given a residence inside the compound, and was a farewell party for one of the Kenyan priests who had completed his time here. We sat in the garden in the familiar white plastic chairs, hidden by the semi-dark-ness, as lamps and electricity outside the living quarters were sparse. Everyone was laughing and drinking, and I was soon passed a plate of what I discovered too late was goat liver. I quickly gulped it down with the help of a warm Tusker. The party was devoid of foreigners save for me; an older British gentlemen wearing an ankle-length, short-sleeved, dazzling white tunic imprinted with a Botticelli painting on the center pouch; my Nep-alese friend; and his friend, Sunil. I sat down next to Sunil and asked him what he did at the camp, at the same time tentatively grabbing a piece of meat from a new plate that was being passed around. It turned out to be the barbequed goat, rubbed with Cajun-like spices and absolutely delicious.

Sunil had spent the last few years in Sri Lanka working as an aid worker, living in one of the compounds run
by the Tamil Tigers, the rebel organization designated
as a terrorist group by thirty-two countries, including
the United States. I asked him what the group was really like.

"Francisco, it is like no other IDP camp you have seen
before," he said, referring to the term "internally displaced people," essentially refugees who had not crossed
a border but had simply migrated within their own country due to violence or natural disasters. "Women can
walk around the camps at night without fear of being
raped. There is no corruption. You are not allowed to
cut down any trees, and they even have a Central Bank!
I remember talking to the Tamil Tiger in charge of economic development, and he said that the Palestinians
did not deserve a state because they had not focused on
building up their society, like they had been doing for
so many years so that by the time they achieved their
independence they would be ready for it!"

Frankly, this account of the Tamil Tigers was at odds
with what the international press had reported up to date.
The Tamil Tigers were founded in 1976 by Velupillai
Prabhakaran, who sought to establish an independent
state for the Tamil (an ethnic group within Sri Lanka)
in northeastern Sri Lanka. The organization was notorious for pioneering the use of suicide belts, developing
the Black Tigers unit (which was dedicated to carrying
out suicide attacks), and utilizing civilians as shields. In
1991 the Tamil Tigers assassinated Indian Prime Minister Rajiv Gandhi, who had earlier sent Indian troops to

Sri Lanka as "peacekeepers" to fight against the Tigers. The Sri Lankan government finally defeated the Tigers on May 17, 2009, assassinating Prabhakaran two days later. News agencies, which were banned from documenting the fighting, heavily criticized the Sri Lankan government for indiscriminately targeting civilians in their quest to defeat the Tamil Tigers.

"And do you know why they were beaten?" Sunil continued. "Because Sonia Gandhi hates them because they murdered her husband in 1991. So once she came to power, India provided the Sri Lankan army with all the weapons and money it needed to defeat the Tamils. It could never have beat them on its own, without India's help."

Sunil popped open another Tusker, and now regaled me with the colorful story of how the President of Ghana had shot his father-in-law in public for being corrupt, and how much better Ghana had gotten since then. As hard as I tried, I was never able to verify this story, but it sure was entertaining.

Finally, a few more beers into the night, I spoke with Sunil about my educational research and asked him if he had any suggestions as to what to do with the idle youth. We brainstormed a few ideas, and then I asked him if these were the same people who were recruited to go fight in Somalia.

He turned to look directly at me and then leaned in conspiratorially. "You know, I've actually done some unofficial research on my own about al-Shabaab recruitment since I arrived. I've even met with a few families who have seven children and had one or two boys who went to fight for them."

"And?" I asked, trying to control my excitement.

"Well, as you know [I didn't], al-Shabaab has thrown out the World Food Program in Somalia and decreed that Somalis must go back to agriculture and start growing their own produce. This obviously has not worked so well, so every day there are three vehicles that cross over from Somalia to pick up supplies from the refugee markets at Ifo, Hagadera, and Daghale," said Sunil, referring to the three sub-camps. "Often they bring over al-Shabaab recruiters, who register as refugees and come live in the camps. I estimate that there are about 100 to 150 recruiters, who typically send twenty to twenty-five new fighters to Somalia each month. They pay them each $500 a month and actually deliver the money regularly. They typically target the idle youth, those not in school or vocational programs, who have arrived since 2007, which we estimate at about 25,000."

He paused, took another long swig of his beer, and added the sentence that made it clear how we could beat al-Shabaab and, for that matter, al-Qaeda. "Understand, though, that they are unable to recruit those children in school, or those who have been here for a few years, because they have developed a different mentality. Anyone who has received even a little education doesn't go with them. So they target the older kids who arrived here post-2007, those who are too old to go to school here and were never able to attend school in Somalia. Al-Shabaab goes to those kids sitting under a tree and bullies them, asking them what they are doing with their life, if they do not want to be real men and fight to provide for their families rather than just wait for a UN handout."

He continued. "We have 1,500 recorded births every month in Dadaab, which means that the real number of children being born could be double that. Add to that number 4,000 new refugees that arrive each month, twenty-percent who are recruitable youths. As the size of the camp increases, it is getting easier for them to recruit fighters."

"And the madrasas? Do they recruit from there as well?" I asked.

"No, no, the madrasas are not a problem—yet. They are just like regular private schools. Then once a month al-Shabaab sends a luxury convoy to pick up all of the recruits and take them back to Somalia to train and fight."

Our Nepalese friend interrupted us at this point, and I imagined there was little else to glean from Sunil, as his eyes had narrowed and become unfocused, betraying the effects of the Kenyan ale. I walked to my room soon after, elated to have gained a better understanding of the problem I had come all this way to research, and accompanied by the sounds of locals clapping and chanting beautiful Kenyan songs in parties around the compound.

* * *

A couple days later I found myself once again at the front of a classroom full of refugee students. I gave a brief explanation of my research to these high school students, and began the line of questioning. "Who do you admire?" I asked.

"The Prophet Muhammad," one student volunteered.

"Why?" I asked, out of habit. After a bout of nervous laughter, and some uncomfortable and some outwardly hostile glances by the students, I realized my faux pas and backtracked. "What I meant is that out of all of his positive qualities and actions, which ones do you admire most?"

The tension in the room dissipated now that it was clear I was not criticizing their religion. Nobody had yet named the Prophet as someone they admired, and I was surprised by the more religious overtones of the high school students versus the younger pupils I had interviewed. Maybe *this* was the root of extremism, the beginning of radicalization, the point where indoctrination began.

"Because he never took revenge on anyone," the student answered, contrary to my expectation and, frankly, to my own understanding of how the Caliphate had been established. Muhammad was usually praised as a brilliant and efficient general whose military victories were responsible for the spread of Islam.

Others chimed in. "Because of his honesty."

"Patience."

"Kindness."

These were adjectives that, in most Western media, were unfortunately not typically associated with the Prophet. Finally, after a few more heroes were named, someone volunteered a shocking answer. "Osama bin Laden."

Snickers could be heard around the room.

I stared at the young man before me, my heart racing. "Why?" I asked.

"Because he is brave. Because he is a great leader who is defending our people against the West."

"Abu Mansoor," added his friend. Abu Mansoor al-Amriki, born Omar Hammami, is a twenty-six-year-old man who grew up in Alabama and was raised by a Southern Baptist mother and a Muslim Syrian father. Up until early high school, he had a fairly normal American life, excelling at academics and soccer and taking a cute girl to Homecoming. Then something went wrong. He became more and more extremist after graduating from high school, and eventually dropped out of college and moved to Canada, where he married a Canadian-Somali. She eventually divorced him because he was unable to keep a job. He was in Cairo for a while learning Arabic, and somehow made his way to Somalia. In October 2007 he appeared for the first time publicly as Abu Mansoor, giving an interview to al-Jazeera as a member of al-Shabaab. In January 2008 he appeared again to explain al-Shabaab's goal to establish an Islamic Caliphate, "from East to West after removing the occupier and killing the apostates." He has since risen quite rapidly in the ranks, and is today considered one of al-Shabaab's top commanders.

At hearing the name of the American commander in al-Shabaab, the rest of the class giggled.

Again, I asked for the student's reasoning.

"Because he is very brave and is helping Somalia," he answered.

Finally, a third voice said, "Abdullahi Yusuf." At the mention of Somalia's ex-president, one of the most hated men among Somali refugees for his creation of the Somali Salvation Democratic Front, a rebel group known for raping and killing civilians, the whole room burst out laughing.

I had just been conned by the president and vice-president of the debate club, who had wanted to see what my reaction would be to these extreme statements. Even the teacher and headmaster, both present in the room, laughed heartily.

Although I felt a combination of silliness and relief at being conned, two characteristics of this particular classroom experience surprised me. First, the fact that so many students had admired the Prophet Muhammad showed a greater degree of religiosity among older students than younger ones. I was heartened to hear them co-opt the parts of the Prophet's life that exemplified the peaceful and forgiving nature of Islam. These aspects of the religion provided comfort to a population that had fled terror and violence. I was encouraged, seeing these students espouse a tolerant interpretation of Islam, instead of the extremist interpretations of al-Shabaab and al-Qaeda, whose suicide bombers had distorted the meaning of jihad and sullied God's name by screaming "Allahu Akbar" (God is Greatest) before massacring civilians.

However, I was also shocked at how comfortable the students who pulled my leg were with the terrorist rhetoric. Was it because they had been subjected to it? Secretly believed it? Or was the mocking of Osama bin Laden and his creed the ultimate method of empowerment? Had his rhetoric sounded so hollow to these children that simply uttering it in a serious manner was enough to ridicule it? How many other communities felt this way?

* * *

The walk from the UNHCR-funded school to the community-run school, through the residential camp of Dagahale, was long and depressing. Since Kenya is located in the southern hemisphere, we were in the middle of winter in Dadaab, and yet I withered under the noon sun and its 100 degree temperature. Though the mornings and nights were punctuated by the odd breeze, the mid-day hours were stifling and unbearable.

Jeremiah, the teacher who was accompanying me, explained to me why the performance of the students had been so poor last year in the primary school national examinations, the ones that decided who made it to secondary school. "Students and teachers cheated every other year that they took the exam. They had received the answer key prior to the exam, and some students paid to receive it. Last year was the first year that no cheating occurred, so even if we have a much smaller class starting high school this year, it is the most prepared class we have ever had."

Dadaab has one of the best educational programs for refugees in the world, and it has generally done an excellent job of training and utilizing refugees to take on leadership and professional roles within the various non-governmental organizations. That said, if we measure success in absolute terms, rather than relative to other refugee camps, the situation is dire. Of 1,000 children who enter first grade in Ifo, only 250 will pass the Kenyan national exam in eighth grade. Of the remaining 750 students who failed this exam, fewer than one hundred will gain spots in the Youth Educational Program that prioritizes teenage mothers and students with disabilities. To reiterate an earlier point, although this way of admitting students is humanitarian in nature and gives everyone a warm fuzzy feeling, it means that if you are a healthy and able male between the ages of fourteen and twenty-four who did not graduate in the top 25 percent of your class, you're shit out of luck.

By now I had received enough information about graduation rates to estimate that out of the students who started first grade in the camp, only 2.5 percent of them would ever graduate from secondary school. This meant that 97.5 percent of all students dropped out of school because they were resettled, married early (affecting only the girls), or most typically, failed out or became disenchanted with the educational system. It was the drop-outs who made up the majority of the youth population that spent its days chewing *qat*, working half-days for the NGOs or working in the market, but mostly just wasting away under the shade of a tree somewhere.

Every year in Ifo, about 600 students finish primary school unsuccessfully and then have little to do throughout their days. If about 75 percent of them are male, that means that every sub-camp spits out about 450 healthy idle males a year, or about 1,350 for all of Dadaab. These numbers have never gone down, merely continued to rise at different rates depending on the levels of violence in Somalia. Thus over the last ten years we have created a population of 13,500 idle, frustrated, and healthy young males. Since Dadaab has been around for close to twenty years (and secondary school education and the YEP program didn't start in full force until the mid-to-late 2000s), it has produced a population closer to 30,000 male youths who are ideal al-Shabaab and al-Qaeda recruiting targets. Especially when you offer them $100 to $500 a month.

The situation will only become direr. Dadaab currently has an estimated population of 275,000 (the unofficial tally is well over 300,000). Every month the Kenyan government registers 1,000 new births and approximately 4,000 new arrivals, which means that every year Dadaab grows by 60,000 new members. These are the official figures, which means that the real numbers are likely higher. If we ignore resettlements and migration away from the camp, which could be significant, the population in the camp will double in five years. Taking in consideration emigration from Dadaab and assuming there is no peace in Somalia, the population will double in ten years. During the severe drought in Somalia of mid-2011, approximately 1,300 Somali refugees were arriving every day, significantly shortening this estimate. It is an understatement to say that the situation is unsustainable. The infrastructure and existing programs in Dadaab will collapse if the population continues to increase in this way. Already there are one hundred children per teacher, a ratio that will only get worse every year.

After visiting so many schools and meeting with hundreds of children, I felt certain that the student population was not radicalized, an effect they all attributed to their education. But did receiving a well-rounded education make the population less likely to be swayed by terrorist recruiters? Was it impossible to prevent recruitment in an idle population desperate for a vocation and income?

Recruitment by al-Shabaab was at an all-time high in 2008 and 2009, and done so openly that recruiters gave speeches to young men in the market, extolling the benefits and glory of their organization. The Kenyan police in the camp would typically be called over by the community leaders to arrest the al-Shabaab members, only to release them a day later—both due to a fear of retaliation and due to corruption.

What had driven al-Shabaab to recruit so brazenly, openly antagonizing an unfriendly government in a country hostile to it? The answer was a secret program by the President of Kenya, who had recruited Kenyan-Somalis in order to train them to fight in Somalia. Faced with this growing threat, al-Shabaab recruiters flooded the camps, stopping this open recruiting policy only after the Kenyan Parliament found out about the President's covert program, protested, and shut down the training.

The night before, in a drunken conversation I had with Kenyan government officials and security personnel who were visiting the camp, I learned that there had been another covert operation run by the Kenyan government. The program had attempted to recruit Somali refugees outright, with the hopes of sending them back to Somalia to defeat al-Shabaab. The drunkest of the officials admitted to me that their biggest mistake, it had now become clear, was circumventing the

Somali sheikhs and community leaders in Dadaab and addressing the youth directly and exclusively. Given how closely knit clans and families are in Dadaab, this tactic had doomed the program from its inception. Today, al-Shabaab recruitment had once again gone underground. It was clear, though, from dozens of conversations I had, that al-Shabaab's twenty- to twenty-five-person monthly recruitment cap was not due to a lack of volunteers in the camp but rather to the organization's budgetary and infrastructure constraints.

These thoughts burdened me as I walked to the community school with Jeremiah, who complained about the dependency the UN had created in this population. "These people's lives are so much better than those in my town in Kenya, Francisco. They do not pay for rent. They get free food. Free education. My family does not even know if they can pay for a meal tomorrow. Here, all the refugees do is keep asking, 'What can you do for me? What else can you give me?'"

This was a common complaint: that the international community and the encampment policy forced long-term refugee populations to lose their drive, stifled any entrepreneurial spirit, and crushed independent will. My guides complained to me that most men in the camp were lazy, spending their days chatting and lounging. It was the women who were responsible for picking up the rations (the WFP ration center was full of women hoisting heavy bags of grain, which they would then trek back to their houses), collecting firewood, cooking, and cleaning. The men's inability to obtain jobs and play the role of provider had created a cadre of men who had come to accept their own futility and given in to a life dependent on the generosity of others. This attitude encouraged the men to marry young (girls were fair game if they were older than twelve) and drop out of school.

Later that day, we came along a group of elders who epitomized, for Jeremiah, his complaints. Many of the old men were toothless, their brown gums now useless after years of chewing *qat*. Their beards, and sometimes heads, were dyed bright orange, in many cases a color more faded and dusty than vibrant. Jeremiah explained that they used a mixture made in part with tree bark, and that the dye denoted status for sheikhs, leaders, and elders. The differences between the generations, those who had grown up in Somalia and those had spent most of their life in Dadaab, were piercingly clear. Most elders did not speak English, or even Arabic, and needed translators to communicate with me. Their questions were less intelligent and creative than those of the youngsters.

To lighten the mood, Jeremiah pointed again to the entourage of children that was following us through the camp. He laughed. "When I was younger, we would always flock to see white people whenever they came to our town. We thought that white people did not have any skin! We thought you wore your flesh inside out! I wonder what these children think of you." We laughed together at this thought. We were walking to a secondary school that had been demanded, organized, and staffed by the refugee community three years ago, after the UN had informed students that there was not enough room to accept all of those who had passed the difficult national exam.

The school building was brand new, with more desks than students and blackboards that hadn't yet been ground down by years of use. Its mere presence, its glistening new paint and tin roofs, were an affront to the very idea of the dependency that Jeremiah had criticized in this population. This structure was a product born of a community that cared for its children. Members of the community even paid the teachers out of their own pockets, rather than wait for UN funds to become available.

Why had the community suddenly cared so much about these particular students? Was it because they had surpassed such onerous obstacles, succeeding in a difficult and highly flawed academic environment, encouraged by the promise of a better future that was then denied to them? Was it because not acting would have forced the children—and their parents—to lose hope? Was it a sense of unfairness that had mobilized the community? This was the best-kept project the community had. This project was a sign that even after years of encampment, and without the promise or likely possibility of their children having a profession upon graduation, Somali refugees had come to value education for their children above all else.

Even here, though, in the crown jewel of refugee education and with significant community buy-in, there was much to be desired. Most teachers had only just graduated from secondary school, had received rudimentary teacher training, and struggled to convey their knowledge to their students. I convened a conference to ask these teachers how to improve the current system, and the now-recurrent theme emerged: We need better training. We want to be better teachers.

Better teachers.

This was the message that I heard and saw most often during this trip.

* * *

It was finally time to speak with the kids lounging under the trees.

I spent the next few days touring the camps again, but this time speaking to the idle youth. I met mostly people who had been in the camp for at least ten years, all of whom pressed me to help them expand their educational opportunities: more programs, more spaces for secondary school students, more teachers. Everyone I met expressed an interest in going back "home," even those who had never been in Somalia or couldn't remember their time there because they had made the arduous trek as babies on their mothers' backs. Out of the dozens of conversations and ad-hoc meetings I had with these idle youths, two young men stand out in my memory. One was a nineteen-year-old Somali man in Hagadera, who had arrived in the camp when he was six years old. In the middle of a conversation about increased levels of violence in the camp, brought on by the arrival of new refugees who had come from Somalia, he added his two cents: "People are not evil by nature. Society makes them evil."

Surprised by what seemed like such a naïve pronouncement, I said that certainly most people were good but some people were innately evil. In spite of all the trauma he had witnessed and undergone, he smiled at me. "No. Society makes them bad. But even the evil men I have met, deep down they are still good." His smile made me feel like a small child, coddled and naïve, spouting a Hobbesian-view of the world I had merely debated in class. This young man had been in contact with pure evil, survived, and still had faith in his fellow man. I felt amazement that someone who had undergone such hardship could maintain a positive view of the innate goodness of humanity.

The other young man I met revolutionized my thinking, and was happy to be quoted by name. Sahal Abdi Hussein was a twenty-year-old man who had dropped out of secondary school "to earn some income in the market." He was the perfect example of a bright, articulate (in English), and healthy young man within the 97.5 percent of the student population who had fallen by the wayside. I explained to him my concern about the high failure rates and asked him why he had dropped out. "I wanted to make money. I did not see a lot of benefit to staying in school for another four years. What would I do when I finished? There are so few scholarships available to graduates who want to study university, so what was the purpose of graduating?"

I pressed him as to what to do with the problem of idle youth in the camp, a large group of whom had now encircled us and did not seem thrilled to be categorized as "idle."

"Should we increase vocational programs?" I asked. "Secondary schools? What do you do with the 97.5 percent?"

"Why is your focus on them?" he demanded. "Why worry about the ones who fail? You should forget about us! You should focus on the 2.5 percent who are intelligent, hardworking, and lucky enough to have made it through!"

He went on. "Let me explain to you what the problem is. The people who made it through and passed secondary school, they all want to go to university. But last year less than thirty students were able to attend. Most of them ended up as teachers, making 5000Ks a month. Why study so hard, then? To become a secondary school teacher? So, people like me are not inspired to continue studying because we see our brightest and hardest-working peers end up with very little for their efforts. What you need to do is make sure that all of the 2.5 percent can go to university, whether it is in Canada, America, or Nairobi!"

He continued, excited that someone was finally listening to the ideas he had given some thought to. "But instead of allowing them to resettle there [outside the camp], make sure they come back to Dadaab for some time. That way, in the summer and for a few years after they graduate, they can come back and help us with *our* university education, become *our* better qualified teachers, act as doctors, set up businesses. And then they could go resettle somewhere else. But the most important thing is that, by rewarding the 2.5 percent, you *inspire* the other 97.5 percent to work harder, to become better students. And then, instead of the UN having to provide everything for us, this 2.5 percent can take better care of everyone else. Focus on them, and things will change."

I was stunned. The idea was excellent, simple, and required fewer resources than any of the other suggestions to improve education and quality of life in the camp. Abdi was one of the students who had failed out of the system, but he was an intelligent and hardworking young man who would have done great things in college. People like him were the future of an independent and peaceful Somalia.

* * *

It rained on my last day in Dadaab. The humongous dark and gray cloud had been hovering over the camp for three full days, and finally let loose warm soft droplets that dried the instant they touched the coarse red sand. I had spent the last few hours at a deserted Club Pumzika, reminiscing and writing, trying to make sense of everything I had learned after meeting so many refugees. The large, harmless insects that thrived around me no longer bothered me. As the raindrops started to fall I initially took cover, protecting these very words that were evidence of an incredible journey. But a few minutes into the rain I entrusted my notebook to Amare, the bartender at Pumzika, and walked around the compound in the drizzle. The raindrops felt good against my face, wiping away some of the dirt and sweat, and quickly drenching my shirt.

I was heartbroken that day, sad to be leaving such a flawed, magical place, but cognizant that there were children in Pakistan and Yemen waiting to be met. New stories to be told. New people to admire. And my conversation with Sahal Abdi Hussein the day before had planted a seed—the beginning of an idea of what I could do to help this population after I had returned home.

As I boarded my last convoy toward the airstrip, the muezzin could be heard from the residential camp, a crackly and distant recording that reverberated the cheap speakers but powerful and beautiful as always. Even here, in the most miserable region of Kenya, it had followed.

* * *

A few days later, showered and cleaner than I had been in a while, I recalled a meeting I had with a UN education officer in Nairobi. She had mentioned that violence was not the only difference between the more recent Somali refugees and the broader refugee population. "Ten years ago, refugees who arrived had some semblance of an education, some background we could build on. Nowadays, it is common to find fourteen-year-old boys, even seventeen-year-olds, who have never attended school. The educational infrastructure in Somalia has been completely obliterated. There is nothing left."

I was sitting at the hotel bar watching a World Cup match as I thought of her comments. I thought back to the previous World Cup, four years ago. I had just graduated from college and had watched most of the games on a tiny color television in a friend's mice-infested apartment in Philadelphia. I remember being terrified because the company I had founded with three engineer friends was facing imminent bankruptcy, a total failure, and I was desperately trying to figure out what to do with my life. Who would have imagined that four years later I would be researching terrorist recruitment on the Somali border?

What had I learned so far from these amazing children? I had learned that virtually all refugees harbored dreams of going home, and that many of them were preparing themselves to help their country. I learned that hope, even if available to only 2.5 percent of the population, was a powerful message that could motivate an entire community. I was made aware that even a highly religious population, where all women covered themselves and everyone admired the Prophet Muhammad, was not a sign of a radicalized population; in fact, this was a population focused on the best aspects of Islam: mercy, patience, and forgiveness. I learned that these children, thousands of miles away from our own, dreamed of and wanted the same things from life: an education, the opportunity to better themselves, the ability to help other people, and the freedom to live a life in peace. A well-rounded education, the British-based Kenyan curriculum, had created in Dadaab a moderate and non-radicalized society.

But why, then, did some young men join al-Shabaab anyway? According to the teachers, workers and youths I had asked, only those who had not been through the school system went back to fight. "Would you go fight with al-Shabaab for a lot of money, Francisco?" one of the idle youths had asked me.

"Of course not," I replied, indignant.

"So why would we?" he answered. "Especially other students who, like you, do not believe in their interpretation of Islam or in the horrible things they are doing in its name?"

It had become clear to me that the establishment of a well-rounded education system was a powerful weapon against radicalization *and* recruitment.

The overpowering message that these children imparted to me was that human beings can remain optimistic even in the direst of circumstances. In spite of the violence these children had experienced and fled, in spite of the violence that followed them into the camp, they still believed in the innate goodness of people. Even though less than 0.01 percent of the entire camp population was given the opportunity to go to college, they still strived so hard to keep this dream alive. The message was clear: Focus on the lucky few, and they can change the world.

I Want to Burn This
Place to Ashes

Peshawar, Pakistan

After a quick twenty-four hours in Jordan, I was once again at the Amman airport, eating a sugary mixed-berry gelato and feeling quite ridiculous in my pale blue *kurta* (a collarless shirt with long sleeves that stretches down past your knees and is common in India and Pakistan) and linen pants. My ex-girlfriend, now living in India, had been kind enough to send them to me so I would "fit in better" on this trip.

Although I felt like a fake dressing like a Pakistani, I had been warned about my dress. Blake, a woman I had met at a conference at school, emailed, "Extremely complex and sensitive out here. My best advice—look Pakistani. Seriously. Extremely seriously. Things have been happening that have not made the news." Hence the attempt at growing a beard, composed of uneven colors and patches of facial hair, which I now sported. Even Fayaz—my "fixer" and translator in Peshawar, who had agreed over email to charge me $8 an hour for his services—advised me to wear Pashtun cultural dress. "I will be happy to gift you a Shalwar Qamees," he wrote to me. "You should not walk around Peshawar looking like an American." I had forgotten to purchase authentic footwear, however, and was thus incongruously wearing my now beat-up boat shoes under the outfit.

In spite of these warnings, and the increasingly bad news of more violence near the area, I did not feel the same debilitating fear that had gripped me before going to Dadaab. I felt that I knew what to expect: the poverty, the shoddy schools, the existence of recruiters from extremist groups. On the flight back to Amman, I had read Dave Eggers' novel *What is the What?*, a story of one of the millions of children who had been displaced or recruited. I found the tale familiar. Just the day before, I had read an article in *The New York Times* about Somali child soldiers, both in al-Shabaab (in which they reportedly comprise up to 80 percent of the fighting force) and in the armed forces of the Transitional Federal Government of Somalia. For many Americans, the term "refugee camp" has become intertwined with the idea of recruitment.

But where were the stories of hope? The stories that shone a light on the 2.5 percent that I had met in Dadaab? The stories that featured the intelligent, hard-working, striving Somali refugee children I had spoken with who clamored only for a better education? More and more I became convinced that people should understand what life is really like for these children, especially those who are sought so assiduously by al-Qaeda and its affiliates.

* * *

As my beard grew, my tan darkened, and my passport was stamped with increasingly controversial visas, security checks at airports became ever more difficult. I had spent two hours being searched and interviewed (through a translator) in the Amman airport, as security officials suspected me of transporting drugs or contacting drug dealers. I could imagine how much more difficult the interrogation would be post-Pakistan. My father had grumbled that upon my safe return to the United States I was going to spend days in the little immigration room being questioned while he waited outside.

The truth was, I *was* worried, but not about Amman or Boston: I was concerned about gaining entry into Pakistan. The government is very particular about any foreigners visiting its displaced persons camps, both because of their conditions and because of the presence of Islamic charities that are fronts for terrorist organizations. Terrorist organizations in Pakistan such as Lashkar-e-Taiba (which is rumored to be trained and funded by the Pakistani Intelligence Service, the ISI, and is the prime suspect in the 2008 Mumbai bombings) have created charitable organizations that provide humanitarian services, making up for the failings of an ineffective government. Lashkar-e-Taiba's charitable organization, Jamaat-ud-Dawa, was banned by the Pakistani government in 2008, and yet still set up shelters and schools to educate and recruit children in the Jalozai IDP camp in early 2009.

Even obtaining a visa to enter the country was a difficult process, and a group of Harvard students had been outright refused entry a few months prior. I had lied to my Pakistani college roommate, telling him I was interested in visiting Pakistan for tourist purposes and convincing him to sponsor my visa application. (He could credibly claim ignorance if anything bad happened while I was in Pakistan or if he was questioned, which is why I kept him in the dark.) I had reserved a room in a run-down guesthouse in Peshawar, the capital of the Khyber-Pakhtunkhwa province on the Afghanistan border, which was an hour away from the Jalozai camp. Only an idiot would stay at the Pearl Hotel, the luxury Western hotel in the city, which was full of military contractors and sketchy foreigners and which had already been the target of two large-scale terrorist attacks. On the other hand, I hoped no one would think of bombing a cheap guesthouse full of middle-class Pakistanis.

Once there, I was supposed to be provided access to the camp by a local doctor, who was apparently friends with the camp administrator. All of these contacts were thanks to Blake Allen, the director of the Pakistani Leadership Institute at Plymouth State University, which each year trains over a hundred Pakistani teachers in a month-long course. Unlike in Kenya, in Pakistan there would be no UN compound, no security convoys, no bars. My transport from Islamabad Airport to Peshawar was being provided by a friend of a friend of mine from school, who was originally from Peshawar and had been the Police Chief there before coming to the United States to earn his masters degree.

Expectedly, and pathetically, the fear and nausea that I felt before Dadaab returned to me on the flight from Abu Dhabi to Pakistan. All of my parents' warnings, even the concerned looks of my friends and their parents, flashed in my head. I was entering the most dangerous country in the world. This designation is based only on the size of its nuclear arsenal and the probability of a weapon falling into the hands of one of its many home-grown terrorist groups. But most of the world's scariest terrorist groups do indeed have representatives in Pakistan. There are, approximately, forty-seven domestic, transnational, and extremist terrorist groups in Pakistan, including: al-Qaeda, Hezb-e-Islami, the Afghan Taliban, the Pakistani Taliban, and Lashkar-e-Taiba. What would they do if they found out I had come here precisely to study how and why children joined extremist groups, the very root of anti-Americanism? Would I be kidnapped like David Rohde, except without the daring escape and the Pulitzer?

The security risks here made al-Shabaab's presence in Dadaab seem almost harmless by comparison. Less than a year ago a Western NGO worker had been force-fully pulled out of his security convoy, paraded around the street for a short while, and then shot dead. For no reason other than the color of his skin and his nationality. This execution had occurred in the middle of a refugee camp.

At ten o'clock in the morning.

Scores of other NGO workers had been targeted and killed in the bombing of the Pearl Hotel, just a few short blocks away from my own guesthouse.

I thought back to the words of my favorite Somali, "People are not evil. Society makes them so." Once again, like my jaunt through the off-limits refugee camp with my sixteen-year-old guide, I was trusting in the innate goodness of strangers.

The stewardess interrupted my thoughts with an offer of food or beverage, both of which I accepted. One benefit of spending so much time flying around the Middle East and its surroundings was the quality of the airplane food: fresh vegetables with little packets of olive oil and lemon juice, curries, tagines, fish in coconut sauce (yum), delicious kebabs, and fluffy chocolate and mango mousses. This was the menu in Coach Class—I can't even begin to imagine what it must be like in Business or First.

* * *

The Islamabad International Airport was renamed the Benazir Bhutto International Airport in June 2008 by Prime Minister Yusuf Raza Gilani. Bhutto was assassinated on December 27, 2007, in the middle of her campaign to become Prime Minister for the third time in her life. Previously she had been ousted from the government on corruption charges and had returned to the country after reaching a deal with then President Pervez Musharraf, who promised her amnesty against other pending corruption charges. After her death, her husband, Gilani, won the election (due almost exclusively to her popularity) and became Prime Minister.

As my plane approached Islamabad I could see very few lights from my window to indicate a thriving urban population, both due to severe electricity shortages in Pakistan and the fact that it was two o'clock in the morning. Once the plane had landed, we descended the rickety staircase to the tarmac and then waited for a bus to pick us up and drive us to immigration. The weather was cool and balmy, accented by a soft breeze that fluttered our *kurtas* and felt refreshing after being cooped up for the last few hours.

I was asked no questions by the clean-shaven and friendly looking immigration officer, who thus saved me from coming up with an intricate story to explain my presence in his country. I blame my easy entry on the idiot grin I made sure to put on when I handed in my passport. As to be expected in a tourist-unfriendly country, there were four immigration officers to deal with Pakistani passport holders and only one for the fifty or so foreigners (some of whom appeared to be planning on backpacking through the country). By the time I finally had my idiot grin captured on their Logitech camera (the same ones used by US Immigration Officers and likely a present of the US government), it was close to 3:30 AM.

After picking up my duffel bag and crossing the final gate, I felt relieved to see a young man holding up a placard with my name on it—only to realize he was accompanied by another more senior looking fellow and a police officer (whose black uniform and beret gave him a scary official look). My heart skipped a beat. Was I already in trouble? Had the government already found out why I was here? It turned out they had all been sent by Asmattullah, my friend's friend from Peshawar, to come get me at the airport and make sure I arrived safely in Peshawar. We were soon seated in a fifteen-year-old black Jeep with a cracked windshield and on our way, a journey that would take us approximately three hours.

As we zoomed past military roadblock after roadblock I felt grateful for the transportation my friend had arranged, the duty-free chocolates I had brought him seeming more and more inadequate as a gift.

The highway from Islamabad to Peshawar was wide and surprisingly free of potholes, and the countryside was a lush green, dotted with picturesque mud huts used to store grain and hay. We spent the drive joking, in English, about the Prime Minister's nickname when he had been the First Husband ("Mr. 10%", for his habit of taking a 10 percent cut of every business deal that took place in Pakistan as a bribe), lambasted George W. Bush, complained about the Pakistani people's unluckiness with politicians despite their own good and gentle nature, concluded how much hotter Indian actresses were than their Pakistani counterparts (their view), and exalted Musharraf as a great leader (who was likely to run again in two years).

As dawn illuminated the road, I was awed by the dump trucks that passed us by, each more striking than the next. They were adorned with vivid colors, including paintings of tigers, birds, and flowing verses of Urdu poetry, the artwork covering every available inch of the outside of the truck. I mentioned this to one of the men, who proudly told me that each owner would spend tens of thousands of dollars to make his truck look beautiful, a source of personal pride. We compared them to the unadorned semitrailers that lumbered past en route to Afghanistan, packed with valuable supplies for the US military. The men mentioned to me that a number of Blackwater contractors were in Peshawar; their offices were near my guesthouse and their presence was vehemently denied by the local government.

As we finally entered Peshawar around seven o'clock in the morning, I looked out the window and saw only men walking the streets, dozens of them jay-walking across the interstate, each and every one of them dressed in the flowing kurta-pajamas. The city itself was dirty, concrete, and depressing. One beautiful fort, the Bala Hisar Fort, built in its current incarnation in the nineteenth century, overlooked the entire city.

Our driver weaved in and out of side roads to reach the University Town residential area where my guest house was located. This section of the city was dotted with large mansions and beautiful walled gardens incongruous with the rest of the city, and my companions told me powerful military officers lived here. My guesthouse was far better than I had imagined, a fortified three-story building with a genial, all-male staff that spoke some broken English. The room that I would call home for the next few weeks was large and full of very old and very dusty furniture, including some heavy curtains that were hanging above my headboard. They looked as though they hadn't been cleaned in ages and I felt menaced enough by any insects potentially inhabiting them that I placed my head at the foot of the bed. I slept fitfully for three hours, plagued by dreams of home.

* * *

After my nap, I went downstairs to the lobby to wait for Fayaz. He ostensibly did not recognize me as a foreigner until I spoke out loud, and immediately requested to have chai in my room while we ironed out the details of his contract and my schedule. We agreed on $80 a day, much more than I would normally have paid a translator, but Fayaz claimed excellent credentials and an ability to navigate the maze that was Pakistan's regional government. He bragged to me that he was a Linguistics professor at the National University of Modern Languages and told me he held the equivalent rank of a Major in the Army because NUML was run by the Army. (In truth, I would later find out, Fayaz taught English as a second language and his equivalent rank was completely fictional.) A good "fixer," however, essentially a local that foreigners hire to get things done, is worth every penny of what was an exorbitant amount of money in Pakistan.

Fayaz (angered that the front desk staff had given him my room number without asking him who he was) complained about the lack of security at my guesthouse, and told me he preferred not to speak English with me in public so as not to attract attention to my foreign-ness. He also warned me against even thinking of leaving my guesthouse alone, even for a short walk to the convenience store next door, as I would attract too much attention and could be shot or kidnapped. I was also explicitly forbidden from taking out my camera to take pictures, as this would signal to the population that I was a foreigner in this city. The trick to surviving in Peshawar was to become invisible, a façade made easier by my kurta, beard, long dark hair, and tan. Indeed, in my entire time in Peshawar, I did not see a single foreigner in the streets.

Fayaz and I left the guesthouse and hailed a minuscule cab, rustier than the horse-driven carriages in Petra, so I could find an ATM to take out money and pay him. The city felt as though at war. Peshawar, in spite of the assurances of the three men who had picked me up at the airport, is only six kilometers away from the former North West Frontier Province. In these lawless tribal areas, Fayaz pleasantly pointed out, "We will both be killed—you because you're a foreigner and I because they'll accuse me of being an informant." The United States Consulate had been attacked again less than a month ago, and none of the diplomats unfortunate enough to be stationed here ever left the compound. Sections of the city, deemed "cantonments," were protected directly by the army, heavily fortified with barriers, and entered and exited through significant roadblocks. These cantonments included all the government buildings, officers' residences, the US consulate, and UN offices. These were the most heavily manned and most protected areas of the city, and thus, those most likely to be attacked.

The roads we drove on were fortified by multiple army checkpoints, all detailed with at least a dozen men with AK-47s and at least one machine gun mounted on a tripod. This first day I was constantly stopped by the military police while riding in taxis and rickshaws (a small three-wheeled vehicle that tops out at 20 mph), and was only saved the nuisance of having to pay constant bribes by the fact that Fayaz had an ID card that said he taught at an army college.

It was during this bank run that I discovered one of the city's most interesting contradictions, however. Even though Fayaz—despite his warnings against revealing my nationality—made the mistake of describing me to the bank workers as an American student who needed to withdraw money, everyone we encountered was extremely helpful. One man refused to let me exchange my dollars with him, directing me instead to a competitor who would give me a better rate. I was surprised at this friendly and hospitable treatment, as I knew that a large part of the population seethed with anti-Americanism. But none of this danger and aggression toward the United States affected the one-on-one conversations I had with tellers and bank managers, even when they could not profit from my business. They did not blame me for the policies of the United States and treated me far better than any bank teller would have in Cambridge, MA.

In the end, I tried three different banks, but the Peshawarian banks were unable to link to my US bank account. I was forced to call my mother and ask her to send me money through Western Union (the one company truly ubiquitous around the world).

After our unsuccessful bank run, we finally got in touch with Dr. Mehran, the contact who would help me get into the displaced persons camps, who told me to call him back in two hours. In the meantime we started strolling toward one of Fayaz's favorite restaurants. On the way, inspired by Anthony Bourdain's book about eating delicious street food around the world (which I had read on the flight), I made Fayaz stop so we could sit in a small bench at the back of a mango stand and eat authentic Pakistani street food. Our meal started with *golgappa*, fried pastry casings filled with chickpeas, which the eater dips into a spicy mix in cold water. As I bit into the first one, dripping with water, the taste was pleasant but funky. The owner of the mango stand kindly offered me a glass of tap water, which I politely declined, hoping to prevent dysentery. I then saw the owner's eight-year-old son dip the empty glass into an open bucket of water, filled from a tap on the wall, and give it to Fayaz. This was the same bucket of water that he would use three minutes later to wash the dishes, his hands, and the mango knife.

Fayaz happily gulped down half the glass and threw the rest back into the same multi-purpose bucket. As I started drinking the freshly made mango juice (fruity and delicious), I realized that the stall owner and his son probably used the same water to make it. The spicy water I'd been dipping the garbanzo puffs in? All the same water. I started sweating harder, my paranoia about getting seriously ill in a city with few modern health facilities exacerbating the 98 degree weather that was already stifling me in my long black kurta. I cursed Anthony Bourdain and his macho bullshit—of course the guy could eat on the streets of Cambodia; he had a whole camera crew and a producer with him, to say nothing of the Travel Channel's budget, which allowed for rushing him to the best hospital should anything go seriously wrong! I, however, was fucked. I had broken the cardinal rule of eating street food: Never drink anything with water and make sure whatever you eat is hot. It being too late now, I kept gulping down the *golgappa* and slurping away at my mango juice in front of the smiling Fayaz (who had offered to pay for this meal and who would be deeply offended if I didn't finish it) and the owner (who would also be offended if I didn't like his food).

After finishing the appetizer and politely refusing seconds, I saw the shawarma cook from next door coming over with our orders. No offense to my Jordanian friends, who I'm sure will be livid to hear this, but it was the best shawarma I had ever tasted. The bread was thick, warm, fluffy, and freshly made; the chicken marinated in a red curry sauce and topped off with onions and chutney; all drizzled with a delicious white mystery sauce that tasted strongly like mayonnaise from heaven. Best of all, it was piping hot, and thus unlikely to kill me.

This whole time I had been looking for an electronics shop where I could buy an adapter for my Blackberry charger, and after our meal I purchased a charger for seven dollars. The shop I bought the converter from was next to Peshawar's "most beautiful mall," a title Fayaz had proudly bestowed on a tiny two-story conglomeration of shops that no self-respecting thirteen-year-old girl would ever hang out in. To make things worse, it was almost pitch black inside.

Pakistan's biggest infrastructure problem is its inability to provide enough electricity to satisfy residential and commercial demand. The government had recently cut the number of working hours for government officials in Peshawar in order to reduce energy consumption. Both the men who picked me up at the airport and Fayaz complained about what a huge problem this presented. There was such an energy shortage that the city's single small mall did not receive enough electricity to keep its main lights on. In fact, major cities in Pakistan suffer from eight hours of brownouts a day, which is both a major infrastructure problem and a blow to national pride.

Rather than messing around with small aid projects in Pakistan and paying off the military, to the tune of over $2 billion dollars a year, the US—if it wants to win the hearts and minds of the people—should build power plants. Building the plants is relatively straightforward, and the results would be tangible for the average Pakistani, with urban centers across the country benefiting from the increase in available power. Rather than waste tax dollars on low-quality products gaudily stamped with the words USA in red, white, and blue, why not bring Pakistanis electricity? That cricket match you're watching? Thank the United States. The refrigerator that allows you to keep meat fresh longer than a day? Ditto. Hell, even the bedroom lights. It would be a constant reminder of our goodwill, and a tangible benefit of the country allying itself with America.

* * *

Next Fayaz and I headed over to one of the cantonments, ready to meet with the bureaucrats in charge of all refugees in Pakistan, almost all of whom are originally from Afghanistan. The thirty-minute drive to the refugee headquarters highlighted some of Peshawar's most interesting quirks. A preponderance of billboards and institutes advertised cheap and long-lasting hair transplants, each with the face of a C-list young male celebrity announcing how the transplants had changed his life. Fayaz confirmed that Pakistani men are very prone to hair loss, so much so that you would think this would be Rogaine's most profitable emerging market. Virtually no women were in the street at this hour, and the few exceptions wore the full *burka*. I continued to be amazed at the beautiful paintings that covered most buses and even three-wheeled rickshaws. The two most common designs on the back panel were a tiger or the face of Captain Sher Khan.

Karnal Sher Khan was an officer in the Pakistani Army during the Kargil conflict of 1999 against India on the Line of Control, the line that divides Kashmir between India and Pakistan. The conflict lasted two months and was caused by Pakistani soldiers and Kashmiri militants, funded by the Pakistani government, who infiltrated positions on the Indian side of the Line of Control and were fought back by the Indians. Khan, born in the Khyber-Pakhtunkhwa province, was posthumously awarded Pakistan's highest military honor, the Nishan-e-Haider, for the bravery he demonstrated during the Kargil battle. The twenty-nine-year-old Army officer apparently single-handedly killed over fifty Indian soldiers and defended five of the Pakistani Army's outposts. What is most astounding about this story is that the Indian Army, in 2009, recommended that the Captain be awarded the Nishar-e-Haider, their way of acknowledging what a tremendous warrior the young man was. The Pakistanis I met also claimed that he was such a respected officer that the Indian Army gave him a large ceremonial burial. In the paintings on the back of trucks and taxis he always appears bloody, holding his machine gun, his teeth bared. The image is a fitting representation of the city's character, as Pashtuns take great pride in their warrior history and the large security presence in Peshawar means you are rarely more than a few feet away from a machine gun in any public place.

We arrived at the Ministry for Refugee Affairs after passing only two military checkpoints, and wandered about in an airy crumbling building that had more plants per floor than entire office buildings in New York. My initial impression of Pakistanis as friendly and helpful was confirmed, as those we met did their best to help us bypass the regular approval procedures, which could take weeks. After being shuttled back and forth between some of the more junior staff, we finally arrived in the office of the Minister, only to be told by his male secretary that we needed to apply for permission first through the Home Secretary and then through the Minister. There then ensued an extended conversation in Urdu, of which I understood only the word "terrorism," and it was agreed that the next day we would go request permission and a security escort for our trips. Fayaz would later tell me that the Minister had refused to let us go into the camp without an escort, citing criminals and Taliban inside the camp who would be only too happy to kidnap or kill me.

Another twenty-minute rickshaw ride later and we arrived at another cantonment and began our long walk toward the compound that housed the military offices in charge of internally displaced persons. (Taxis weren't allowed inside any of the checkpoints, so we had to walk from that point onward.) Fayaz's officious manner was unsuccessful at getting us past the security gate, which was located next to a freshly painted old Indian tank that had been captured during the 1965 war, and I gingerly elbowed him aside to plead my own case. After convincing the security officers that I was in fact a student, I handed them my passport and student ID and waited an additional forty-five minutes while they cleared us. I took advantage of the wait to email my Dadaab contacts to ask whether they could put me in touch with anyone from the UNHCR in Peshawar.

The military police finally let us through, and we were escorted past low-rise buildings and expansive, vibrantly green fields with dozens of gardeners laboriously watering multi-colored flowers. The compound was even more escapist than I had envisioned, a lush paradise removed from the loud and dusty chaos that was Peshawar. We were escorted to an Officers' Club that was neither opulent nor run down, and met a friendly young captain in knee-high boots and fatigues who interviewed me briefly and then peppered Fayaz with questions about our relationship. Fayaz made a failed attempt at camaraderie by highlighting his stint as a professor in NUML, the military-run university in Peshawar, and his brother's job in the Air Force. What was most striking about this meeting was the level of respect Fayaz accorded the young captain, in spite of his low rank, based simply on his membership in the Pakistani Army, and the derision the captain exuded at Fayaz's decision not to join the Army. The Pakistani Army was clearly far more respected than the local government. The captain soon left us in the dark room—even here electricity was used sparingly—and returned thirty minutes later with the signature necessary to give me access to the Jalozai camp. One signature down, two more to go.

The next trip to the Ministry of Afghan Refugees would have to wait until tomorrow, though, as we had reached the magical hour of 4 o'clock, when every self-respecting civil servant pretends to work for an additional thirty minutes before heading home. Fayaz dropped me off at the guesthouse, and I was soon eating the worst chicken biryani of my life, with burnt rice, large cloves, and fatty chicken, made all the worse by warm raita, the yoghurt and cucumber sauce that is usually served chilled. My meetings that day had highlighted how different Pakistan was from the UN camp in Kenya. The day, which had begun so well, had left me with a feeling of exhaustion and dread, burdened by constant reminders of the violence that surrounded me. The guesthouse room, which had earlier seemed so much grander than its counterpart in Dadaab, felt dirty and oppressive, with dusty carpets and cigarette burns on the cheap couch. But despite my morose attitude, the day had been quite productive. After throwing away the chicken, I began the interminable wait alone in my room until nine o'clock the next morning, when Fayaz would come pick me up and I would be allowed out again.

* * *

As Fayaz had described it to me that morning, the local population classified the existing terrorist threat as three-fold. There exists the anti-USA/Pakistani government contingent, made up primarily of the Pakistani and Afghan Taliban, who have been strengthened, both financially and operationally, by al-Qaeda. The Durand line, the official border that separates Pakistan from Afghanistan, runs for over 1,600 miles and was initially established by Henry Mortimer Durand, the then British Foreign Secretary, in 1893. In reality, the border is porous enough, and the areas on both sides sufficiently autonomous, that there is no real distinction between the two countries. Cousins, and even brothers, live on opposite sides of the border, which they frequently cross. The former Northwest Frontier Province, located on the border with Afghanistan and now legally referred to as the Khyber-Pakhtunkhwa Province (though all of the license plates and signs on government buildings still refer to NWFP), and the refugee camps within it serve as ideal hiding places for criminals and terrorists alike. Peshawar itself is surrounded on its northern, eastern, and western borders by lawless territories ruled by very angry and very violent tribesmen who have been effectively independent of any central government since the British Mandate. (The only direction you could reasonably go toward, without expecting to be kidnapped or killed, would be south and then east, toward the capital.) Until very recently, Pakistan had been happy to leave these regions autonomous and let discontent fester unperturbed.

The second of the presumed terrorists, as defined by the locals, are the groups funded by the Pakistani government to fight against India. Not all of these groups can be controlled. (Pakistanis point to the 2008 Mumbai attacks as proof of their autonomy.) The most prominent among this group is Lashkar-e-Taiba, an Islamist militant organization created by Zafar Iqbal and Hafiz Muhammad Saeed in Afghanistan, which is now headquartered in Pakistan and is almost certainly supported by the ISI. Though the locals to whom I spoke assume (correctly, I imagine) that the ISI continues to fund almost all these groups, all echoed support for the continuation of this policy. Although most Pakistanis I spoke with readily admitted that it is precisely this type of funding of non-state actors that led to these groups' ability to wage terror in Peshawar, they praised the ISI fervently. As one fellow put it, "If it weren't for the ISI, these animals [the terrorist organizations] would have come into our houses and killed everyone! The [ISI is] doing a great job!" With all due respect to this gentleman, if it weren't for the ISI, these groups wouldn't exist in their current form. The relationship between non-state actors and the ISI has existed for many decades now, and was heavily utilized by the United States during the Cold War as the CIA funneled hundreds of millions of dollars to the mujahideen so that they could wage war against the Soviets in Afghanistan. (For more on this, I refer you to the excellent book *Charlie Wilson's War*, which is much better than the movie.)

The third contingent the Pakistanis mentioned, and the one least talked about internationally, is comprised of Indian-funded terrorist groups that operate in Pakistan, hoping to destabilize the government. Personally, if I were India the last thing I would want to do would be to further destabilize my neighbor, who at the moment has at least a few dozen nuclear weapons and hosts a number of terrorist groups that want nothing else than to wipe my major cities off the map. However, from the Pakistani view, since Pakistan funds terrorist groups against India, why wouldn't India fund terrorist groups against Pakistan? The possibility seems plausible enough when you think about it in those terms. Mind you, Pakistan abounds with conspiracy theories that cover a wide spectrum. My favorite is that the Russians are, or were, funding the Afghan Taliban to fight against the United States army after the American-led invasion of Afghanistan, to get back at us for doing the same thing to them in the 1980s. Again, it sounds perfectly plausible, the mark of a good conspiracy theory. My second favorite is that investors in Dubai fund terrorist attacks in Pakistan because it helps the Dubai Stock Exchange rise and keeps the Karachi Stock Exchange down, as investors flee Pakistan to invest in Dubai instead. This seems a little more farfetched.

Popular support for a lot of these terrorist groups, especially Osama bin Laden and al-Qaeda, was initially quite high, even after the September 11 attacks, and capitalized on the anti-American feelings in the area. To be fair, Pakistanis attribute a lot of these anti-American feelings to the 180-degree turn US foreign policy toward their country took after the Soviet Union fell apart. Throughout the Cold War, Pakistan was a staunch ally of the US, helping us defeat the Soviet Union in Afghanistan, and serving as an effective counterpoint to Soviet influence in the region, especially against India. However, once the Cold War was over, not only did the

US government stop giving aid to Pakistan, it went so far as to censure Pakistan for producing nuclear weapons (a program, developed in response to India's successful test of a nuclear weapon in 1974, which we had been aware of for years) and forced sanctions on the country. I imagine the Pakistanis felt used and abused at this point, akin to a scorned and discarded lover who had hoped for better treatment. These sanctions and our frosty relationship disappeared virtually overnight once the War on Terror began, with President George W. Bush famously stating, "President Musharraf, he's still tight with us on the war against terror, and that's what I appreciate." Given this history, it is difficult to blame the Pakistanis for being wary of our cooperation today, in the firm belief that our support of them is not sincere but rather rooted only in our national security concerns and will dry up as soon as the threat has evaporated.

However, even though a vibrant anti-Americanism still permeates Pakistani society (a 2010 Pew Research poll noted that close to 60 percent of Pakistanis view the US as an "enemy"), this anti-Americanism has not translated into higher support for all terrorist organizations. Rather, their public support has decreased substantially as they have rained terror on major cities. The same poll states that only 18 percent and 15 percent of Pakistanis have a favorable opinion of al-Qaeda and the Taliban, respectively. In fact, Pakistan has suffered extensive trauma from terrorist attacks within its own borders. In 2009 and 2010, over 4,700 terrorist, insurgent, or sectarian attacks were recorded. These attacks killed over 5,900 people and injured more than 9,500.

In those two years, 139 suicide bombings killed approximately 2,500 people. Needless to say, most people now support the Pakistani army's attempt to eradicate some of the terrorist groups in Swat and Waziristan and bring the former Federally Administered Tribal Areas (FATA) under its control.

* * *

In order to gain access to the refugee camps I needed three signatures from three distinct agencies, including the military signature I had already received. The agencies would then be able to provide security and transportation. I spent the next day driving back and forth between the Defense Colony, a protected enclave where rich people and some military officers lived, and the civilian offices of those in charge of Afghan refugees (which they estimated to number over 2.7 million).

The army in Pakistan, and especially in Peshawar, is omnipresent and all-powerful in many respects. Whereas the civilian offices had only a few roadblocks, some police, and dreary dark offices, the military compounds had extremely heavy security, far more luxurious offices, and vast, perfectly manicured lawns with beautiful flowers—an especially expensive proposition in such arid weather. In spite of the presence of computers, though, I had yet to find an office in which the computer was turned on, with all of the writing and signing of documents taking place on paper. The most senior bureaucrats, whose offices included perks like windows and air-conditioners, didn't even have computers on their desks.

Half of the men I met (I saw no women working at any of the offices I visited) had long beards, and the rest sported either groomed beards or trimmed mustaches. It was rare to see a clean-shaven face.

After eight hours of groveling and shuttling back and forth, I had little to show for my efforts except for a stern warning about the likelihood of my getting shot at or kidnapped inside the camps and a chastised Fayaz, who had been screamed at for taking me around Peshawar in an open taxi given how dangerous the city was. Another civil servant advised me not to leave the hotel at the same time every day and to vary my daily routine as much as possible.

One particular civil servant, with brilliant green eyes (not that uncommon in the region), and a young son with the fortune to have inherited them, had behind his desk a large black and white picture of a young man sitting in a chair. The young man was not particularly dark skinned, looked to be in his early twenties, and was sitting with one leg over the other, showing off a pair of shiny white lace-up shoes, which must have been all the rage sixty years ago, and perfectly manicured hands. He looked like a nice young man from the early twentieth century.

"Who is that?" I whispered to Fayaz. He looked at me incredulously, as though I were a complete dolt.

"Quaid-e-Azam, obviously."

Blank stare on my part.

"The founder of Pakistan!" he exclaimed.

"Oh!" Aha! I could finally stop staring at him stupidly, as I knew enough Pakistani history to know that another guy called Jinnah was also involved. "But why doesn't he have a picture of Jinnah instead?" I asked smugly, showing off my knowledge of his country's history.

"That *is* Muhammad Ali Jinnah. Quaid-e-Azam means greatest leader."

Ah yes, I was definitely back in the idiot category.

I was shocked. I had always imagined Jinnah as a hulk of a man, with a thick bushy mustache, hands that could crush a small man's skull, and army fatigues! *This* was the founder of Pakistan? This boy with pouty lips, a snazzy three-piece suit, and a manicure? This was the leader of a nation known, in part, for its aggression and violent ethnic divisions? He was the one who had the character to bring these factions together?

Muhammad Ali Jinnah was born in December 1876 in Karachi, Pakistan (then part of British India) to a rich family, and would go on to study law in England. (At age nineteen, he was the youngest Indian to be called to the bar.) After his father's business went into bankruptcy, he returned to British India, where he practiced law in the city of Bombay (today Mumbai) and became active in politics. He joined the Indian National Congress, then the largest Indian political organization, where he rose to prominence. Unlike Gandhi, Jinnah spoke mostly English, preferred to dress in Western clothing, and prophetically warned in 1920, upon his resignation from the Indian National Congress, that Gandhi's method of mass struggle could lead to divisions between Hindus and Muslims. Throughout his life he had been a great supporter of establishing a joint Muslim-Hindu state independent from Great Britain, and in 1934 he returned to Pakistan from a sojourn in London to head the Muslim League and became the first Governor General of Pakistan in August 1947. He would die one year later at the age of seventy-one after having established Pakistan as an independent Muslim state and overseeing one of the largest population migrations in history. (An estimated 12 million people were displaced during the partition of India and Pakistan, with up to one million people killed in the interim.) He is by far the most admired man in Pakistan, the reverence in which he is held being almost fanatical in nature.

I looked away from the picture and realized that the Pakistani kurta was different from the one I was wearing in more ways than I had previously noticed. In addition to having a proper shirt collar, the kurta also had sleeves that were identical to those of a dress shirt, with regular cuffs and buttons. The civil servant in front of me was even wearing French cuffs. The only difference between a kurta and a dress shirt was that Pakistani kurtas did not button all the way down and extended to the wearer's knees, like a dress. It is a creative merging of Western and local fashion concepts.

On the way back from his office, after a fruitless and extremely frustrating day, we passed by the remains of Kachagarhi camp, a former Afghan refugee camp. The government had recently forcefully resettled its population (50 percent to other camps, 50 percent back to Afghanistan), and the UNHCR had partially destroyed their makeshift homes so that no new tenants could move in. The refugees here had lived in small mud huts, rather than tents or huts made out of trash, and the ruins of the huts remained. I thought back to the twig walls and rusted tin roofs of Dadaab's dwellings and tried to imagine who lived better. If all went well, I would soon find out.

We passed by a Kentucky Fried Chicken that had been shut down, and Fayaz told me that in spite of its popularity the chain had been forced to close due to continued threats by terrorists. People had stopped going for fear of being bombed or targeted for patronizing a Western chain.

I commented to Fayaz that I was impressed my TV had cable, even a pirated version of HBO with commercial breaks.

"Ah yes, even I have hundreds of channels at home," he said. "But there is no cable in my village, or in the towns outside Peshawar."

"Well, that makes sense. They're poor and probably don't have any electricity, I imagine."

"Not just that," he retorted, "the politicians back the religious leaders, who do not allow cable in the villages. They think it is corrupting the population." This type of paternalism was common in Pakistan, where theaters were allowed to show violent and gruesome action scenes but heavily censored depictions of two people kissing.

For fun, I asked Fayaz if there were any bars in the city. Unamused, he answered that there were in fact none in Peshawar, and that there was only one coffee house in the entire city that the "upper class" frequented.

This type of comment had become an annoying characteristic of my translator, who constantly tried to portray himself as important and well-off in front of me. He also had the habit of chewing loudly with his mouth open, throwing trash out of moving vehicles, and every now and then rubbing the sleeves of my kurta between his thumb and forefinger, as though implicitly criticizing the material. The last two days in particular had been spent in bureaucratic hell, crisscrossing Peshawar as we traveled between government offices, both civil and military, all in the hopes of gaining access to the camps and the protection of a security convoy. I was already looking forward to a weekend break without Fayaz, although I couldn't possibly imagine what I would do stuck in my room for forty-eight hours straight.

Finally back in my room I took stock of how much my living situation had deteriorated. The bed sheets were stained (they had always been stained, but I had only begun to mind it today), and it seemed that making the bed (i.e., putting the translucent sheet that was given to me on top of the ultra-thin sheet that covered the mattress) was not part of housekeeping duties, although I was secretly glad no one was overtly entering my room while I was away. Obviously the one towel I had was never going to be exchanged for a new one. And then, just as I was lying down in bed to zone out for a few hours, the last straw occurred:

I saw a bed bug on my sheets. The moldy old curtains and decrepit mattress was probably teeming with them.

The Pearl Continental, bomb blasts or not, looked infinitely more appealing at this moment.

* * *

The food at the guest house had gotten exponentially worse since my arrival until it was bad to the point of comedy. Confined to my room after Fayaz dropped me off in the late afternoon until he came by the next day, I was forced to eat it every night. Hence, these first few days, I had selected for all dinners and snacks the most edible item on the guest house menu, their gruesome club sandwich. This sandwich was a concoction of ultrathin untoasted white bread with cucumbers, mayonnaise that tasted as though it had been doctored with sugar, three small pieces of chicken, and some sad, soggy fries. The ketchup also tasted as though the cook had poured a few packets of Sweet n' Low into the bottle to shake things up.

These stomach-roiling experiences with Western food in Pakistan were not limited to the guest house. Every official I had visited over these past few days had been kind enough to offer me lukewarm tea, in spite of the fact that most of their offices lacked air-conditioning and we were all sweating through our shirts in 100 degree weather. I had been told that drinking a hot beverage in scalding weather cools you off, but in my experiences this idea was absolutely untrue; if anything, you sweated a little more profusely while you drank the tea and then went back to your usual slow roast.

Why had the sub-continentals first started drinking tea? Likely because their countries had been colonized by the British, who most likely continued their tea-drinking tradition in spite of the sweltering heat. I imagined that in those days drinking tea became associated with prestige, something the wealthy foreigners did, and the colonized man emulated them. I had asked Fayaz why so many of the billboards in Peshawar were written in English, instead of Urdu (the national language) or Pashto (the local dialect), to which he had replied, "Because it looks prettier than Urdu. Plus, the upper classes all speak English, and people want to feel like they are part of the upper class."

Why would people continue to drink a steaming hot beverage when already their country felt like a sauna? Probably because it still made them feel refined, even if they secretly hated the taste of tea. And why did I believe the locals secretly hated the taste of tea? Because virtually all the tea I had been served had too much milk and a heart-stopping amount of sugar. The extremely sweet, milky, and lukewarm mixture resembled nothing like a good cup of tea.

This was one of the quite probably idiotic theories that had come to me during one of the many interminable hours I spent cooped up in my room, either hoping to fall asleep or waiting for Fayaz to come pick me up.

After having spent the last two days shuttling between painfully inefficient offices, and being heavily reprimanded for appearing in public so often by some of the bureaucrats, I decided to spend the next morning at the UNHCR headquarters while Fayaz went back to get our travel permits. Although we had finally received the dual military permits necessary to visit the IDP camps in Jalozai, Fayaz was told that I was denied access to the Afghan refugee camps for security reasons: a local NGO worker (one of many that year) had been kidnapped the day before. The view was that if a local had been kidnapped, then a foreigner, even dressed in a dashing Pakistani outfit, stood no chance of surviving.

Fayaz called Nasir, my contact at the UNHCR, to relay the news. Nasir, seeing how upset I was, offered to put me in touch with other non-governmental organizations in the area so that I could bypass official channels and ride with them to the camps, taking advantage of their existing security convoys and permits. I immediately took him up on the offer, surprised that he was willing to be so accommodating. I was grateful and suspicious at the same time. (I had become far more paranoid since I had arrived.)

Prior to Fayaz's unpleasant phone call, I had been studying the history of the Afghan refugee program in Pakistan. There have been three broad migrations of Afghan refugees to Pakistan: in the 1970s due to the conflict with the USSR; in the 1990s due to the Taliban and civil war; and in 2002-03 due to the American-led invasion of Afghanistan. The UN estimates that over the past twenty-five years approximately one third of the Afghan population became refugees at one point, and that Pakistan has hosted between 5 and 7 million Afghans and Iran 3 to 4 million.

Given the cultural similarities between Afghan Pashtuns and Pakistani Pashtuns (they're indistinguishable to a foreigner), Pakistan had an open-door policy when the first Afghan refugees started coming over the border in 1970, fleeing the Soviet Union's scorched-earth policy and the firebombing of entire villages. Even today, Pakistan, unlike Kenya, does not have an encampment policy and

Afghans are allowed to work and live outside designated camps. In many cases, Afghans provide cheap labor and take on odd jobs. Refugee children are even allowed to attend public schools, so long as space is available. (Although all this sounds too good to be true, key sources verified this access policy.)

To understand the scope of the refugee migration and the challenges it engenders, take note that the BEfAR Program (Basic Education for Afghan Refugees), remains the largest refugee education project in the world. The Afghan schools within the refugee camps do not follow the Pakistani curriculum, but rather a version of the Afghan curriculum that was appended in the 1980s by researchers at the University of Nebraska, Omaha. In fact, many of these camps were heavily funded by the United States in the 1980s, when they were used as training and staging grounds for the mujahideen fighting against the Soviet Union in Afghanistan. The Soviet Union was forced to withdraw from Afghanistan by February 1989, and by the early 1990s, after the USSR had collapsed and in combination with donor fatigue, funding began to dry up quickly for the Afghan refugee program. By 1995, food rations to the refugees were stopped and Afghans were forced to fend for themselves. There are divergent opinions as to the effect this had on the refugee population, with some UNHCR employees stating it had little effect and others arguing it was crippling to these societies. Either way, the end of US funding made it more likely that refugee children would be taken out of school earlier to provide for their families. Girls are taken out of school even earlier than boys, with the largest drop-out occurring after the first and second years of education, when the girls become old enough to start helping around the house.

Initially, Afghans refused to send their daughters to school, both because there had been no schools for girls in Afghanistan and because of serious security concerns. Today, approximately 31 percent of students are girls, a percentage that drops to a depressing 8 percent by the sixth grade. Even more discouraging is the concept of *amaanat*, which was described to me as the idea that your daughter is not really your child, as it is just a matter of time before she gets married and becomes part of another family. Essentially, she is "borrowed" until she gets to her "real home," that of her husband. Consequently, parents are not incentivized to invest in their female children, which leads to the boys in the family receiving more food, better clothes, and more education. A large percentage of refugee girls are married between the ages of eleven and twelve. In the Federally Administered Tribal Areas (FATA), the area where most Afghan refugees have settled, literacy rates are the lowest in the country, with female literacy hovering around 5 percent.

The prayer call startled me from my research, and Nasir came into the room to drive me back to my guesthouse. Unlike in Jordan, it was common in Peshawar to see private and public employees pray after each call, wash their hands and feet (ablutions), face Mecca, and place their foreheads to the mat.

At the guesthouse I met Fayaz, who looked delighted that we could go to Jalozai on Monday and Tuesday. As for the Afghan refugee camps to which I had been denied access, the ministry had graciously offered to transport a few teachers and students to the civil offices so I could interview them there. Fayaz looked positively charmed with himself for having secured this offer.

I, however, was furious. Months of background research, clearing tremendous safety and bureaucratic hurdles at Harvard, putting my life at risk just by being here, and alienating my parents with my stubbornness and high risk tolerance—all for nothing. Not seeing the camps and having the government pick and choose who I could speak with was as good as never coming here in the first place; the research would be worthless. I needed to get to the camps.

In the back of my mind a small voice urged caution. I had spent the day working in an empty office, the walls of which were covered by pictures of UN employees who had been targeted by terrorists and had given up their lives while trying to help Peshawar's Afghan refugees. I began to worry, as I became more agitated with Fayaz for his almost total failure as a fixer, that I wasn't accurately measuring the very real danger I was putting myself in. Maybe I wasn't thinking clearly anymore, my brains addled after what felt like weeks cooped up in my increasingly unbearable room, which had still not been cleaned and had taken on the stench of a high school locker room.

Before I could get a word out, Fayaz complained about what a long day he'd had, saying he was tired. This was too much for me, my temper exacerbated by his snobby attitude and nonchalance over the failings of the past two days.

"You're tired? You're tired!" I shouted at him. "I've spent months preparing this trip, getting the visas, developing the contacts, putting my life in danger by showing my silly foreign face all around town, all for nothing! What was the point of coming all the way over here if I can't even visit the camps!"

Fayaz blanched at my anger.

"And we're not going to Jalozai on Monday, we're going tomorrow!"

"But what about security?" Fayaz asked, worried and confused.

"Fuck security! We'll show up, show the two documents, and ask for a cop to follow us around."

"But how will we get to Jalozai without a security convoy?"

"We're taking a fucking cab, Fayaz, that's how. Call the guy from your village who drives a taxi, tell him we're hiring him tomorrow."

Was I being irrational? Absolutely. Was I putting both our lives in danger? Definitely. But I felt that once I was back in the camps, surrounded by all those children I had come to care about so desperately, I would feel centered again. I would refocus on what was important, the reason I had come all this way in the first place.

"Why can we not go on Monday and Tuesday instead?" Fayaz continued.

"Because I'm going to go visit other refugee camps with some NGOs—unofficially, of course."

Fayaz looked as though I had just punched him in the groin.

Upon seeing this reaction, I told him, "Don't worry, you're not coming. My friends said they didn't have any room in the convoy." In fact, I had only been told that I would not need a translator and I easily could have asked for a spot for Fayaz. I just wanted a break from his ineptitude, his snobbery, his constant fearfulness. He looked even worse now, sweating profusely in the air-conditioned room and mumbling.

"What did you say?" I asked.

"So you will not be needing me on these days, then?" he asked, as reality slowly dawned on him.

"Nope."

"But . . . but I stayed in Peshawar for you! I could have been in Lahore for the summer!"

So that was why he had looked so grief-stricken! His foreign golden goose had stopped laying dollars and the dreams he had of making close to $1,000 disappeared. I felt sorry for him, but I was tired of his bullshit and inability to get things done. He had advertised himself as an all-powerful "fixer," like local Vaseline. But nothing had been greased, and more and more I felt like he was an impediment to my research here. Both military permits to Jalozai had been received thanks to my contacts, and how good could those possibly be? His famed Rolodex had yielded us zilch.

And then he said something quite unexpected.

"But, Francisco, if anything happens to you on Monday or Tuesday, the first person the police is going to come looking for is me! I'm going to be held responsible for your safety if anything happens. They're going to think that I planned it!"

Though he was quite comfortable talking about something awful happening to me, he was frantic at the thought of the potential repercussions for him. I was too flabbergasted to become angrier at him and simply sat there, mouth wide open in shock.

"You have to understand," he continued, "we have applied for permission jointly with the government, so they think I am going to be with you the entire time!"

After more protesting on his part, it emerged that Fayaz wanted a letter stating that he was no longer employed. "I would still be working with you; this is just in case anything happens."

I explained to him that letter or no letter, if anything happened to me he would still be the first person to be arrested and tortured for information. He remained unconvinced, and I agreed to type and print out the letter, on the understanding that I was terminating his employment in its totality, after he promised to go to the Ministry one last time on Monday.

Now that his salary depended on us getting access to the camps, he became more creative and offered to try and bribe one of the bureaucrats. But it was too little, too late. I told him that I had already secured access to the camps in Peshawar, and that what I really needed was access to Shamshatoo.

Shamshatoo, the most dangerous camp in Peshawar, is an independent camp that takes no outside funds, permits no NGO or Pakistani presence, and is run by Gulbuddin Hekmatyar and Hezb-i-Islami. Gulbuddin Hekmatyar is one of the original mujahideen funded by the CIA and the Pakistani ISI to fight against the

Soviets. In 1975 he founded Hezb-i-Islami, which initially grew out of the Muslim Youth Organization, a group that had been founded earlier in Kabul by students as a means of countering Communist influence in their country. He played a leading role in the Afghan civil war after the defeat of the Soviet Union (he was Afghanistan's Prime Minister in 1993, 1994, and 1996), and since the US-led invasion of Afghanistan has fought viciously against US troops there. In February 2003, the State Department gave him the notorious designation of Specially Designated Global Terrorist, inducting him into a group populated with people like Osama bin Laden and Ayman al-Zawahiri (al-Qaeda's Number Two). The original Hezb-i-Islami party split in 1979, and the United States now makes the distinction between Hezb-i-Islami Gulbuddin (HIG) and Hezb-i-Islami, which is a political party in Afghanistan.

Dr. Mehran, my contact for the camps in Jalozai, arrived in the room shortly after I had finished typing and signing the letter for Fayaz. After a brief introduction (it was the first time we had met), he quickly called the principal of a primary school in Jalozai and arranged for me to visit six classes on Saturday and afterward meet with a group of teachers there. Tired of the room service food, I asked him to accompany me outside to buy some food from the market nearby. He asked me if I left the guesthouse at night, laughed, and told me it was a very good idea to stay inside if I didn't want to get kidnapped. "Why don't you just order a pizza? We have Pizza Hut in Pakistan!"

Images of a thin crust super supreme flooded my senses, infinitely more delicious than the soggy fries and sugary sandwiches to which I had gotten accustomed.

Mehran gladly called Pizza Hut for me from his cell phone, and asked me, "Which one do you want to order?"

"Super supreme!"

Silence on the other line.

"Umm... they have chicken tikka, fajita, or veggie."

Images of greasy pepperoni faded fast as I realized that, Pizza Hut or not, I was still in a Muslim country that didn't serve pork. "Chicken fajita!"

Forty minutes and $5.75 later, I received an individual-sized pizza with chunks of chicken embedded with hot pepper seeds (*really* hot pepper seeds), green peppers, and onion. Three slices into the six-slice pizza my stomach began to feel queasy, and within three hours it seemed I had finally contracted a tourist's greatest enemy: traveler's diarrhea.

Diarrhea or not, tomorrow I was finally getting to the camps, and I was thrilled beyond belief. Little did I know that I was heading toward my first death threat of the trip.

* * *

I groggily woke up to heavy banging on my door, only to find Fayaz smiling at my entryway; I thought he was showing up at 8 and he thought we had agreed on a 7 AM departure. I could feel the three hours of sleep weigh on my eyelids, and took a hurried cold shower. (Did I forget to mention that there was no hot water in the guesthouse?) Jalozai turned out to be thirty minutes away, rather than the ninety minutes Fayaz had advertised (probably to get a higher fee for the driver, who would then pay off Fayaz).

"Oops! That is because I was estimating the time differential with public transport!" he feigned.

We had never taken public transportation and it had been clear from the beginning that we would be hiring a taxi. My anger at being so brazenly overcharged evaporated almost immediately, however, as I stared out the window and once again saw the familiar blue and white UN emblem on the plastic coverings that served as walls in the camp. From the car I could see the tops of tents, hundreds upon hundreds of them stretching as far as the eye could see. This is what I had expected Dadaab to look like, a transient place for people who expected to go home.

Jalozai was initially established in the early 1980s as an Afghan refugee camp, and held up to 70,000 refugees at its peak. After the US-led invasion of Afghanistan in October 2001, the Pakistani Government founded an additional camp next to it, commonly referred to as New Jalozai, to accommodate the influx of Afghan refugees. After the fall of the Taliban, however, most of these refugees returned home or were forcefully relocated by the Pakistani Army, which then closed down Old Jalozai (in part at the request of the United States). Jalozai today serves exclusively as an internally displaced persons (IDP) camp for the Pakistanis who were displaced by the Army's incursion into the Swat and Bajaur provinces. Virtually all of the two million-plus displaced persons from Swat have returned home (a success of which the Pakistani Government is rightly proud). Jalozai currently holds upward of 100,000 displaced persons, mostly from the province of Bajaur. One of the displaced Bajauris explained to me: "We were all initially supportive of the Taliban. But then they started killing us and attacking us from one side, and then the Pakistani Army started firebombing our villages from the other side. We were squeezed out and forced to come live here."

I was startled to see a group of women in full burkas pass us by, casually carrying heavy loads on their heads and shoulders under the relentless attention of the scorching sun. I saw a number of small children with the stunning honey-colored skin and brilliant green eyes that characterizes some Afghans. They were some of the most beautiful people I had ever seen, with breathtaking features.

"I thought the Afghans were forced out. So why are there so many still here?"

"They're not Afghans, Francisco. They're Pakistanis from the tribal areas, the border regions. They look the same."

"You mean Pakistani women also wear the full burka?"

"In these villages they do," replied Fayaz. "Some people have suggested that Pashtun women must wear the burka because they are so beautiful, you know?"

This rationale made me nauseous, both because it exonerated men from their actions since they "couldn't control themselves in front of such beautiful women" and chastised the women for being beautiful, something over which they had no control.

My stomach ache worsened and, still regretting the chicken fajita pizza decision of the night before, I looked for the closest possible bathroom. We continued to drive past multiple signs designating the different blocks, and showed our military documentation at the entrance to Section 6. We were assigned a guard with a gun, and then got out of the car to meet the camp administrator. After accepting his offer for tea in the 100 degree weather (mine without milk or sugar, which always elicited a laugh), I asked for the nearest restroom.

I was directed to what would most accurately be described as a hole in the ground inside a wooden tool shed—as to be expected in the middle of a refugee camp. Only after I had squatted and relieved myself did I realize that nowhere in the outhouse was there any toilet paper, just a bucket with water. I had been warned about this common practice but had never encountered it until now. I will spare you the details of this moment, but afterward I finally understood why the left hand is so taboo at the dinner table in many societies.

I waddled back to the impromptu meeting and asked what everyone was laughing about. They had been laughing at our policeman, who had apparently never shot the gun he had been assigned. *This* was the security everybody had been so adamant I get?

The camp administrator gave me a quick summary of camp statistics (10 policemen, 150 local guys with guns, 22,449 families, 111,452 individuals, and 17 schools) and informed me that the camp had no electricity. The camp administration offices were made up of dilapidated tents and surrounded by barbed wire, which I was told was to protect the only generator in the camp. On the way to the school, we passed the marketplace, teeming with people and filled with far more stalls than Dadaab, including loads of fresh fruits and vegetables. Being located near a city, rather than in the middle of nowhere in Kenya, obviously paid off.

The schools in Jalozai, however, made Dadaab look like real luxury. There were no real classrooms, only white tarps held up by long wooden sticks of uneven sizes. Each tent had only one small chalkboard, and although the official student to teacher ratio was 1 to 45, the social studies teacher taught 150 students at once, three grades at the same time. There was no food program, and classes ran only from 8 AM to 12 PM. The only positive, and shocking, statistic was that the textbook to student ratio was 1 to 1. UNICEF and the Pakistani government had coordinated their actions so that every child was given a bag with textbooks, notebooks, and writing utensils. Out of the 100 or so students I met that day, all of them sitting cross-legged on the ground, all of them had textbooks in front of them. In addition, all of the teachers had gone through the one-year formal teacher training program, a requirement in order for them to be teachers in the camp.

This did not mean, however, that they were good teachers. The Pakistani teaching methodology was based on rote memorization, not on understanding, and thus the teachers practiced this outdated teaching methodology. The easiest way for them to "teach" the students was to force them to chant, in unison, new concepts over and over again until they had been memorized.

What was incredible about this camp, and all of the camps I had visited thus far, was that in spite of the failings of the educational systems and the extraordinary challenges faced by the educators, these camps presented an incredible opportunity to educate properly the children they housed. As a teacher mentioned, "You know what is good about this is that in Bajaur these girls did not get an education. Here, even if they drop out after one or two years, at least they have been exposed to more knowledge than they would have been back home. Maybe they will even form a school for their daughters."

His comment reinforced an opinion I had been developing for some time: These temporary and long-term crises that brought so many people so close together presented an invaluable opportunity for the United States to educate and instill our values in a rural population. These are populations that have historically been too dispersed, too far removed from cities, or simply too ignored by their own governments to receive any education. During crises, however, these populations often live close together for months and even years, providing an opportunity to educate and influence large swaths of people who were previously unreachable. Imagine a program in which skilled teachers taught refugees from radical populations (from countries such as Somalia, Afghanistan, Pakistan) some of the values associated with a well-rounded education and consistent with our beliefs.

Once these refugees are able to return to their rural villages, they will carry with them these new ideas—ideas that will help minimize the ideological space for extremism to flourish. A broader understanding of the world and the differences that exist in it could only mitigate the threat of radicalization in (mostly) Muslim villages around the world. Islam is a religion that espouses patience, mercy, and tolerance, values that can be taught to refugee children in a culturally sensitive way. Yes, refugee and IDP children are a tragedy, but they also represent a latent opportunity to curb anti-Americanism in the most troubled regions—the regions that typically provide al-Qaeda and its allies with its most willing recruits.

* * *

I stepped into the tent and introduced myself to the male children. The schools were not co-ed, and only female teachers could teach the girls. The boys regarded me with suspicion and fear—until I smiled. A few of them giggled and most of them smiled right back. Then I began with the first and second graders, asking them who they admired (a difficult concept to grasp made almost impossible through Fayaz's translation), and heard Quaid-e-Azam a few times, along with a few famous cricket players. Cricket is Pakistan's national sport. The children all wanted to grow up to be teachers, doctors, and, as in Dadaab, pilots. It seemed the draw of flying away from all of this misery was a common theme among refugee children.

The real shock came when I asked them what their favorite subject was. "English!" they yelled, virtually all at once. English was the overwhelming favorite for older boys and even girls, who I interviewed next, although Islamic Studies came a close second with females. The girls were in general far more religious than their male counterparts, and a number of the girls stated that they wanted to become religious scholars when they grew up. Interestingly, the place of female scholars in Islam, especially in the study of the *hadiths* (the sayings and actions of the Prophet Muhammad, which are used frequently as a basis for Islamic law), has been important since the death of the Prophet, as his wives played a major role in recording and explaining *hadiths*. When I asked if I could take a picture of the refugee girls, they all yelled, "No!" I deferred to their wishes, but, curious, asked them why not. I had taken pictures before of female Muslim students. "Because it's a sin," a few of the girls replied, their peers nodding in agreement. In fact, most of the girls who wanted to be religious scholars mentioned "entry into heaven" as their main motivator. It was clear that religious indoctrination, and the consequent fear of being a bad Muslim, began very early in this society.

Afterward, I spent a few hours speaking with the teachers, who told me that most boys dropped out to go help their parents work in the big cities, either begging or doing menial jobs. Although most girls married between the ages of fourteen and sixteen, after age ten their movement became heavily restricted and they were not allowed to leave their houses alone. Although this is purportedly for security purposes, it seems to contribute to a vicious cycle of rape and violence in the community in which men charge that any girl out alone and not fully covered by the heavy *burka* is tempting them.

I asked the teachers whether they had problems with idle youth, who appeared to be less numerous here than in Dadaab, since as Pakistanis they were allowed to look for jobs. The teachers confirmed that they weren't as big of an issue, and I followed up with questions about Taliban recruitment in the camp, especially in relation to young men who were unemployed. They responded that, although most of the refugees had supported the Taliban, they had been driven from their homes precisely because of this hospitality, their communities pummeled by US drone strikes, Taliban attacks in the community against the Pakistani government, and then the Pakistani army incursion. Now, almost all of the refugees professed their hatred of the Taliban because of the civilian casualties it had inflicted on their communities, and the teachers said that there was no recruitment in this camp, in part bolstered by the presence of the ISI in Jalozai.

Before leaving I told the teachers to ask me any questions they had, encouraging them to ask me anything. After a few generic questions about my background and research study, they set their sights on a far more personal subject. "Well, we all really like you, and we think you are a very nice man and think what you are doing is very good," Fayaz translated, "but we want to know if you will do *kalma*?"

"*Kalma*?" I asked.

"You know, *la illaha illa Allah*, become Muslim," Fayaz explained.

The *kalma* refers to the statement, *"La illaha illa Allah, wa Muhammad rasoolu Allah,"* which translates roughly to, "There is no God but Allah, and Muhammad is his Prophet." The *shahada* refers to the declaration of your belief in the Islamic religion. Converting to Islam is a straightforward process: All it requires is for you to recite the *kalma* once, truly believing it, either alone or in front of others. One single honest repetition is all that is required to become a Muslim.

"Because that way you can go to Heaven," Fayaz finished translating for the teachers.

I was flattered that they liked me enough to try and convince me to convert to Islam and save my soul. Religion was a defining characteristic of their lives, and since it was very clear to them that I was an infidel, they truly believed I would burn in hell. I tried tactfully to explain to them that I had been raised Catholic, opting to omit my own internal struggles with my religion after the most recent pedophilia scandals and the Vatican's disgusting response to them, and thanked them for their concern. They seemed genuinely disappointed, but all gave me warm farewells.

As I left the camp, the children swarmed me, jostling to get close, all smiles now. Although they were beautiful and wonderful kids, they were not as well off as the refugee children in Dadaab. They were much dirtier, both their faces and bodies; their clothes were ragged and ripped; and they were all a little thinner and shorter than their African counterparts.

As Fayaz and I left the group and approached the car, an older and visibly angry man approached us. The inexperienced policeman tensed up as the stranger got closer and started screaming at us. The man calmed down a bit, and after an intense ten-minute conversation in Pashto between the man and Fayaz, punctuated by more yelling and finger-pointing my way, we finally boarded the car.

"What did he say?" I asked Fayaz.

"Not now. Not here," he grimaced.

Before we drove away, the man approached us again with another few heated pronouncements to make. He banged the window, and pointed at me again. We finally drove off, Fayaz sweaty and pale from the encounter. Once out of the camp and back on the main road, Fayaz explained, "He said he wanted to burn everything around him to the ground, including all the foreigners. The second time around he said he wanted to burn you to ashes." He exhaled, calming down a bit. "Thank God that is over! I was so worried about visiting Jalozai camp that I could not sleep at all last night!"

* * *

Pakistani, and especially Pashtun, hospitality is famous for its sincerity and expansive nature. I didn't need a fixer in Peshawar, I needed a friend. Nasir, my contact at the UNHCR, had become that friend, breaking through the impenetrable red tape of the Pakistani bureaucracy, and using his own connections to bolster my case. Now that he was on my side, Fayaz and I parted ways for good that afternoon. It turned out that Nasir was good friends with Fazal Rabbi, the deputy in charge of education at the Ministry for Afghan Refugees. Nasir and Fazal were both rotund and sported thin black moustaches above their slender lips. Fazal was always impeccably dressed in a shining white kurta with gold cufflinks and maintained an air of bureaucratic importance. Unlike Nasir, however, he had succumbed to one of the many billboards in Peshawar and had lacquered black hair that sprouted from his scalp in perfectly symmetrical rows. Nasir was more jovial, although he was constantly preoccupied and could at times withdraw during a conversation as yet another worry crept into his balding head. Nasir and Fazal invited me to dinner, saving me from the torture of another guesthouse club sandwich, and we went out to Shiraz, one of the more famous restaurants in Peshawar.

The restaurant was housed in a tall two-story building off the side of the main highway, its shiny white façade dulled by years of heavy dust storms. We parked in the small lot that ran in front of the restaurant and got out of Fazal's white pick-up truck. As we walked toward the entrance, I didn't think twice about the metal detector and guards posted at the door. The restaurant was divided into three sections: a buffet room upstairs, which was very popular and almost always fully booked; a ground floor section for families; and the main dining room, where we sat, which was populated exclusively by men. The food was inexpensive (my hosts refused to let me pay), plentiful, and delicious. We ordered two kinds of fatty, spicy, roasted mutton, which we ate with our hands, a mouthwatering chicken *biryani*, homemade *nan* bread, a buttery and dark red chicken curry, tender kebabs with a refreshing yoghurt sauce, and homemade *raita*. I enjoyed myself immensely, in spite of the long silences and difficulty understanding Fazal, but I pitied the young unmarried men around us, conscious of their inevitable sexual repression from living in a conservative society where socializing between the sexes was so frowned upon.

During our dinner there were two short power outages, common at night in Pakistan, but it only took a few seconds for the restaurant's generator to kick in. I could imagine the havoc electricity shortages must wreak on large factories and government ministries. Perhaps this was the reason federal employees weren't fond of using their computers.

On the ride back I lamented to myself that I could not see the stars in the Peshawar sky, covered as it was by pollution, and thought back to Dadaab, cradled under a breathtaking pitch black sky dotted with hundreds of brilliant stars, and the children I had met there. Were *they* better off, in spite of being forced to remain in the camp and live in that stifling, desolate place? They certainly looked healthier and better cared for. By not having an encampment policy, was the Pakistani government allowed to wash its hands of the problem? Instead of doing more, could the Pakistani government simply expect the Afghan refugees to find work and support their families?

I remembered a discussion I had had earlier that day at my guesthouse. Blake had offered to put me in touch with a middle-aged doctor, Usman, who worked in the internally displaced persons camps, and after emailing each other back and forth a few times while I was in the US, Usman had come to my guest house that day to introduce himself. He had done most of his research on health issues that affected the displaced persons, and we both deplored the existing situation. Because he had been my initial primary contact in Peshawar and had recommended Fayaz, I explained to him how worried Fayaz had been about his liability with the ISI should anything happen to me. At this mention of the intelligence service, Usman replied, "Yes, they probably called him to warn him. They've already contacted me and asked me what you were doing here."

I was stunned. Not by the fact that the ISI had questioned one of my contacts here—after all, few foreigners ever came to Peshawar in general and refugee camps were a sensitive subject in particular. Rather, I was stunned that the intelligence service had contacted Usman out of all people. I had never met Usman until that afternoon, had spoken to him on the phone only once, and had depended on other contacts in Peshawar for transportation and security clearances. The only real exchanges we'd had had been over email. I immediately developed a newfound respect for the ISI, an organization I had previously considered brutish and outdated. My emails and text messages were obviously being monitored.

I mentioned this realization to Nasir, who was driving. "Oh, yes, I'm actually good friends with the agent in charge of all the guesthouses in Peshawar. I'm sure he'll be calling me any day now to ask about you. They're probably watching you." I felt oddly, and probably stupidly, comforted by this notion of an invisible protector.

I still couldn't imagine what the ISI had said to Fayaz. No wonder he had been so spooked.

Back at the guesthouse I ordered some black tea to help with digesting the massive dinner, and was cranky but unsurprised to receive chai with lukewarm milk instead. I poured it out, not bothering to complain, and heard a rap at my door. Surely it couldn't be the waiter, who had just come in. I figured if it was someone who had come to kidnap me or someone from the ISI, they would both get in anyway, so I gingerly opened the door. I found the night manager, sweaty and nervous, tremblingly holding a copy of his resume complete with his picture (a common addition in developing countries) and informing me that he would return in fifteen minutes to talk. I assumed he wanted some professional advice, and I made a few brief comments on his resume, trying to help him make it more professional. Once he returned, I sat him down and tried to go through the suggestions with him. But it became clear that he was wholly uninterested in my opinion of his resume. Instead he said, "I see a lot of people from UNHCR coming here. You get me a job there?"

I tried to explain that I had no influence at the UN-HCR, but encouraged him to fix the resume and hand it to Nasir next time he came by. He left disillusioned, to say the least, and I doubted he would ever find the courage to hand it to Nasir directly. The mutton grumbled uncomfortably in my stomach and I spent a painful, sleepless, and sweaty night trying to digest it. Dinner had been so delicious, though, that the stomach problems were well worth it.

* * *

Nasir had arranged for me to attend a celebration for World Refugee Day at an Afghan refugee primary school the next day. On the way over we drove next to an irrigation canal full of dirty brown water, where children from the slums and Afghan refugee children who lived nearby swam to cool off. A tiny compound surrounded by mud walls housed the school of over five hundred students. Inside there were no classrooms, only tents. Children sat cross-legged in the dirt as their professors struggled to teach them with a tiny and crumbling blackboard. Today classes had been suspended for the celebration, which was attended by community elders, teachers, and parents. The adults were all men (the school was all-male), and most wore the traditional white Afghan cap embroidered with white flowers or a white turban. Long white beards were de rigeur, but most of the elders looked dusty, tired, and weighed down. The celebration was held in the small courtyard, which was set up with dozens of white plastic fold-out chairs. To the left were plastic tables with lemonade, tea, and cookies. There was no stage, only a space in the front where children and adults would present.

In between speeches in Pashto, a choir of boys came up to the front and sang one of the four (or more) national anthems of Afghanistan in Pashto. It seemed that even on the subject of Afghanistan's national anthem there was discord. The children looked unhappy as they sang, and the child soloist sang in a desperate, high-pitched voice. Overall, the experience was surreal and depressing.

The main speech included significant reading from the Quran, highlighting the fact that Muhammad himself was a refugee in Medina at one point. The few words I recognized in Pashto were *jihad* and *mujahideen*, both of which came up numerous times. When I asked the friendly teacher that Nasir had provided me as a guide, he said the speaker was thanking Pakistan for its generosity. I didn't believe him, but didn't want to cause trouble by asking other people.

After the closing prayer, everyone raised their palms toward the heavens and repeated "Amen" a few times. Amen? I confirmed with my guide that it was in fact "Amen" being said, and he said it was their way of saying thanks.

After the speeches, I asked the teacher about security issues at the school, and he explained that the situation had improved dramatically over the past few months, pulling up his left sleeve as proof. His hand was withered and frail, and I could clearly see the crude skin grafts that had patched up what had probably been very large chunks of missing flesh. He had been a bystander on the main road, the same one I traveled on every day, when a car bomb had exploded. "No more bombs anymore," he said, smiling weakly. He warned me of the dangers of going to the Chakdara camp, three hours away on an unsafe road and surrounded by a hostile population, a destination I had assumed would be the highlight of my trip.

I was back in my room by noon, part of a miscommunication, and realized I was late for a meeting with Fazal Rabbi in his office at the Ministry. I called Nasir, hoping to arrange transport, and he told me to hail a cab.

Alone.

Off the street.

"Hayatabad. Phase 5. Ministry for Afghan Refugees. Don't pay more than 80 rupees." He hung up.

I stared at the silent receiver. "But what about security precautions?" I thought. The threat of being kidnapped? Should I just ignore his advice and stay in the guesthouse?

At the thought of spending the next twenty hours in my room, watching reruns of old movies, the right decision seemed obvious.

I said a little prayer, asked the security guard at the guest house to hail me a cab (the driver subsequently charging me double the price Nasir had quoted, all told an extra $1), and hopped in. Without anyone to speak to, I actively looked out the windows for the first time. Mango stands were ubiquitous, full of bright yellow specimens about to burst and batches of fat green ones with a more acidic taste. Large bloody legs of lamb were hanging from the outside of butcher shops, covered in flies feasting on the raw meat. (A friend of mine later told me you should never buy meat that the flies weren't swarming, because that showed it wasn't fresh.) I saw children working, especially near hardware and mechanic shops, and I wondered whether that was due to summer vacation or a prevalence of child labor.

The driver turned around and asked me something in Pashto. I replied with a blank expression. A few seconds later he pulled over at one of the military checkpoints on the road, presumably to ask whether any of the guards spoke English. One approached our cab and asked me where I was going. "Phase 5, Hayatabad," I said proudly. "Yes, yes, you are already here. What block, though?" I gave him the same blank look I had given the taxi driver a few seconds ago. "Well, where are you trying to go?" "The Ministry of Afghan Refugees."

His turn at the blank expression. He said a few words to the driver, who then went straight for a while until we reached another checkpoint. Same procedure. Same blank stares. We repeated this exercise four more times, alternatively asking students and guards, until we finally reached the place. The driver gave me a big toothless grin and two thumbs up. I couldn't help but laugh, shake his hand, and give him a big tip (which he refused, happy to take only 200 rupees, a little over $2.25).

This was my third time in the Ministry, but oh! how different it was now that I had gone to dinner with Fazal! I was almost immediately ushered into the Chief Commissioner's office, an eerily quiet, cool, and beautifully wallpapered abode. I spent about three minutes explaining my research until he was thoroughly bored, and then he pressed a button on his desk, calling in his terrified (male, of course) assistant. He barked a few orders, then turned to me and said, "Ok. You can go to the camps." I had spent the last four days attempting to get permission, and now it had all been accomplished in less than four minutes. This was the power of hospitality in Peshawar.

On the way back I again jumped into a street taxi, this one heavily run down and manned by an especially angry looking driver. We spent thirty minutes on the way back, far longer than it had taken me to get to the

Ministry, until he pulled over and announced, "Abdara Road."

There had obviously been a misunderstanding.

The driver waved over a perfect stranger who was walking nearby, and who happened to speak perfect English. I explained to him that I had wanted to go to "Old Bara Road, not Abdara Road." He conveyed this to the cab driver, who angrily explained that it had not been his fault, that in fact we were very far away from my guesthouse, and that he wanted an additional hundred rupees ($1.15) to take me there. I quickly agreed, thanked the friendly stranger profusely, and we spent the next twenty minutes maneuvering through traffic.

I hadn't realized how dusty the city was, but my face and hair were caked by this point and I could see the locals covering their faces with handkerchiefs as the afternoon winds picked up. Still totally lost, the driver stopped again and again to ask for directions. At one point, frustrated, I showed him the address on my room key, which he stared at blankly before growing even angrier. Of course he was illiterate and here I was, crassly rubbing it in his face. I felt like an insensitive foreigner. From the window I saw a KFC that had not been shut down. It was open, and flanked by three security guards, a metal detector, and concrete barriers all around it to prevent car bombs.

The driver started stopping every few seconds to ask directions from guards, military police, and young men with skullcaps and long beards, motioning for me to show them my room key with the address on it. At one point one of the conservative-looking students with a beard and a skullcap actually boarded my taxi, holding my key in his hands. I became afraid. I was utterly alone, could not communicate with anyone, and had just given a stranger my room key. I felt careless, naïve, and scared. For all I knew he was now telling the driver to take me to a Taliban safe house. He suddenly jumped out of the vehicle, and I lost sight of him. "I guess I definitely have to move guesthouses now," I thought to myself. I thanked God that I always carried my cash and passport with me, just in case I needed to get out of the country in a hurry.

The student reappeared next to a security guard, who it turned out had been giving him directions, and who pointed us in the right direction. We finally arrived at my guest house, and I was more relieved than I probably should have been, given that I had not been in any real danger. In fact, I was amazed to realize that out of the two dozen people who my driver had stopped and I had spoken to in English, none of them had been hostile toward me in any way. Some were curious as to what a silly foreigner was doing in the back of a taxi, but all were friendly, helpful, and smiling.

Emboldened by my recent adventure, I dropped off my cash and passport in the room, and headed out into the street again to the nearby open marketplace. I hadn't eaten anything all day, and although my stomach was feeling better, the mere thought of dinner at the guesthouse brought on feelings of nausea. I walked for half a mile or so, drawing as little attention to myself as possible with my authentic Pakistani dress (one of Fayaz's old outfits, actually), looking mostly at the ground. I didn't catch any stares and happily walked into a bakery, where I bought a mouthwatering sugar and coconut donut and some Mountain Dew. Things were finally starting to look up.

* * *

I met an amazing man the next day. Gul Muhammad Afridi looks older than his age, his dark complexion and deep wrinkles offsetting powerful green eyes. He is an Afghan refugee who came to Peshawar many years ago and now runs fifty-four schools around the city. A couple years before, dismayed by the lack of quality teachers available to Afghans and aware of the inexistence of teacher training programs, he opened a two-year training college for Afghan refugees. He was unable to find NGOs that would give him grants, or get the Pakistani or Afghan governments to fund him. So he sold his house, and used the capital to pay forty teachers and rent a modest building. As of January 2010, he didn't charge his students a fee for attendance, paying everything out of his own pocket. Most remarkable about this teacher training school, however, is that it trains over four hundred female student teachers, approximately 80 percent of the student body. The women I met that day were intelligent, motivated, and more inspiring individually than anyone I had ever met before. Their lives, their very presence at this school, were a testament to the human spirit, to the ability of people to persevere in the face of adversity.

As inspiring as these women were, unfortunately, they represented a minuscule minority of the female Afghan population, unique both because of their parents' relative open-mindedness and their financial ability to stay in school. Few of them had grown up in rural refugee camps, and most lived in urban centers in Peshawar. While to a foreigner the distinctions between urban Afghan female refugees and their rural counterparts in Bajaur (the conservative Pakistani province on the Afghan border) are unrecognizable, once I sat down with these women I realized that these small differences make all the difference in the world. The women I met were let out of the house, despite being more than ten years old. They had completed twelve years of study. Although eighteen to twenty years old, most of them remained unmarried. In public, both groups may wear *burkas* and full veils, trappings I saw these students put on before emerging from the building. In private, however, these urban women keep their *hejabs* on but almost all uncover their faces, displaying their uncommon and enigmatic beauty. Most Afghan women would never show their faces to a man outside their family.

Every day is a struggle for these women, as they're teased and harassed on the way to and from school. People leer and taunt them, men at times envious that they are receiving education or are employed, or simply disgusted that they walk the streets alone, without male accompaniment. Every day these amazing women fear that these taunts will turn into physical violence, or worse, an acid attack meant to destroy their faces. And yet, every day they walk, take a bus or taxi, all because they would like to graduate and inspire other students to achieve what they soon will. But each year they have to convince their families to allow them to return to school, an exhausting ordeal. The barriers aren't institutional in nature as much as they are social, the women forced to argue against their uncles, fathers, grandfathers, and even neighbors to come to school.

I pressed these women about their culture, trying to understand why men were so afraid of women leaving their houses alone. What did they fear so much that they kept these wonderful women locked up? After discounting standard answers like religion, culture, and poverty, I tried to dig deeper. A common thread began to emerge, as more and more of the student teachers touched upon the idea of honor and the fear that women were dishonoring their family by leaving the house alone. But why were men afraid that women would dishonor them? Was it because they were afraid of the behavior of other men? Did the men believe that, once a woman left the house unsupervised, she would go gallivanting around with strange men?

During my conversation with these sixty women, facilitated and translated by a young woman training to be an English teacher, I realized that this was the only contact I had had with the opposite sex since my arrival. This two-hour conversation with female students was probably more contact than the average Afghan man had ever had with women outside of his family. I was saddened by this lack of communication between the sexes, an impasse that invariably led to rumor-mongering, misunderstandings, and an inability to understand each other. The most devastating aspect of this lack of communication was that it severely restrained women from achieving their potential and made it impossible for Afghanistan, and parts of Pakistan, to progress. The female students expressed an intense and overwhelming sense of frustration, each standing and delivering loud, clear, and harsh speeches arguing against the obstacles in their paths, the injustice of their gender.

Ironically, the only two professions the community viewed favorably for women to pursue, education and medicine, both required higher-level degrees. Because women were not allowed to perform more menial jobs, and only the most desperate would beg on the street, contributing to the household income in a meaningful way was impossible for them without a proper education. Even with this economic incentive, large and at times insurmountable obstacles remained. No wonder Gul Muhammad had been passionate enough to sell his house.

Back in Gul's office, in customary Pashtun form, I was offered pastries, potato samosas (think fried potato dumplings), and the drink I'd come most to dread: lukewarm tea with milk. My aversion to warm milk was such that my parents would use it when I had food poisoning in order to induce vomiting. I first tried to ignore it, focusing instead on the samosas and Mountain Dew. But the chai remained, ever so lukewarm in the 100 degree weather. (I would later find out that it had been, at 107 degrees, the hottest day of the year.) As we got up to leave, my hosts caught sight of the tea.

"No, no, wait. Francisco has not finished his tea!"

I tried to make excuses about the weather, already sweating profusely, and still not having acclimated to the idea of hot drinks in hot weather.

"Do not worry, at first you will feel hot, but then it will cool you off in fifteen minutes!"

I took a deep breath and chugged the tea all at once. Fifteen minutes later I felt just as hot as I had before, but didn't have the heart to tell anyone.

Our next stop would be the Ministry for Afghan Refugees, where the offices felt like an oven because the government had banned the use of air-conditioning to save on electricity. On the drive over, I thought back to the female students I had just met. Even though only a minority had been born in Afghanistan, since most of their parents had emigrated to Pakistan in the 1980s, all of them wanted to return there. This was the same case as the refugees in Dadaab, where Somalis born in the camps longed for a land they had never lived in. I thought back to the earlier celebration, a few days ago, when the Afghan children had sung the various Afghani national anthems. I realized that this ceremony was part of the conditioning by their society and the host government to train them to be homesick for a home they had never known, to fuel an allegiance to a country they could only imagine.

I had asked these women about their educational history with an ulterior motive, hoping to confirm an inkling. None of their schools had had desks. All had sat in classes with at least fifty students. Student to textbook ratios had typically been four to one. But, confirming my earlier supposition, they all praised the quality of their teachers and the important role a good teacher had played in their lives.

"We did not need more textbooks because the teacher would come over and explain to us the problems," said one.

"Yes, it was very hot, but we liked paying attention to her," chimed another.

"She really cared about us."

In spite of their different backgrounds and experiences, their success and desire to continue studying attested to the power of a committed and well-trained individual. The idea for the Winning the Minds Foundation was becoming clearer and clearer in my mind.

* * *

Back at another teacher training institute, this one composed of male students but founded by another amazing Afghan woman, I glanced upward to see Hamid Karzai's smug face on the wall behind her desk. I couldn't help myself and asked outright why she kept his picture in her office. She shrugged. Here they were, scrounging by on a few thousand dollars a year to run a teacher college with over five hundred students, and gloating over them with his idiotic smile and much mocked cap (Afghans had stopped wearing it since he took it up as part of his "man of the people" uniform) was a man responsible for squandering and stealing billions of dollars of American taxpayers' money that we had dumped into Afghanistan since September 11, 2001. The outcome could have been so different for a country filled with such amazing and dynamic people. But instead, the United States was stuck supporting a corrupt, inept, and selfish president

who had surrounded himself with drug lords and pe-
dophiles, and then threatened to defect to the Taliban.
Afghanistan, and all of the NATO troops who risked
their lives there, deserved better. Why bother dealing
with Karzai and his cronies, who lacked legitimacy and
served as a key recruiting tool for the Taliban? Why
not build a civil society based on local non-governmental
organizations like these, taking advantage of people who
actually loved their country and cared for their people,
rather than throwing good money after bad?

As I said my goodbyes to the headmistress and her
students, they insisted on having a teacher accompany
me back to my guest house, a little over two miles away.
I agreed, grateful for the company, but then saw the
headmistress give 200 rupees to the teacher and immediately protested. I could accept food and drinks
from struggling Afghans out of politeness, but would
absolutely not allow her to pay for my taxi. She insisted
(it was becoming clear that this was not a woman with
whom you disagreed easily), in spite of having already
given me a beautiful table linen as a gift. I protested
again to no avail. To my delight, a student offered to
drive me home instead. I quickly accepted, happy to
find a face-saving compromise, and then saw him point
at his rusted moped. I took a deep breath, aware that
this was the only compromise, as I would not take cash
from these wonderful people.

The bike sagged dangerously low with my weight on
it, and my helmetless driver, Mujtaba, looked back over
his shoulder.

"Don't hold on to me, I don't like it. Hold on to the back handlebars."

It was absolutely terrifying to be riding on the back of the bike, which swerved dangerously as Mujtaba tried to adjust to the added 200 lbs on the turns. Mujtaba agreed to be my translator and guide for the next day, and the ride got worse as he took out his cell phone and attempted to type in my phone number while driving down the highway. I felt like a true Pakistani, riding on the back of his rusted bike without anyone giving me a second glance. I prayed the entire ride back, arguably the scariest fifteen minutes of my time in Peshawar.

* * *

Once back, I washed up a bit, drank some water, and headed out in Nasir's car to the UNHCR headquarters for an official celebration of World Refugee Day. As expected, a smattering of local celebrities, none of whom I recognized, were inside the UN compound, as well at the Head Commissioner for Afghan Refugees and the UN country head. I arrived in tandem with a young US Foreign Service officer, the poor guy emerging from the comfort of the air-conditioned bulletproof Suburban clad in a black suit and tie that soon showed sweat marks. I felt genuinely sorry for the man, who was probably my age, living in constant fear here, and cooped up in the US Consulate all the time. To make matters worse, he was generally ignored by the locals at the party. This was probably not the life he had envisioned when he joined the Foreign Service.

The myriad speeches, all fortunately short, included a taped video by the Head of the UNHCR (who quoted an estimate that there are over 50 million refugees around the world) and a nonsensical fifteen-second announcement by Angelina Jolie wearing bangs. The Pakistani Commissioner's speech was noteworthy for his constant reference to the Afghans as "our brothers." He said, "Our economy is not strong, but we have never turned our backs on our brothers. We will always support them."

This relative openness of the Pakistani government and its people to accepting refugees was a message I had been hearing from Afghans and Pakistanis alike since I had arrived. They all referenced the many cultural similarities between Afghan and Pakistani Pashtuns. As I spent more time in Peshawar, however, I would begin to see cracks in the façade of unity, especially as I began to spend more time with Afghan refugees who served as my interpreters. If you were Afghan, your car would be stopped. You would be asked for your papers. If you had all of them, you paid a small bribe. If you didn't, you paid a bigger bribe. Walking alone on the street as an Afghan refugee? Pay a bribe. Walking with a group of male friends? Pay a bribe. Walking with your wife? Nobody bothered you.

The refugee men I spoke with told me that Pashtun men respected women too much to harass your wife. They went so far as to say that women in Afghan refugee camps could walk alone on the roads without fear, a notion somewhat contradicted by the requirement to keep your wife indoors at all times. This was the complicated and fascinating notion of respect for women practiced

by these men, who held women in such high regard and
yet did not really treat them as individuals who deserved
the same rights as men. The men all vowed to protect
women, but at the same time smothered their potential.

Later I met with a Pashtun acquaintance to talk about
his culture and its attitude toward women. The young
man I spoke with came from a college educated family
(his brothers and father had all obtained a university
degree), was finishing his masters and applying for a Ful-
bright fellowship. In spite of telling me that he believed
in the intellectual parity of men and women, he stated,
"The best thing a woman can do is produce a good son."

I was shocked, his response unexpected given his educational background. "But what about their intellectual
potential?" I asked. "You're saying the best thing a
woman can do with her life is give birth to, and raise, a
son. Right?

"Yes."

"But what about Marie Curie?" I asked him. "You
want to study oncology in the United States, so you should
understand. If Curie had dedicated herself solely to bearing children we would have never discovered radioactiv-
ity! The world would be worse off and millions more
would have died and been unable to benefit from her
experiments! Just imagine how many other brilliant
women today there are who are forced to dedicate their
lives to bearing children, their talent wasting away."

He seemed stumped at this response and we started
talking about the few women in his graduate school
classes. "We do not want our women to be too educated
either," he told me. "For example, I love a girl in my class.

But I know I will never marry her. She is too educated. She would not be docile—she would not obey me! A girl who is less educated will more likely do what I say. Also, I do not want my wife to work, and the more educated she is, the more she will want to work."

"But what if what you say, or what you want, is wrong?" I asked. "Don't you want a wife who can tell you?" He didn't respond to this, which I took to mean no. "For example, imagine one of your daughters needs heart surgery. If women aren't educated, then who will perform the operation on your daughter's, or your wife's, chest? A man?"

He visibly shuddered at the thought.

I continued. "You yourself told me that the best surgeon in Peshawar was Ghani Khan's daughter! If you were in an accident, would you prefer she operate on you or a less talented man?"

"But even she does not shake men's hands!" he proclaimed, satisfied that he had made a point.

"What are you afraid of if your wife leaves the house or goes to school? Or if someone sees her face? Why keep them locked up?"

"Because of my honor!" he exclaimed, raising his voice. "She may talk to someone! She may meet someone! Do you not feel a pain in your heart if your girlfriend is spending time with another man?"

I laughed, conceding that he had a point. "Of course I do! We call it jealousy in the States. But I trust my girlfriend," I told him.

Of course he didn't trust women, though. How could he if he had never spent time with one who wasn't a part of his family? Most Pashtun men I had met had no interaction with women in their daily lives. There were no friendships, dates, or relationships with the opposite sex, so how could they ever learn to understand them? The restrictions imposed on Pashtun women were, I believed, based on a projection of men's own insecurities.

A Pashtun joke holds that a teacher was once explaining the concept of heaven to a group of Pashtun men. "Everything is calm and plentiful. People live at peace with one another," the teacher described.

A young Pashtun stood up and asked, "Sir, so will my cousin also be there so I can compete against him?"

"No, everything is plentiful so there is no need to compete."

"And will I have the taste of revenge in my throat, ready to defend my honor?"

"No, no, everything there is calm. There is no need for revenge, as you will be done no wrong."

"And sir," continued the student, "will I be given my weapons so I can fight my enemies?"

The teacher, a bit more exasperated now, answered, "You will have no enemies, and thus no need for weapons!"

"Sir," retorted the student, "then you can keep your heaven! I would rather live in hell and live like a Pashtun man should, with his weapons, his revenge, and his competition!"

I'd been told the joke does a good job of describing the Pashtun male, because it highlights the constant struggle to defend one's honor, a paranoia that forces men to defend against all slights, both real and imagined. After speaking with so many men over the past two weeks, I had come to believe it was this underlying paranoia that set the foundation for many of the constrictive practices imposed on Pashtun women.

* * *

As I've mentioned before, the Pashtun culture, the largest minority in Afghanistan and the predominant group in the Khyber-Pakhtunkhwa province, has a wonderful notion of hospitality. The downside to this custom is that it sometimes forces poverty-stricken people to offer, in order to protect their honor, what they cannot afford to give away. This type of self-sacrifice ranges from paying for your drinks and taxis, in spite of your repeated objections, to offering you food when their own family may go hungry. It is unfathomable for me to imagine sacrificing my own well-being, or my family's, for the benefit of a stranger. And yet this is precisely what makes Pashtun hospitality so unique and, at times, so painful to accept.

The Hazana refugee camp, within the Peshawar city limits, houses over two hundred extended families, or about twenty-four thousand people. There are no borders to separate the camp from the surrounding slums, no military or police presence, and the main entrance is a narrow alleyway with an unpaved road. Rather than being distinguishable from the surrounding slums, the camp, like virtually all other camps inside Peshawar, is itself a slum. A small river runs through and adjacent to the community, emanating a stench of sewage and shit. The children are dirty, viscerally poor, and almost all jump into the putrid water to cool off. The youngest stand naked on the dirt road, protected by their older siblings.

These children were the first people I saw in the camp, almost as though they were an informal welcome committee. Our driver parked the car nearby, unable to drive any further, and Mujtaba and I crossed a rickety wooden bridge, strengthened by newly nailed floorboards and hemp. As the bridge swayed side to side during our crossing, the children paid scant attention to us. They yelled and giggled, jumping off the ropes into the dirty river. Once safely across we found the school building closed and padlocked. I would later find out that no one had been informed of our visit, and thus two strangers had simply shown up in a refugee camp, unannounced and without security, asking to see the school and speak with the headmaster. I felt comforted by the fact that Mujtaba was also an Afghan refugee, even if he did live outside the camps.

"Well, since we're already here, let's take a tour of the camp," I told Muj. He turned to look at me as though I had just asked him if he'd like to accompany me on an afternoon stroll through a landmine field.

"No. These people will not like us walking in their camp." He was serious, and scared. He beckoned some of the children, who upon seeing my total incompetence with their language, indulged me with the most popular English phrase of the trip: "Hello! I am fine! I am fine!" Giggling, they scurried away, but not before Muj had asked them to bring the school watchman over. The old man arrived, exchanged a few words with Muj, and then used his cellphone to call the headmaster.

"He did not answer," Muj told me, "so we are going to his house instead."

That seemed both perfectly inappropriate and reasonable. We crossed the bridge again and entered another small and narrow dirt road, surrounded by mud brick walls. Unlike Jalozai, these camps had a feel of permanence about them—well, as permanent as mud walls can be. On our way we encountered more children, most who ran away or poked their heads behind the sheets and tarps that served as doors in the camp. As we got deeper into the camp, the number of puddles of sewage increased, dark green and moldy, festering under the midday sun.

We arrived at a covered entryway, where we waited while a little girl went in with the school watchman to decide our fate. It seemed that they approved of our presence, for after a few minutes they pulled aside the sheet for us to go through. Once inside, we were brought to the corner room of the compound, where I found six men and two boys diligently working on sewing machines, making vests. The principal was sitting in a corner and welcomed us with cold water, which I was always apprehensive about drinking, though it felt delicious and cooling as it traveled down my throat.

The sewing studio we were in had a thatched roof but was missing two walls, and opened up to the river and a small forest with thin trees nearby. We spent an hour talking about the subjects taught at the school (Pashto, English, Dari, Science, Math, History, Geography, Islamic Studies, and Quranic memorization), the dropout rate (girls usually completed eighth grade and then dropped out because they weren't allowed to travel outside the camp to attend high school), and teachers (about half were Pakistani, all had completed high school, and none were professionally trained). As always, no classes were co-ed. The headmaster estimated the literacy rate in the camp to be 30 percent.

As we got up to leave, the principal stopped us and began to insist that we eat with them. I refused, concerned about taking food away from people who needed it more than I did. Muj translated my polite refusal. The principal insisted. I lied and said we were late for a meeting. He continued to insist. This went on for a full fifteen minutes, until Muj explained to me that it was an insult for me not to accept this man's food, as though it weren't good enough for me. "Of course that isn't the case!" I wanted to reply angrily. "I just don't want to eat their food when I know their children are hungry!" I refrained from telling him either, though, afraid that one of the teachers understood more English than he was letting on. With the promise to myself that I would only eat two bites, we moved to a cool mud room, where we sat on the floor as they started bringing in dishes. Now that I had sat down, I realized I couldn't eat only two bites without insulting them further. I was stuck.

And thus the feast began. They brought out freshly made round nans, heaping plates of rice with chopped tomato and red onion to go with it, tender goat meat, the best eggplant dish I had ever tasted, roasted peppers, chickpeas in a tangy olive oil, and an Afghan version of ratatouille. There were three plates of each dish, an overwhelming amount of food for only eight men. The food was delicious, the dishes the most sumptuous I had tasted since I had begun my trip, and I ate heartily, hating myself a bit more after each bite and feeling extraordinarily guilty. To make matters worse, I am left-handed and had been putting my left hand into communal dishes until the Pakistani next to me finally reprimanded me and explained that in Muslim countries you should never touch food with your left hand. I had fortunately only soiled the delicious chickpea and eggplant dishes, which now no one would touch. I made an uncomfortable truce with my soul by eating more of the vegetables, which I knew were the cheapest items to buy. There was very little talking at the meal.

Toward the end I thanked the old principal again and again, finally enveloping his small frame in a bear hug. We left the camp, hours later than expected, and headed back to my guesthouse in a rickshaw taxi. (The driver had left to go pick up Nasir's wife.) Mujtaba flattered me enormously on the ride back, telling me how much the men at lunch had liked me, even after understanding that I was only a student and couldn't really help them.

* * *

Before I knew it, my time in Peshawar had come to a close, the last few days punctuated by meetings with faceless bureaucrats and new problems related to my visits to the camps. Another local NGO worker had been kidnapped and killed recently, and the Ministry became even more skittish about my visits to the refugee camps, cancelling my existing visitation permits. The trip to Pakistan overall had been somewhat frustrating, plagued by bureaucratic obstacles, false starts, and countless hours cooped up in my room. Although my access to the teachers and elders had been plentiful, in comparison to Dadaab I had been provided with much less access to the children, which made it very difficult to gain a solid understanding of how radicalized the population really was, or if in fact any recruitment took place. The invisible but yet very real presence of the ISI made it all the more difficult to speak openly about a subject that was already so taboo.

The biggest disappointment had occurred during my final two days in Peshawar, when I was twice denied access to the Shamshatoo camp. The first rejection came through official channels, on the grounds that the Pakistani government couldn't provide adequate security for me inside the camp. The second rejection was the most heartbreaking, as a female graduate student I had met asked her father whether he could show me around the camp. After two days of deliberation he rejected my request, insisting that even though he lived in the camp, visiting was too dangerous for a foreigner—an argument he made clear by explaining that two Pakistanis had disappeared from inside the camp a week before.

The Shamshatoo camp is a refugee camp situated on the outskirts of Peshawar. It is perfectly self-contained, receives no UN or NGO aid, and strongly discourages visitors. The best way to think about it is as a separate country within Pakistan, similar to some of the Hezbollah-run refugee camps in Lebanon. The reason I make this analogy to the militant organization is because Shamshatoo is run by Hezb-i-Islami, the Afghan chapter of the Muslim Brotherhood. Hezb-i-Islami was founded in 1975 in Pakistan by Gulbuddin Hekmatyar as an organization to fight the Soviet-backed government of Afghanistan. Gulbuddin, like other mujahideen in the 1980s, was funded by the CIA and directed by the Pakistani government, which informed him where he could set up camp and where his followers could live in Peshawar. During the Soviet invasion of Afghanistan, Gulbuddin used Shamshatoo as a launching pad for cross-border raids, retreating to the safety of his camp after the attacks. Today, Shamshatoo is once again a launching pad for Hezb-i-Islami's attacks against US troops in Afghanistan.

None of this is groundbreaking intelligence, mind you, as the United States is keenly aware of Shamshatoo's role as a safe haven for terrorists—so much so that a few years ago the United States government asked the Pakistanis to close down the camp. The Pakistani government instead shut down the Jalozai camp for Afghan refugees, turning it into an internally displaced persons camp and cannibalizing a significant ISI presence that the government had developed there. The message was clear: We're not going anywhere near Gulbuddin Hekmatyar's camp.

On the ride back from another refugee camp, Gul Muhammad, the founder of the women's teacher training schools, took me on a tour of the most famous bomb blast sites in Peshawar. We started with the former ISI regional headquarters, from which the Pakistani government had funded and influenced the Taliban. The building had been three stories tall and covered half a city block. Only the barest skeleton of the building remained, as the blast had destroyed the front half of the building and collapsed most of what remained. "Big bomb!" exclaimed Gul. "Whole city trembled." The attack, which took place in November 2009, had killed over fifteen agents and wounded dozens more. The ruins had not yet been demolished due to a lack of government funds.

Next we passed the Peshawar High Court, which even on a Saturday had a line of hundreds of people snaking through its corridors and out the main gate. The Court had been successfully targeted in 2007 (one killed, eight wounded), and again in 2008 and 2009. It now boasted multiple concrete barriers and a strong military presence.

Finally, we drove past the Pearl Continental Hotel, a massive white building removed from the main road by a hundred feet and a parking lot, which looked visibly more luxurious and welcoming to foreigners than any other building in Peshawar. It had been successfully targeted in 2009 (seventeen killed, sixty wounded), effectively ending the United States government's plans to buy the building and host its consulate there. Even now it looked incongruous in the city, white and shiny against the dirty and dull background that was Peshawar. A friend of mine would later tell me that the restaurant and hotel were virtually deserted these days, a side-effect of being the most conspicuous building in a time of war.

Despite the setbacks, the highlight of my time here remained the first trip to Jalozai and my conversation with the hundred IDP students, and their teachers, from the province of Bajaur. Here had been a clear example of the ability of societies to change and the positive effects that could be wrought from a crisis situation. Prior to their fleeing the violence in Bajaur, most of these students hadn't ever attended a school. Their parents did not emphasize or even expect that their daughters be educated. Now that they were living in a camp so far away from home, reliant on the government and international organizations, they had acquiesced to having their daughters be educated. Years from now, when the situation has stabilized enough for these families to go home, will they go back to their old ways? Will the mothers and daughters be content with a life of ignorance, now that they have been exposed to the benefits of education? Will those young girls who were educated be comfortable refusing their daughters the same opportunity in the future?

I believe that these experiences, and the happiness and benefits that education has already brought to these families, has forever changed this society. I don't believe they will ever be able to go back to a society that restricts education based on gender, even if women are forced to host secret classes in their homes. The other message that had been just as vibrant in Peshawar as in Dadaab was the ability of the human spirit to persevere and even flourish in times of extreme difficulty. Although the refugees I had met had varied opinions on the situation in Afghanistan, all of them were extraordinarily hopeful that their own situation would improve. All of them harbored dreams of a better future, and worked hard to get closer to that vision. It seemed to me that even in the direst of circumstances, human beings would retain the ability to be hopeful and dream of a better life.

* * *

Since I had become bold, or stupid, enough to walk around the area near my hotel, the food had improved dramatically. Fresh donuts with pieces of roasted coconut, sizzling hot samosas bought off of a genial old man on the street, and mango milkshakes had become a daily routine. During my walks around the University Town area, I noticed for the first time the disproportionate quantity of mansions near me, all protected by high cement walls—and the biggest reinforced with a few armed guards. Were these the homes of the famous rich Afghan refugees that Pakistanis had enviously spoken to me about?

On my last day in Peshawar I visited the school of what I later realized was one of the richest Afghans in the community. (This was not hard to deduce, as the guy unabashedly bragged to me about his wealth.) Although I found him arrogant and rude (he was used to shouting loudly at his staff, to the point that I finally asked him not to interrupt me while I was speaking), he ran 160 schools in Afghanistan and was relatively well versed in the political situation there. He was adamant about providing a college education to his graduates, arguing that rather than focusing on getting to higher literacy rates we should focus on making sure that high school graduates could attend university. "For every college graduate you fund, he can take care and educate one hundred illiterate children!" he proclaimed.

Although this was an exaggeration, he did have a point, as long as you could convince those who received a scholarship to give back to their communities. What I'd found over the past few weeks in Pakistan was that the schools' higher graduation rates in comparison to Dadaab were not merely due to lower standards or more textbooks but also to the higher degree of community involvement in the students' education. Some headmasters charged parents a nominal fee for their children to attend school just to make sure that the families were engaged. In many cases the community would pay the teachers' salaries when the non-governmental organizations were late to do so, and fund the costs of building new classrooms. Children were sometimes forced by their parents to attend tutoring, which was organized by the older students.

The rich school owner interrupted me again, and motioned for one of his students to bring him his laptop. Another student translated that he wanted to show me a documentary he had made, which he bragged had cost him over $30,000 to produce. The video was amateurish and unsteady, taped using a hidden camera, and consisted primarily of interviews and conversations with opium farmers and government officials about the drug trade. "Offered to pay one million dollars for all copies, the Minister, and I said no! This is my art!" bragged the man.

Although he claimed the video had a few salacious comments that could embarrass some Afghan government officials, it was all in Pashto and largely uninteresting. "Twelfth grade, twelfth grade!" he yelled as he pointed excitedly at the screen as a small-time opium farmer spoke. He was trying to explain that this young farmer had finished high school, but had been forced to grow poppy because he remained poor and relatively uneducated. If only the farmer had been given a university scholarship, his life would have been different. "Farmers grow opium because they're not educated!" he argued. Even though I agreed that the young man's life would have been better had he received a university degree (hard to argue with that point), the idea that opium farmers grew poppy because they were uneducated was ludicrous. I interrupted him, and disagreed.

Most people aren't aware of this, but poppy is not a particularly profitable or efficient crop for farmers to grow in Afghanistan. On average, Afghan farmers receive less than 1 percent of all profits from the heroin trade. Per kilo of poppy paste, extracted by making a small incision on the poppy flower head, which then oozes out a brownish red thick paste, the farmer receives only $40 (based on November 2009 prices). Over 300 poppy heads are needed to make one kilo, requiring about 3,700 square feet of farmland. Onions, on the other hand, are less labor intensive and more profitable for the Afghan farmer to grow. So why don't the farmers grow onions instead of poppy? It must be because they're uneducated, right? Wrong.

Afghan farmers grow poppy because of security and corruption problems. Let's ignore those farmers forced to grow poppy by the Taliban and Afghan politicians for a moment, and focus on those who independently choose to harvest poppy. Imagine for a second that you're a farmer in Afghanistan who lives a few hours away from the nearest big city, where you can sell your goods. You decide to grow onions for the season, spend your savings buying some seeds, and put in your hard work. Between your hard work and good fortune, you get a beautiful crop of onions. You and your sons pile them up on a donkey carriage or rent a car, and start off toward the city. Along the way you may or may not be mugged by the police, the army, the Taliban, or just random criminals, who will take away your money and your crop. If fortune continues to smile upon you and you don't get mugged, you're certainly going to have to pass a number of official and unofficial "checkpoints," where in order to get through you're going to have to bribe the police, the army, some bureaucrats, some Taliban, and some warlords. (Let's hope you don't have to pass through all of their checkpoints.) By the time you reach the market, if you reach the market, you have to pay an additional tax on the crop to the officials at the market, and the profit you were hoping to make from selling your onions has evaporated thanks to all of the bribes you had pay. You're probably operating at a loss now. And this is before you're forced to travel back and go through the same ordeal.

Compare this to the idea of growing opium. Typically, the person who wants you to grow opium will also give you a loan so that you can feed and clothe your family during the winter. Once you've harvested the poppy, you don't have to deliver it anywhere, as someone will come pick it up from you. So, even if in gross terms you make less money growing poppy than onions, which one would you rather grow?

I had finally shut up the rich guy with this explanation, debunking his spurious correlation between poppy farmers and education. He stared at me for a few seconds, seemingly impressed that I knew this. After a few seconds of this golden silence, he pointed at the screen again and proudly yelled, "Taliban!"

Finally! This was a perfect segue to ask him about recruitment. I questioned him about the relationship between the Taliban and the refugee camps here, brazenly asking whether he knew of any recruitment that took place. In his view the Taliban was not actively recruiting from the refugee camps, but he knew of a few students who had decided to leave Pakistan and go back to Afghanistan to join the Taliban—few, he stressed. Mostly, he explained, the Taliban recruited younger children whose impoverished parents couldn't afford to feed them. I asked how much of a difference it made if a potential recruit was educated or not. "Depends," he answered. "If he only knows Quran, then no difference. But if he has proper education—history, geography, science, math— then very difficult to recruit." He explained to me that most Taliban were uneducated, many illiterate, and that it was difficult for an educated young man to cope with that type of environment. Other Talibs would typically view him with suspicion. "Education opens their minds, makes it more difficult to join Taliban," he concluded.

I was thousands of miles away from Dadaab, with a population that was ethnically and culturally different, and yet the same message emerged. Obtaining a well-rounded education, even for those students who were poor, made extremism and recruitment far less likely. It was an eye-opening message, one that pointed to a consistent and inexpensive way to reduce radicalization.

Given the limited resources of the United States, and the myriad number of failing states around the world that were harboring increasingly more anti-American and more radicalized populations, it is impossible to engage in counterinsurgency campaigns everywhere. But here was a clear strategy that could address some of our national security interests at a fraction of the cost of a full counterinsurgency strategy. By spending our money educating these children, we reduced the support and space for al-Qaeda to operate in, directly addressing our fears of ungoverned spaces. The problem isn't that these spaces are ungoverned—large parts of the world are—but that they are susceptible to an extremist ideology. Our programs could counter this susceptibility and make these environments more hostile to extremist ideologies. Perhaps this was the sustainable strategy that we could support across administrations, without worrying about bankrupting the country or having to set timelines.

That final night Asmattullah, the man who had been gracious enough to provide transportation from Islamabad to Peshawar and back, took me out for a farewell dinner with his friends. Like most group meals I had attended in Peshawar, this dinner did not feature much conversation, a factor of the culture or perhaps due to my presence. The meal, as I had now become accustomed to, was delicious and consisted of only two dishes: roasted lamb and lamb with oil and tomato. It is a testament to the quality of the ingredients that the lamb with a little oil, tomato, and pepper is to this day the best lamb I have ever tasted.

* * *

I left Peshawar on a Saturday morning, finally whipping out my camera on the drive out and making up for lost opportunities by shooting indiscriminately from the car window, annoying a whole host of unwilling subjects.

The Akora camp, founded in the early 1980s, hosts approximately eighty-one thousand individuals, or about six thousand families. It was the only rural camp I had secured permission to visit, and I was planning on stopping by on the way to Islamabad. As we got closer to the camp, I could feel a marked difference between the urban and rural dwellings. Although the buildings were also made of mud walls, and the half-naked children still swam in dirty water, the community seemed marginally better off, everything a bit cleaner. Here the refugees grew most of their own vegetables in surrounding fields.

Once there I met Rahmat Muhammad, the proud father of thirteen children, happy husband of two wives, and the only reason girls in Akora receive any education. In spite of being a polygamist, Rahmat is deeply passionate about education for women, so much so that ten years ago he had taken on the entire Council of Camp Elders and built a school for girls with his own savings. Since women had not received education in the camp for over twenty years, he was forced to hire Pakistani teachers to make up for the lack of educated women in the camp who could serve as educators. Many of the teachers initially worked for free, happy to help the girls learn. What is most surprising about the Akora camp, though, is that for the first ten years of its existence the Council of Elders prohibited even boys from receiving education. The elders thought that education would make the students "bad Muslims." It wasn't until after these elders started dying off that schools were set up in the camp.

Rahmat's two schools have over six hundred female students, most of whom drop out after finishing primary school. They spend Saturday mornings learning how to make beautiful beaded shirts, one of which they gave me as a gift, and sometimes receive a sewing machine as a graduation present so that they can make the shirts at home. Girls here typically get married between the ages of fifteen and sixteen, but some as young as twelve or thirteen. First-time grooms are usually seventeen, but, like Rahmat's brother, can be as young as fifteen. Given that the girls at the school were in their early teens, I wasn't allowed to ask them any questions directly, and handed my list of questions to their female teacher. As expected by now, they all wanted to grow up to be doctors, teachers, and even pilots.

Over our lunch at a highway stop (which consisted of fried ground lamb meat patties, rice, and warm nan and which of course I was frustratingly not allowed to pay for), Rahmat mentioned that in spite of all of the obstacles he had faced, and even the enduring opposition of some of the elders, progress was being made. He was hopeful about the future, but cautioned me that change for girls in Afghanistan was generational in nature—in effect, one had to wait until the older generation began to die off so that the younger and slightly less conservative men could begin to make better decisions that affected the community.

"But what will happen when they return to their villages in Afghanistan?" I asked him.

"Progress continues!" he said excitedly. "Some of our students teach other girls how to read and write in their homes!"

The lessons of the displaced Pakistanis from the Jalozai camp seemed to be universal in nature. As long as these women did not return to an extremely restrictive society (similar to the society that the Taliban had engendered prior to 9/11), they would strive to continue their education and pass on their knowledge to the new generation.

I said goodbye to Rahmat and happily took with me a set of letters he wanted me to mail to a woman in California who had come to visit him and helped pay for new classrooms and sewing machines.

* * *

Once in Islamabad, I was again reminded of how proud Pakistanis are of having Kentucky Fried Chicken in their country. Upon my arrival the manager at my new guesthouse made sure to point out the fact that I was within walking distance of a KFC. (Or maybe he just thought I looked like a picky eater.) After my coming from Peshawar, Islamabad felt almost inauthentic, with half of the men in the streets wearing Western clothing and all of the shops you would expect to find in any major city. Alike Peshawar, however, you would be hard pressed to find public trashcans anywhere, and people here were also fond of throwing half-liter bottles of Mountain Dew out the windows of moving vehicles. After all of the Mountain Dew I alone had drunk since my arrival, it added up to a lot of empty bottles in the streets.

Refusing to bow to the stereotype of Americans eating fast food abroad, I walked around the neighborhood looking for a local restaurant. I found a semi-deserted snack stand nearby, cluelessly called "Munchies," and ordered the two most local-sounding items on the menu: chicken *parata* roll and *samosa chaat*. The result was disappointingly awful, the chicken dry and old and the soggy samosas filled with little potato and fried in oil that tasted as though it hadn't been changed since Munchies' inauguration in 1982. I went back to the guest room, happy for the change of scenery but strangely missing Peshawar. The power went out, temporarily bathing the room in darkness while the generator was powered up. At least the power outages were here to remind me that I was still in Pakistan, capital city or not.

* * *

My last night in Pakistan I had a farewell dinner with a couple government officials, most of whom had been working on the border areas and the refugee crises for decades. At my insistence we went to an Afghan restaurant, a generally dumb idea on my part given the happy memories I had from the refugee camps and the excellent food the inhabitants had given me. In comparison, and in large part because that emotional connection was missing, the food was lackluster.

Once we got into the rice, I once more brought up the subject of Shamshatoo and Gulbuddin Hekmatyar, an increasingly fascinating figure in Afghanistan's recent history. I followed my inquiry with a question about Afghan unity, explaining to the officials my experiences listening to various "national anthems" and asking whether Afghanistan was really a country. The graybeard of the group replied, "In 1995 a lot of the Taliban were Pashtuns, even though the movement was not originally started by Pashtuns, and the intelligence community at large thought it was some sort of Pashtun movement. After pressing our contacts in Afghanistan for more information, we realized that, in fact, the Pashtun nationalists were dead-set against the Taliban, who were actually trying to destroy their culture."

Another member of the group added, "It was confusing for a lot of people. Nobody really knew what was going on. Then we realized that [Ahmad Shah] Masoud was amassing a pretty strong army of Uzbeks and Tajiks, and we decided to approach Gulbuddin, whom we considered a Pashtun leader, to see if he could harness a Pashtun-based militia that we could fund as a counterpart to Masoud."

Ahmad Shah Masoud was a former engineering student at Kabul University who became one of the key *mujahideen* commanders against the Soviet Union, a distinction that earned him the nickname "The Lion of Panjshir." He was briefly the Minister of Defense in 1992, and then after the rise of the Taliban launched what became known as the Northern Alliance. In a stroke of strategic genius, al-Qaeda agents murdered him two days before 9/11, wiping out the most importance opposition leader against the Taliban and the man who purportedly had enough credibility to unite Afghanistan under his command. Had he survived the attack, he would have most likely become the United States government's top choice to lead Afghanistan.

The official continued, "We went to meet with Gulbuddin in Jalalabad in September 1995, and I still remember his response to our proposition that he lead a Pashtun-based movement. 'First, I am a Muslim. Second, I am a Muslim. Third, I am an Afghan. What is this Pashtun bullshit?' We were all stunned back then, but we learned something very valuable: People have historically tried, always unsuccessfully, to break up Afghanistan. You could probably get an Afghan to kill his brother over the control of Kabul, but it is impossible to break it up."

"Plus, the Afghans are so proud of themselves that they even look down on us as Pakistanis!" interrupted the elder. Then he leaned in conspiratorially and told me a history that on its own would have made to the trip to Pakistan worth it. He began, "In 1995 and 1996 the Taliban decided to make its way to Kabul and claim the capital city. They decided to go via Nangarhar, even though their entire military forces were composed of one jeep and one truck of soldiers, and fight first against Haji Zaman's two thousand fighters. Not a single shot was fired and Zaman ended up living in Paris. The Taliban then took Jalalabad, again without firing a single shot, and Haji [Abdul] Qadir and his family ended up in Germany and Australia. Commander Zardad, who was expected to give the Taliban the most resistance, didn't issue a single order to attack. He went to live in London."

"But why didn't the *mujahideen* fight back? Why didn't they resist the Taliban?" I asked incredulously, feeling stupid for not making the connection myself.

"Ah... wait, Francisco. That is the point of this story. All the *mujahideen* ended up in European capitals," he continued. "After 9/11 and the American invasion, Haji Zaman [Ghamsharik] came back from Paris and became the Commander of the Tora Bora operation [an operation in which the American military asked Zaman and Abdul Qadir to fight against the Taliban in the Tora Bora mountains in November 2001]. Haji Qadir became the Vice-President of Afghanistan, after coming back from Germany." He paused, both to collect his thoughts and to allow me to take in everything he had just said. "Now let us go back to 1995 for a bit. Two US senators and two congressmen, among them one Samoan [presumably Faleomavaega Eni Fa'aua'a Hunkin, the Democratic Representative for American Samoa], came to visit the Kacha Garhi refugee camp. We arranged for them to meet the elders and community leaders, and the Samoan stood up to give a speech. This is the story he recounted:

> There is a gentleman in a European capital who is very fond of smoking. He is especially fond of a gold cigarette case, which he always carries in the right-hand side pocket of his suit jacket. On this particular day he had a meeting with a group of journalists and decided to wear a new suit. He was unable to place the gold cigarette case in the usual side pocket, as it was still stitched shut, and decided instead to put it in his inside breast pocket.

During the meeting with the journalists, it turned out that they were actually a group of assassins who attempted to stab him in the heart, an attempt that was foiled only by the presence of the case. This man is Zahir Shah, the former King of Afghanistan. God wanted him to survive because he still has a role to play in Afghanistan. God has sent down his angels, the Taliban, to defeat the infidels, the *mujahideen*, so he can go back home.

The elders erupted, furious at the American-Samoan. They protested that they hadn't spent their life fighting in order to put the King back on top. The Samoan raised his hands to quiet the gathering and smiling explained, 'The King is terminally ill. He will be dead in six months [Zahir Shah actually survived another twelve years and died in 2007]. You will have elections soon thereafter, and you will be free to choose who will rule your country. Afghanistan will have a democracy.'"

At this point the official smiled at my obvious confusion, lit a cigarette, and gave me some time to process all this new information. He took a couple of long drags, exhaling powerfully through his nostrils, and switched tracks. "The Taliban first sprung up in a southern village in Afghanistan. The warlord in charge of the village was a pedophile who liked young boys. One day he kidnapped two young girls, cut their hair, and dressed them up in boys' clothes. He raped them so savagely that one girl died. The Mullah of the town mosque heard about this and rounded up a few of his students, hence the name Taliban [Talib means student in Arabic]. They killed the guards, overpowered the commander, and beat him to death. This is how the Taliban were born. We [the Pakistani government] liked this organization. We thought it would work well in Afghanistan. So we started to fund and help the Taliban. Francisco," he said, making sure he still had my undivided attention, "the reason the *mujahideen* didn't fight the Taliban is because we, including the United States, paid them off. We gave all of them asylum in Europe and a lot of money in exchange for allowing a Taliban victory. We created the Taliban." He squashed his cigarette in the ashtray and lit up another one.

"At the same time that we were supporting the Taliban, however, there was a big crackdown against fundamentalists by Middle Eastern dictators in Algiers, Tunisia, and Egypt. A lot of the extremists fled their countries and moved to Europe, but the hardliners all came to Afghanistan, spearheaded by Osama bin Laden and al-Qaeda. You have to understand that the Taliban were uneducated, illiterate, and ill-equipped, and were suddenly joined by these battle-hardened, well-educated, well-trained, and well-funded Arabs. Although the Taliban had strength in numbers, it became clear that the new Arabs could overpower the Taliban leadership easily. The Taliban thus became hostage to al-Qaeda and to Osama, who took advantage of his power to target his archenemy, the United States, a country the Taliban hadn't really cared about. That, Francisco, is why the Taliban was able to take over Afghanistan and why, in spite of our initial support for them, 9/11 happened." He stubbed out his cigarette and ordered the check.

Don't blame the United States, blame Saudi Arabia!

Sana'a, Aden and Kharaz (Yemen)

"Welcome to Yemen, where the women wear bags and the men chew shrubs."

— Female British Journalist (who for obvious reasons wished to remain anonymous)

This conversation, the facts of which were later verified to me as mostly true, and its implications kept me awake that last night in Pakistan. Before I had time to digest it all, though, I was back in Amman and then, finally, off to Yemen.

The by-now familiar fear consumed me at the Cairo airport, via Sana'a. I tried to remind myself that this feeling of fear was expected, that it always happened. I tried to rationalize it away, telling myself that Peshawar was far more dangerous than Aden, the city in southern Yemen I would be visiting. Deep down, though, I knew this was untrue. This feeling was reinforced by the security guards and Cairo airport personnel, who were unable to contain their shock and surprise every time I mentioned my destination, likely thinking, "*This* is the idiot who wants to go to Yemen?" This sense of foreboding was worsened by the fact that it had taken me four months to obtain this visa, almost as though the same luck that had made it possible for this trip to happen was now deserting me so that I couldn't make it to Yemen.

The visa had taken so long to get that, up until twenty-four hours before, it had been officially denied and I had almost purchased a ticket to visit Lebanon instead.

Yemen has one of the most restrictive visa issuance policies in the world. First, the visa is only good for three months after its issuance, so I waited until early April to apply for it—hoping to time its arrival with my scheduled trip in early July. I read the list of requirements too late, however, and scrambled to make an appointment for a physical so that my doctor could give me a special letter certifying that I did not have influenza and was generally healthy. In addition, I was told I needed a special research permit from the Yemeni government since I was researching refugee camps, but that in order to apply for this permit I would have to be accredited as an academic by a research institution in Yemen.

Since I didn't know anyone in Yemen at the time, I reached out to a professor at Harvard who had done research there, hoping he could help me with the process. I still had almost two months before I was expected to leave Boston and start the trip, ostensibly more than enough time to fulfill all the visa requirements. The most succinct summary of the professor's reply was, "You're fucked. You need at least three months to apply, and I doubt the government will give you permission to research anything on refugees." He suggested I get in touch with the American Institute for Yemeni Studies (AIYS), the only research outfit for foreigners in Sana'a.

After I gave AIYS a call and paid my $10 membership fee, which accredited me as a member in good standing, the Institute agreed to provide me with a letter that I could present to the Yemeni Embassy in Washington, DC. However, before the Institute staff could write their formal letter of recommendation they had to receive a paper copy of my research proposal at their offices in Sana'a. (It's not cheap, or secure, as I would later find out, to FedEx anything to Yemen.) Three weeks later I finally received my letter and called the Yemeni Embassy to make sure I had all the proper documentation before sending in the application. "Yes. Absolutely," the official replied over the phone. I paid an additional $80 to expedite my application (two weeks to go before my flight), and was repeatedly promised that I would receive my passport by Tuesday at the latest. (I left Thursday.)

In a stroke of bad luck, the US Postal Service lost my passport on the way to DC, but was able to find it and deliver it to the Embassy with only a twenty-four-hour delay. I called the Yemeni Embassy on Monday to confirm that everything was in order.

"Yes, yes. No problems."

I called on Tuesday.

"Sorry, slight delay. But no problems, I will send it out to you Wednesday," the clerk said.

"But I'm leaving on Thursday!" I told her, worried that now I would be unable to make any of the trip happen without my passport.

"Yes, yes, no problems, though. We send it express. Before 9 AM. Yes, yes."

I called them back on Wednesday morning.

They couldn't find my passport.

After thirty minutes of prodding, cajoling, and very targeted shouting, they finally found it.

And the visa?

"Oh, we cannot give you a visa!"

What?

"Yes, yes, this letter you sent from AIYS is not suffi-cient. You need someone in Sana'a to go to the Ministry of the Interior to formally submit a letter of invitation. Then, if the Ministry of the Interior approves it, they send it to the Ministry of Foreign Affairs. If they approve it, they send an official letter to our Embassy directing us to grant you a visa. If we like your application," she added.

I was furious. "Why wasn't any of this explained to me three weeks ago?"

"Well, we did not look at your application until today," she responded without a trace of shame or surprise, as though I should have expected this from the start.

After extracting more repeated promises that I would be sent my passport by express mail that day, I ended up receiving it three hours before my flight, after waiting on my doorstep for the postman. I can honestly say I've never been happier to see a postman in my life.

I ditched the idea of applying for a research permit and decided to apply for a tourist visa. Once in Am-man, I called the Yemeni Embassy there, only to be told that I needed to obtain a certificate of health from the Jordanian government, and a letter from my embassy requesting that the Yemeni Embassy grant me a visa and stating that I was a citizen in good standing. As you now know, I went to have blood drawn in Amman before going to Kenya, and then, in the interim forty-eight hours I spent in Amman before leaving for Pakistan, I was told by the Yemenis that I still needed the letter of invitation to be presented in Sana'a—even if it was just for a tourist visa.

I decided to switch tracks and signed up for Arabic classes in July in Sana'a. I figured receiving a student visa would be easier than obtaining a tourist one, and once in Yemen I could figure out how to get to the refugee camps. Usually, the language school could have requested my visa, but the week prior to my application thirty foreigners had been arrested in Sana'a for attempting to join al-Qaeda in the Arabian Peninsula—all of them having entered Yemen on student visas under the pretense of wanting to study Arabic. The government had immediately stopped accepting letters of invitation from language schools. To make matters worse, I'd visited the Yemeni Embassy in Amman only to find that no one in the entire embassy staff spoke a single word of English. I had been forced to call Abboud, my wonderful Jordanian friend who was hosting me, so that he could communicate for me.

The big break finally came when a Yemeni student at Harvard, who happened to work at one of the centers funding this trip, put me in touch with his cousin in Sana'a. Now we were going to get somewhere, I thought. We did. After a week spent in Amman, visiting the Embassy every day and haranguing the staff for up to five hours daily, I received a letter. I was being invited to come to Yemen by the Ministry of Water. As usual, it seemed the only way to get things done in an expeditious manner was to do it extra-officially: either through bribes or friendships. So far, friendships had sufficed.

Now, finally sitting on the dinky plane from Cairo to Sana'a (which resembled more a Greyhound bus from

Trenton to Atlantic City than an international flight), I realized that although I was going to get in, I had no permission to go to the refugee camps. I was showing up in Yemen hoping to get permission to enter areas restricted by the military. As the plane took off, the loudspeakers played a chanted prayer from the Quran. I was finally going to Yemen.

* * *

My Yemeni friends once explained to me that, up until a few years ago, when they told people where they were from they were considered "interesting" and "exotic." Sadly, since the increased attention their country has received over the past two years, in large part due to the unsuccessful Christmas Day bomber (who was trained in Yemen), most people now shudder and eye them suspiciously. To be fair, Yemen is a very troubled country, to the point that the vast majority of scholars who study it don't question *if* it will collapse, but rather *when* it will disintegrate. Even most Yemenis I met agreed with this depressing prognostication.

Yemen has been the poorest country in the Middle East for decades. Over 50 percent of its population suffers from malnutrition, 43 percent of the population lives below the poverty line, and the country has a 40 percent unemployment rate. The country's meager economy, with a GDP of around $28 billion, depends heavily on revenue from its oil fields, which account for approximately 70 percent of GDP. Unfortunately, the country's oil production has decreased by a fourth in the past few years, and the country is expected to run out of oil by 2017. More alarmingly, only one fifth of Yemenis have access to safe drinking water, groundwater is being depleted five times faster than it is being restored, and it is expected that Sana'a will run out of water in less than ten years. To make matters even worse, Yemen's problems are exacerbated by a youth bulge, since nearly half of the population is under the age of fifteen and youth unemployment rates are double the adult rate. And that just covers the economic problems.

From the terrorism perspective, intelligence agencies believe that al-Qaeda has had a presence in Yemen since 1992, when it targeted American military personnel at the Gold Mohur Hotel in Aden. In October 2000 Yemen served as the base from which the U.S.S. Cole was attacked. The situation worsened after 9/11 as al-Qaeda began targeting Saudi Arabia, which led to a Saudi clamp down on these terrorists, almost all of whom fled to Yemen. Despite an increased level of cooperation between the American, Saudi, and Yemeni governments on counterterrorism, twenty-three senior members of al-Qaeda, including Nasir al-Wuhayshi, Osama bin Laden's former secretary, escaped from a Yemeni prison in February 2006. It is widely believed that the prisoners escaped with the help of Yemen's Political Security Organization, the country's domestic intelligence agency.

Al-Wuhayshi, a citizen of Yemen, is the leader of al-Qaeda in the Arabian Peninsula (AQAP), an organization the CIA has designated as the most dangerous al-Qaeda branch in the world. In January 2009 al-Wuhayshi brought together the formerly separate al-Qaeda

Yemen and al-Qaeda Saudi Arabia to form AQAP. As the Yemeni government targeted the group more openly (helped in large part by a US military presence), the group shifted its attention from Saudi Arabia to Western targets. AQAP claimed responsibility for recruiting and training Umar Farouk Abdulmutallab, the unsuccessful Christmas Day bomber, and for the most recent attacks on the US Embassy in Sana'a.

In response to this failed attack, both the Yemeni and American governments carried out missile strikes on AQAP training camps in the provinces of Saada and Abyan, killing several dozen militants. Unfortunately, these drone strikes may have strengthened the group's resolve and the strikes' civilian casualties increased the group's support among the local population. Other intelligence officials believe that the Yemeni government colludes with AQAP at times, using AQAP foot soldiers to battle Houthi rebels in the North. "Yemen is Pakistan in the heart of the Arab world," one official said. "You have military and government collusion with al Qaeda, peace agreements, budding terror camps, and the export of jihad to neighboring countries."

To make matters even more complicated, Yemen's Muslim population is split between Shiites in the north and Sunni (and to some extent Salafi) in the South. Yemeni Shiites are part of a brand of Shiism known as Zaidism, named for Imam Zayd ibn 'Ali. Their main difference with other sects of Shiism has to do with their recognition of Zayd, rather than Muhammad al-Baqir, as the fifth Imam—which is why they are also known as "fivers" among the Shiite. In the northern part of the country, fol-

lowers of the Shiite cleric Hussein Badr Eddin al-Houthi
have engaged in persistent rebellion against the Yemeni
government since September 2004, when, following three
months of conflict, Yemeni government forces killed al-
Houthi and several dozen of his followers. Prior to al-
Houthi's death, most of the protests had been mild, held at
mosques and directed against the United States and Israel.
After his death, though, the protests escalated into a full-
fledged armed conflict between the rebel and government
forces, which lasted on and off until July 2010, when an
uneasy truce was reached between the two groups. This
all changed with the advent of the Arab Spring in Yemen,
when hundreds of thousands of Yemenis protested against
President Saleh in early 2011. By mid-2011 the protests
persisted, as President Saleh continued to refuse to step
down, but the Houthis had taken advantage of the security vacuum and established a semi-autonomous region in
northern Yemen. The Yemeni government accused Iran of
arming the Shiite rebels, which both Iran and the Houthis
vehemently denied. In turn, the Houthis accused Saudi
Arabia of allowing the Yemeni government to launch attacks on them from Saudi soil and of paying Yemeni tribes
to fight against them. By mid-2011 the violence had created
over a quarter of a million displaced persons in the North.

Finally, to make things really interesting, al-Shabaab
(the same organization that has overrun Somalia and is
recruiting refugees in Dadaab) announced in early 2010
that it would send fighters across the Gulf of Aden in
exchange for AQAP militants joining the fight in Somalia.

* * *

I woke up as the pilot announced our descent into Sana'a. I hurried to look out the window, but was disappointed to see a dusty city filled with short mud buildings. Desert all around. If I hadn't known I was flying into the capital city, I would have been surprised that a town this small had an airport. Sana'a in fact has a population of around 2 million people, and is located 7,500 feet above sea-level, making it one of the highest altitude capital cities in the world.

Once we landed, I was escorted into the notorious little room the Political Security Office (Yemen's scary domestic intelligence service) presided over in the airport, flagged by the immigration officer who saw my Pakistani visa. (I couldn't wait to get a new passport, as even the entries into Amman had become filled with hour-long interviews in their little room.) I tried my best to look like a bumbling tourist and told the officer I had spent time visiting Islamabad as a tourist. Once he asked who I was visiting in Yemen, I mentioned Fadhl al-Aryani's name.

"al-Aryani?" he repeated.

"Na'am," I nodded, smiling. He handed me back my passport and waved me away. I would later find out that Fadhl, and his cousin at Harvard, were related to the former Prime Minister of Yemen and the leader of the opposition. No wonder my travels had gotten so much easier once he got involved.

The rest of the airport made regional airports in the Dominican Republic look glamorous by comparison. There was only one terminal and two rusted conveyor belts, only one of which was functioning. This conveyor belt was so old and haphazard that every sixth suitcase would fall off, only to be retrieved by one of the security guards at a leisurely pace twenty minutes later. Given that I had spent a twenty-hour layover in Cairo (a choice between that or a sixteen-hour layover in Bahrain), I had every expectation that my bag would not arrive with me, my inconspicuous and unrecognizable black duffel lost somewhere in the ether between the two cities.

So I was unsurprised when my bag did not appear on the rusty conveyer belt. However, in a stroke of good luck, I found it lying next to a deserted baggage claim counter. It had apparently flown in on an earlier flight. I looked for a currency exchange counter in the airport, but could only find one open and its staff was unable to exchange $300 because they didn't have enough cash on them. I exchanged only $100, or about 22,000 Yemeni rials. Since the largest denomination bill I ever saw while in Yemen was 1000 rials, or a little more than $4, I ended up stuffing my pants with a thick sheaf of bills that made loose jeans look French they become so tight. If you visit, don't bother using an American wallet—you'll soon be unable to fold it in half.

The taxis at the airport were relatively new, far better than those in Peshawar, and I soon found myself riding a new white and yellow model. On the drive toward Old Sana'a, which up until a few decades ago was the only part of Sana'a that existed, I saw dozens of ruined buildings and empty lots strewn with modern ruins and debris all around. It was as though the city had never fully recovered from a war or had left the damage visible for all to see. I was surprised that not a single building was over four stories high.

Continuing to look out the window, I noticed that the few women I saw on the street were dressed head to toe in black, half of them showing off their eyes, half of them wearing thin black veils that covered their faces completely. Fortunately for them, compared to the women in *burkas* in Peshawar, the temperature in Sana'a only ranges from 45 to 85 degrees year-round rather than the 110 degrees more common in Pakistan. Instead of burkas, Yemeni women generally wear *abayas*, a long black dress with long black sleeves and head and face coverings. All of the women I saw wore black gloves as well. About half the men in Sana'a wear the traditional *futa*, effectively a really long shirt, underneath which they sometimes wear pants, sometimes not. Over the *futa* they wear a belt with a holster for their dagger, which they carry in front, and a sports coat on top of it all. It is a fascinating combination of Yemeni and Western fashion, and there does not seem to be any rhyme or reason as to what color or style of blazer should go over the *futa*. I saw everything from a five-button bright orange blazer to a dark blue velour. The driver happily pointed out how everyone chewed *qat*, but warned me that whisky was illegal.

Indeed, virtually every man I saw on the road had a bulge, sometimes of grotesque size, of *qat* leaves in his cheek, with the vivid green juice at times dribbling out of the corner of his mouth. Every man in Yemen chews *qat*—from the President to the guy who shines his shoes. (According to the various men I asked, only a very small percentage of women do as well.) Most men in Yemen chew *qat* every day. Three hundred and sixty-five days a year. In rural areas, most people start chewing at noon; in Aden, 3 or 4 PM was more common—except during Ramadan, when they only start chewing after breaking their daily fasts at sundown.

Qat is a green plant that can grow between four and ten feet in height, can be harvested up to four times a year, may take up to eight years to reach its full height, and requires little maintenance other than sunshine and water. People have been chewing its leaves for centuries, allowing the juices to seep into their bloodstreams through their gums and cheeks. The result is a feeling of alertness that is supposed to be similar to the effects of an amphetamine, as well as euphoria and a loss of appetite. The British Medical Journal "Lancet" rates it as the least harmful drug studied with a low level of dependency. Yemen is the largest producer and consumer of *qat* in the world.

The problem with *qat* is the effect it has on Yemenis' income, productivity, and potential for future social upheaval. For example, the average taxi driver in Aden, someone who is considered middle class, makes about 6000 riyals a day. On average, he spends about 1000 riyals, every day, on *qat*. Assuming he works six days a week but chews seven days a week, he spends almost 20 percent of his weekly income chewing leaves. This means that low to middle class sectors of the Yemeni population spend 15 to 60 percent of their income on *qat*, which also happens to create anorexic effects that in turn reduce their food intake. While *qat* accounts for 6 percent of GDP, over a third of agricultural GDP, and provides employment for one in every seven working Yemenis, the World Bank estimates that under one fifth of Yemenis end up going into debt to finance their *qat* habit.

In addition to requiring money that could be spent on food, clothes, or education, *qat* is a huge hit to productivity in Yemen. While it's entirely possible to work while chewing *qat* (virtually all of my taxi drivers past noon did), the fact is most people stop working once they start chewing. Chewing *qat* marks the beginning of the social day, during which people sit around and chew together. Worse, *qat* usually leaves these guys wired up, and they are unable to fall asleep until two, three, or four in the morning, which means that most people don't get to work until noon. Try and get a cab before 8 o'clock in the morning and the driver will charge you triple—no negotiating. And you'll have the company of one seriously cranky driver, I assure you.

Finally, and most worryingly, Yemen is a country that is fast running out of water—some estimate the water supply will be gone as early as ten years from now. The Carnegie Endowment for International Peace estimates that 80 percent of all conflicts in Yemen have been over water. *Qat* is an extremely thirsty plant, consuming far more water than wheat does, for example. It's also far more lucrative, however, which means more farmers are incentivized to grow *qat* over food. As potable water starts to run out, *qat* is likely to become a lot more expensive. And the first people to be affected will be the poorest Yemenis, already at the fringes of society, ignored by a government they despise. And what will happen when they can't afford their daily fix? When the middle class is forced to choose between *qat* and food? You're going to have a very angry population, who already dislikes the government, start demanding some serious change. Given the lack of electoral accountability of the government, this anger will probably be channeled through protests and violence, drawing the country into even greater chaos.

The Arab Spring, with its revolutions in Egypt and Tunisia, inspired hundreds of thousands of Yemenis to take to the streets, triggering the kind of upheaval that will be seen again during an acute *qat* and water crisis. Most tellingly, during the first month and a half of the Arab Spring in Yemen, the government provided protesters with free *qat* as a means to subdue the population. It worked initially, as many of the protests puttered out after dissidents spent only a few hours shouting slogans and then retired into their shady tents to chew. This all changed after President Saleh's security forces shot more than fifty protesters using snipers stationed in the buildings around Change Square.

When I talked to Yemenis about the *qat* problem they invariably brought up alcohol as the counterfactual. Unlike alcohol, they say, *qat* does not make you aggressive. You always know what you're doing, and you're always in control. All good points, I assured them, but they still don't address the problem of what will happen in ten years. At this, the Yemenis usually shrugged and popped another stem into their mouths.

* * *

The taxi dropped me off in Old Sana'a at the Burj-e-Salaam Hotel, which charged an exorbitant $85 a night but looked very pretty from the outside and not too dilapidated from the inside. I was fortunately not staying there, but had instead arranged to crash with a school friend who had been doing research in Sana'a for the past three weeks.

Dan, the guy I was staying with, is an all-around fantastic guy with a booming laugh and a warm personality. Unfortunately, the poor guy had been conned by a Harvard professor into attempting to do research on democracy in Yemen, a solidly authoritarian state that had been under the iron-first rule of President Ali Abdullah Saleh for the past thirty-two years. No, the research had not been going well. You try and get real data on rigged elections and see how far it gets you. At least as a foreigner he was less likely to be jailed and tortured to death than a local doing the same research. Sadly for Dan, he was unable to go back to Yemen in the summer of 2011 and take in all of the pro-democracy protests, as Saleh's government had rounded up and expelled all foreign journalists a few months before and refused to issue any visas to Westerners.

I met Dan at the hotel and we started walking toward the six-bedroom and five-floor house in which he was living. Now that we were in Old Sana'a, it was as though we were in a different city altogether from the one I had landed in. Imagine a small Italian town with narrow cobblestone alleys, intricately painted and well-kept short buildings that loom over you, and the delicious smells of fresh bread and roasted meats wafting through the air.

Only one car, if that, can fit in an alley. Now imagine this wonderful European town without a single tourist or annoying shops selling kitschy, overpriced items made in China. That was Old Sana'a. It was breathtaking. Generations of people had been living here, in these same buildings, uninterrupted for hundreds of years. The city, which has been declared a World Heritage site by UNESCO, has been inhabited for over 2,500 years. Its oldest buildings have been standing for 1,000 years. If you took away the satellite dishes dotting random buildings, there would be little difference between today's Old Sana'a and that of hundreds of years ago. It is one of the most incredible places you could ever visit.

As we walked through the narrow streets, small children stopped and screamed "Welcome!" at us in English, and most young bearded men smiled. The children begged me to take pictures of them, and laughed hysterically when I showed them the results. I was surprised by the friendliness of the Yemenis toward Americans even though the United States supported the much-disliked Saleh government and every now and then used drones to target terrorists (inevitably killing civilians).

Starving, I bought a shawarma off the street. It was delicious and, rather than served in the typical Arabic flatbread, was served in a rectangular-shaped bread like a hot dog bun. Yemen is famous for its breads and its honey (which can cost up to $150 for two pounds), and this particular bread was like Texas toast, thick and crispy on the outside and delicious and fluffy on the inside. In addition to a large thin white bread and the thicker Arabic bread, Yemenis also make a square bread with a hard crust. They call it *qadm*, the word for foot in Arabic, as it was apparently a staple of the Ottoman foot soldier's diet.

Before going out to dinner we stopped by a "pool hall," effectively a room in an alley with two very worn pool tables and some crooked sticks. Once again, everyone was extremely welcoming, to the point of refusing to allow us to pay for the bottle of water they brought us. I inquired at what age children started chewing qat, as everyone in the room was munching away, and was sadly introduced to a six-year-old boy in the corner who beamed at me with bright green teeth.

We then met up with David, the American editor of the English-language magazine "Yemen Today," who had been here for over two years and boasted about being the only foreigner in Sana'a dating a Yemeni girl. We stood out like sore thumbs in our jeans and T-shirts, and yet were walking freely around the food market at night. I asked them how safe Sana'a was, and they both agreed it was extremely safe for tourists. Even the foreigners who were kidnapped by tribes were treated well, subjected to good food and multi-hour *qat*-chewing marathons.

We sat down at a local restaurant with benches on the street and split three dishes of omelet with tomatoes and spices, beans with bell peppers, and the most delicious grilled chopped liver that would have put any New York deli to shame. All accompanied by large, thin, freshly baked flatbreads, a feast for which we each paid less than a $1. I asked Dan and David, if Sana'a was so safe, what about all of these terrorist attacks? They laughed and regaled me with the story of the suicide bomber who had targeted the British ambassador (the bomber had thrown himself at the ambassador's car and detonated himself; his head had ended up in a clothes basin on a woman's rooftop), and the multiple attacks against the US Embassy (which had been forced to close down for two days in early January because of credible al-Qaeda threats). It seemed extremists made a clear distinction between foreign tourists in Sana'a and those foreigners working in Yemen in an official capacity. Although there were constant threats, and regular attacks, on Western government buildings and diplomats, all the expats I met felt free to walk around, day and night, live and interact with the population, all without worry or a security presence.

Afterward we went to smoke hookah with a larger group of expats, most of whom, if I were to be unkind, could be described as social misfits. (Ever wonder where that lonely guy from the high school cafeteria ended up?) Some had been here for a while, working for non-governmental organizations; others had spent less time here and were doing research for their theses. I met a graduate student from the School of Oriental and African Studies (SOAS), part of the University of London, a school best known for graduating somewhat left-leaning hippies happy to live in huts and heal the world. This grad student was doing some fascinating research in Yemen. Apparently, after the Lebanese army expelled the Palestinian Liberation Organization (PLO) in 1991, a group of the hardcore fighters and their families came to Sana'a to set up a new camp. The PLO rented a plot of land for them from the Kuwaiti Investment Company that owned it in Yemen. The Palestinian refugees had never left, and ten years ago, when the official contract expired, they refused to be forced off the land. To complicate matters further, the Yemeni government was now contesting the ownership the Kuwaiti company had of the land in the first place—which resulted in the Palestinians not having to pay rent to anyone over the past ten years. The quarrel was still ongoing, although the Yemeni government had allowed the refugees to attend their schools and work. This grad student's research was based on this group's partial integration into Yemeni society.

Charlotte, a recently arrived French girl, had been part of a musical troupe before deciding it wasn't for her and moving to Sana'a. She had been here twice before and thought it would be a good place to "find herself" and write a movie script. Only four pages of the script had been written, however, as she had started dating "the most attractive man I've ever gone out with" and other than sex had gotten little else done in her month-long stay. The conversation soon turned to her boyfriend's sex life, as he had admitted to Charlotte that he had slept with seven women in the past ten months, since his arrival in Yemen. In a huge bruise to David's fragile ego, one of his conquests had included a Yemeni girl. David immediately asked Charlotte how her boyfriend had accomplished such a feat, his face incredulous. "They are neighbors in the same building," she responded. "Apparently they bumped into each other on the stairs, and then one day she came over to ask for something. She invited him over, fed him, and then told him he could sleep there if he wanted to. So he did."

David, in his desperation and seemingly unaware of the embarrassment he was causing himself, demanded to know the lurid details of the encounter: quality of the woman in question, positions they had engaged in, frequency, etc. After all of his requests had been shot down, he turned away, crestfallen and upset that someone else had achieved the feat of which he was most proud.

We paid the bill and left the hookah bar, on our way to a legendary underground club where we could watch the World Cup match and where there supposedly was a fully stocked bar. "It's been given a special exemption by the President," I was assured by another expat. On the taxi ride back David, perhaps to overcompensate for his earlier inadequacy, regaled us with a story about how he had briefly met Umar Farouk Abdulmutallab, the unsuccessful Christmas Day bomber, who had told our blond friend upon meeting him, "Convert and be saved," apparently the greeting used by Muslim conquerors in past centuries. He then told us a story about a group of Marines who had gotten beaten up at a bar by Russian mobsters, who warned them to "stay inside the Embassy." I'm not exactly sure what the mobsters were doing in Yemen, mind you, as there wasn't exactly a thriving drug export market or prostitution ring that I knew of.

The taxi passed through a deserted checkpoint, the concrete barriers a now-familiar characteristic of my trip, and we got out in front of a fairly glamorous looking marble building with white Christmas lights strung on its façade. The parking lot was full of new cars and more than one Mercedes. The foyer looked like a nice four-star hotel, with two pretty Ethiopian receptionists who escorted us to a wooden staircase in the left-hand corner. One brisk pat down and one metal detector later we arrived in a dimly lit basement filled with cigarette smoke and about a hundred expats.

Along the walls were small framed paintings of half-nude women from the eighteenth century in poses that I imagine would have been considered quite racy back then. There was in fact a full bar, although the prices were outrageous by Yemeni standards: six dollars for a beer (of which they had a wide range) and ten dollars for a Chivas on the rocks. There was rum, gin, vodka, and three different brands of tequila. It was, quite frankly, not a bad place at all, and one expats clearly came to to let loose, as evidenced by the regular downing of whiskey drinks around me. A good looking girl from Pittsburgh started talking to me and joked about setting up a travel agency that would help tourists get kidnapped by tribes. "It sounds pretty awesome, if you ask me," she told me. "Chew some good *qat*, practice your Arabic, and you've got a cool story to tell!"

Sana'a was a much different place than I had expected, and I relished the freedom that I had here to walk around the city and still feel safe. I could see why so many people enjoyed learning Arabic here and were content to spend a few months in the country. The house I was staying in had a kitchen stocked with American processed foods (including Kraft Mac and Cheese), a beautiful rooftop overlooking all of Old Sana'a, and a large room with a flatscreen TV and dozens of cushions, complemented by the thousand channels we received from our pirated satellite. Best of all, you could rent one of the six rooms for $200 a month. This wasn't so bad after all.

* * *

I woke up the next day excited to walk around and emboldened enough by people's friendliness the day before to bring out my Canon and rock the tourist look. The dull stomachaches, a friendly reminder of the parasites my Western stomach was fighting in Peshawar, had returned. This late in the game, though, I vowed to continue eating the delicious street food until my body got used to it or left me dead and dried out on a toilet somewhere. I had *qadm* with egg, potato, and spices for breakfast ($.25) and got lost for a while in the Old City. Children and old men would shout *"Sura!"* (the word for picture in Arabic) at me, and I was delighted to oblige over and over again. Only the youngest uncovered girls would ask for pictures, however, and I made sure to give a wide berth whenever a fully covered woman walked past. As I walked away from the *souk*, the nearby market filled with freshly baked bread, qat, tomatoes, dates, endless spices, and beautiful colored dresses that I imagined women wore underneath their black *abayas*, I saw a friendly eight-year-old boy backing out a truck from a narrow alley—in the driver's seat.

I quickly got out of his way and ambled over to the main road (one of only two paved ones), ready to feel the exhilaration of jaywalking in Yemen. Crossing the road is a dangerous and invigorating sport here, with most cars stopping one or two inches short of running you over outright and a few high-quality drivers simply swerving merely to graze you with a side mirror.

After walking for about an hour and constantly asking for directions, I finally arrived at a travel agency where I could purchase my ticket to Aden. Aden is the city nearest to the Somali refugee camps where AQAP had set up a recruiting network. The travel agency was housed in a short two-story building with brown marble floors and a small office upstairs. I had stupidly forgotten my passport, and thus had no form of ID, but the friendly travel agent easily waved the requirement. After paying for my plane ticket in dollars, I started to walk back toward Old Sana'a and found an Arab Bank ATM that subsequently dispensed to me crisp $100 bills, Vegas-style. Unlike Pakistan or even Nairobi, the ATM was outside of the bank building, in the street, and there was no scary looking guy with a machine gun guarding it. I wondered how much longer this safety could last, especially in the poorest country in the Middle East. The disparity seemed so striking: One could take out the equivalent of Yemen's GDP per capita, in crisp dollar bills from an ATM that was unguarded, while a large minority of the population was starving. Why wasn't there more petty crime? Especially in a culture where guns and knives were so prevalent? Did the National Rifle Association have a point when arguing that if everyone had a gun the world would see less crime?

Back in Old Sana'a I saw two children wrestling on the street and fighting over a gun. As I got closer I was stunned to see that it was a real gun the kids were playing with, at times trying to pull the jammed trigger at each

221

other. The gun was unloaded, which is why the trigger had jammed, but I was still shaken to see the children handling it. Stories of the Yemeni temper abounded, with an expat that night recounting a car crash he had witnessed outside his office window. The two men had gotten out of their cars, exchanged words, done the "let me see how close I can get to your face without kissing you" manly gesture, and then proceeded to duke it out. One of the men took out his *jambiya*, the Yemeni knife that men traditionally wear across their waists, and started slashing at the unarmed man, who reacted by jumping out of the way and then bear-hugging the guy. After they were separated, the knifeless man disappeared for a bit, only to return swinging a thick stick violently at the other man's head. "Don't worry, though," the expat reassured me, "the knives are usually blunt. You're only in trouble if they get to stab you, but slashing is usually harmless."

Dan and I had dinner that night at *Souk al-Milh*, an outdoor food market populated with stalls where you could walk around the different vendors, order food, and then wait at one of the dozens of communal tables while the food was brought to you. Again, Dan and I were the only foreigners in the market, and yet the only distinction that was made between us and the locals was the occasional beggar coming to our table. We ate another delicious dinner of freshly squeezed, foamy lemon juice with sugar (which would become my staple drink in Yemen), kebabs with a spicy tomato sauce on the side, *qadm* bread, garbanzo beans (which were so good that I wasn't even bothered by the cockroach I spotted in that stall—the first one I'd seen all trip), and brown beans with peppers.

I mentioned to Dan my surprise at the low level of petty crime in Sana'a and my experience at the dollar-dispensing ATM. He told me his theory: "It's because Yemenis have such a strong family structure. If you're an orphan there are a myriad aunts and uncles to take care of you, and even if you're not, there's a strong family network that looks over you at all times. For example, if right now you and I were in downtown Detroit we would not be safe as strangers in the neighborhood, walking around at one o'clock in the morning. We'd be mugged almost immediately. Here that doesn't happen, in part because the family is so intertwined with the community that everyone could quickly pinpoint who was responsible and exact punishment. I'd guess it also has to do with a stronger covenant of hospitality as well, where even as outsiders we are offered some modicum of protection simply for being guests in the neighborhood."

In fact, strangers regularly went out of their way to help us. We were living in an area of town with middle-class Yemeni families for whom a $400 camera could make a significant difference in the quality of their lives. Yet strangers ran after us to return our cellphones and cameras when we forgot them. More than once I'd misunderstood 50 riyals for 500, and each time the vendors would give me back my bill and correct me rather than take advantage of me. I encountered nothing but friendliness and openness from this population, never suspicion or resentment.

After dinner we headed to another expat's house in the Old City, where people were determinedly enjoying three bottles of warm, cheap vodka that they had smuggled into the country. There was a latent and powerful sexual tension in the expat community here, a sense of needy desperation. Newcomers were ogled lasciviously, out of a hunger both for physical intimacy and for a sense of normal interaction with the opposite sex. And yet because there were so few potential partners available, almost all had quickly become engaged in relationships. You could see the forced relationships that had become a staple of the foreign community here, where commitments frequently occurred out of desperation or resignation. A good looking American girl, annoyed by her meeker British boyfriend, stared longingly at a tall handsome American across the room. He in turn seemed ashamed of his overweight Bulgarian girlfriend, who was clearly in love with him, rejecting her ever more open and Smirnoff-fueled advances. Fed up, he finally stood up and outright sat apart from the poor girlfriend, who was left longing for his affection.

I soon got into an argument with the host because I disparaged the most recent *New York Times* article on Yemen, a ten-page spread titled, "Is Yemen the next Afghanistan?" Most of the guests consisted of freelance journalists and aspiring writers, and the host had spent time with Robert Worth, the *New York Times* journalist who had written the article, and defended his piece. I told him I was furious that the piece touched only on the negative aspects of Yemen, of which there were a great deal, but failed to mention any of the positive attributes of this wonderful society. The article had highlighted the three South Korean tourists who had been targeted by a suicide bomber, the kidnapping of Western tourists, and how traveling around the country was so unsafe that he couldn't go meet any of the tribal elders and they had all been forced to come to Sana'a for interviews.

Worth had failed to mention how safe Sana'a was for tourists, or how the vast majority of kidnapped Western-ers were treated well and returned unharmed after a few days with the tribes. He had also made the situation sound as terrible as Peshawar, a city that was patently unsafe for tourists who weren't camouflaged in local garb and were camera-less, which was generally the impres-sion that Western media outlets perpetuated of Yemen. After having spent some time in Peshawar, I could see the huge differences in the security situation between the two and it bothered me immensely that the two cit-ies, and countries, were so commonly lumped together. This was a recurring problem for Yemen, and a number of reporters I had spoken to mentioned that major news outlets had a storyline they were forced to heel to—Ye-men as a dangerous failed state, run by al-Qaeda and rife with anti-Americanism—and that stories that disputed this view were simply not published. On the positive side, Worth's article had made an excellent point that supported my experiences thus far and highlighted the key link between radicalization and education. He wrote:

But the tribesmen of Rafadh continued to shelter Quso and his men and not just because of their shared hatred of the government. Quso had offered

225

to supply teachers for the village school. Local families knew he was with Al Qaeda but welcomed the news for a simple reason: there were no teachers in the school at all. "The people were saying, 'We would rather have our kids get an Al Qaeda education than be illiterate,' " Jifri told me. After hearing about Quso's offer, Jifri went to officials in Sana and delivered a blunt message: "Right now you have one Al Qaeda guy in Rafadh, tomorrow you will have 700."

Initially, Jifri said, the government refused to provide teachers, saying any town that was willing to accept help from Al Qaeda was beneath contempt. Finally, they relented.

"The government agreed to send 6 teachers," Jifri told me. "Fahd (Quso) brought 16."

We said our goodbyes a little past one o'clock in the morning and hailed a cab off the street. Our taxi driver, driving down the paved road that divided the Old City in half, happily pointed out how good the road was and how it was paid for by the United States. This was the third time a taxi driver had pointed out the new road, always mentioning that it had been funded by Americans. As with Pakistan and its energy needs, I once again realized that large projects that were very visible to the population and benefitted a large number of people, even in a small way, were a much more effective way of fighting anti-Americanism than smaller health and economic development projects. The positive publicity these large projects generated was a force multiplier of sorts, as people in Hodeida and Aden would also hear about the road and its positive connotation. I am not arguing that a road is a more important, or even a more helpful, project for the Yemeni population than a rural hospital or an agricultural training center outside of Sana'a. I am arguing, however, that large-scale visible infrastructure projects serve US interests more effectively than smaller projects, and help burnish America's image abroad.

The taxi finally dropped us off, two Americans and a British girl, all sticking out like sore thumbs in the early morning hours and yet safe as we made our way through the empty streets and dark alleys of the Old City on our way home.

* * *

It rained heavily in Sana'a the next day, a cold and unexpectedly chilly storm that lasted a few hours and flooded the main thoroughfare in the Old City. Last time the road had flooded seventy-nine people had died, most who, under the influence of *qat*, thought they could simply swim across the road to the other side of the city—only to be immediately pulled under by the strong current and knocked unconscious by any amount of debris being carried with the current. I ventured out anyway, excited to see *Baab il-Yemen* (The Door of Yemen), the main entrance to the city walls that used to enclose the Old City. After asking for directions from a family of ten, who insisted on me taking multiple pictures they would never receive, I ended up stuck with three adorable mini-guides who brought me to the *Baab*. The leader of this ad-hoc group was sixteen, looked twelve, and was happily married with two children.

The *Baab* itself was a disappointment, smaller than expected, not particularly intricate or beautiful, and crowded with *souk* vendors. I entered a couple of stores that sold honey, Yemeni's proudest product, and was shocked to see that the prices ranged from $30 to $60 per kilo (or about $15 to $30 per pound). I later checked with my Yemeni friends and they told me that these were in fact "real" prices, not jacked up particularly high for a foreigner, and that the high-quality honey was well worth them. I left the *souk* to go to Hadda, the newer and richer part of Sana'a, a charmless industrial expanse with big houses and Western-style coffee shops. Prices for honey here increased up to $150 per kilo, and I happily accepted a free taste of a store's premium honey. It was unctuous and wonderful, dark colored and heavy, but surprisingly light on the palate, with a long finish and an intense "best maple syrup/happy memories of warm pancakes" taste.

That day I had finally gotten in touch with Fadhl, the man who had been kind enough to facilitate my visa through the Ministry of Water, and was anxiously waiting to meet him at an upscale coffee shop. Dan joined me and we soon met Fadhl and his group of friends, who drove up in a shiny new SUV and joined us for a quick lunch on what passes for fast food in Sana'a: whole roasted chicken, kebabs, *mtabel* (a roasted eggplant dip), and fresh lime juice. Since alcohol is restricted in Yemen, Fadhl and his friend invited Dan and me to a *qat* chew, the equivalent of Yemenis getting to know you over a beer. After a few phone calls it became clear that their houses were unavailable or full of their parents' guests, and I was happy to offer them my temporary house as an alternative location for the chew.

In advance of my first *qat* chew, Fadhl and his friends accompanied me to the most expensive *qat* souk in the city, where I paid an exorbitant $12 for a small bag full of fresh looking stems with baby leaves—apparently two positive characteristics an amateur should look for when buying *qat* (which has to be chewed fresh or it loses its effect). Next time you're in Yemen buying *qat*, make sure that you purchase stems that look fresh, akin to buying herbs at the super market, and that the size of the leaves is small, as bigger and more mature plants are less tender. Based on these characteristics, my friends assured me that I had purchased high-quality stuff.

A *qat* chew is essentially an occasion on which a medium to large group of men sit around on comfortable cushions on the floor and shoot the shit for four to ten hours. Somehow, *qat* makes this bearable, even enjoyable, akin to meeting up with your best friends over a few drinks. People take the individual *qat* stems from their baggies, break off the driest and lowest part of the stem, and pick off the largest leaves. They usually don't wash the *qat* because the pesticides give it an extra kick. They then proceed to insert the dirty stems into their mouths, chewing them a few times to release the juices, and then pack them into a little ball that they place inside their cheeks (like chewing tobacco). The juices are then released into your mouth and absorbed through your gums and cheek into your bloodstream.

The taste of *qat* leaves was bitter and chemical, my cheek stretched painfully and hurt after a few hours (it remained tender for days afterward), and all I got for my troubles was a mild headache and a feeling of confusion followed by a tempered euphoria as the caffeine kicked in. I found it to be much ado about nothing, and I would choose a warm beer over chewing shrubs any day.

The social aspect of chewing *qat*, however, was far more exciting. I was finally here, at one of the famous *qat* chews, in my very own *mafrouj*, an entire floor in the house that had been dedicated to comfortable cushions and low-rise chairs, surrounded by a new group of Yemeni friends. I mentioned my honey experiences of the day, which elicited much praise of their national product, and floated the idea that we should get Congress to approve duty-free Yemeni honey imports into the United States in exchange for certain tribes withdrawing their support for al-Qaeda. I thought it a brilliant idea, but it created a few giggles among the group as they explained to me how al-Qaeda used the honey business as a front and money laundering operation, sometimes simply as a way to generate support among the farmers.

"You would essentially be funding al-Qaeda with that idea. Even if you weren't, Baba Saleh [Papa Saleh, a nickname for the president] would end up with the profits anyway. He's got his fingers stuck in everything."

"You have to understand, Francisco," another chimed in. "Fifty years ago Yemen was not like this. Yemenis

were not as conservative. Our women weren't fully covered. My mother's friends used to come visit and wear
mini-skirts in the 1960s without a problem. They weren't
harassed. The al-Qaeda ideology of violence, little tolerance, and hatred toward foreigners is antithetical to core
Yemeni values of openness and hospitality."

The only expat of the group, who had been here for
thirty years, then added, "Unlike other Arab nations,
there is not a sense of insecurity among the Yemenis.
They do not feel the illegitimacy of the Saudis, or the
confusion of the Jordanians with their large Palestinian population. They are very clear as to what being a
Yemeni is, and don't need to cling to an extremist Wahhabi ideology to cement their sense of identity." There
were murmurs of assent around the room.

A little background on Saudi Arabia and Wahhabism
is in order at this point. Abdul Aziz al-Saud was the first
king of what today is known as Saudi Arabia, a nation
he founded and unified under his rule in 1932. Twenty
years before this, he formed a religious militia by the
name of *Ikhwan* ("Brothers" in Arabic), a movement
made up primarily of Bedouin tribes that was dedicated
to the purification and unification of Islam. Saud would
eventually go to war against this element of his military
in 1930, after they accused him of religious laxity, but
he benefited greatly from their help and organization in
his conquest of the western region of Hejaz, bordered by
the Red Sea, in 1926.

In 1915, a few years after creating this religious militia, Ibn Saud signed the Treaty of Darin with the British government, which made the territory under the

House of Saud a British protectorate in exchange for Ibn Saud waging war against Ibn Rashid, who was an ally of the Ottomans during World War I. Saud would eventually defeat Ibn Rashid, doubling his territory and renegotiating the treaty with the British, and then in 1925 would conquer the holy city of Mecca, the Prophet Muhammad's birthplace. After the founding of the Saudi Arabian state in 1932, oil was discovered in vast quantities in 1938. All of Saudi Arabia's rulers since have been sons of Abdul Aziz al-Saud, and the United States has largely supported the monarchy since the end of World War II.

Wahhabism is one of the strictest interpretations of Islam and was originally advocated by the scholar Muhammad ibn Abd-al-Wahhab in the eighteenth century. Generally considered extremist in nature, it was initially only followed by a small minority within the Muslim world. However, it is the dominant sect of Islam in Saudi Arabia. After Saudi Arabia began exploiting its oil resources and receiving significant revenue, the country was able to export this interpretation of Islam more aggressively, by building mosques and schools that rejected a more tolerant interpretation of Islam and helped indoctrinate children with more extremist, less tolerant views from a very young age. It is estimated that between 1990 and 2000 Saudi Arabia, through its network of charities that promote this interpretation of Islam, spent around seventy billion dollars from government sources on humanitarian aid and the dissemination of Islam. A Saudi weekly reported that through these contributions an estimated 1500 mosques, 210 Islamic centers, 202 Islamic colleges, and over 2000 schools were built all over the world.

This funding continues today, both by Wahhabi Imams funded by the Saudi Royal family and directly by the Saudi Royal family as a way to make amends for their increasingly un-Islamic reputation. Though the royal family has come to be known for lavish spending and excess, they are the protectors of Mecca and Medina, the two holiest cities in Islam, and are thus beholden to act in a conservative and religious manner in order to continue to be accepted by the Imams as the cities' legitimate protectors. In order to maintain this hold on power, for example, they allow representatives of the Committee for the Promotion of Virtue and the Prevention of Vice to beat women in Saudi Arabia who are dressed "inappropriately," enforce one of the strictest interpretations of sharia law (though the majority of the royal family does not believe in it or adhere to it in private), and continue to fund extremist elements within their country so that they may export their ideology without destabilizing the country too much. This was the environment that created Osama bin Laden and his followers (who now vow to overthrow the Saudi monarchy) and is one of the world's most famous acts of hypocrisy today.

A Yemeni NGO worker who had spent the last few years in remote villages interjected, "We're not like the Saudis, who are a bunch of fucking Bedouins without a culture—we have a culture that has developed over thousands of years. Forget America, Saudi Arabia is the devil incarnate in the Middle East. Wahhabism is really the enemy. It's a Saudi-funded cancer that has brainwashed our people into following an angrier, more conservative, chauvinist, and intolerant version of Islam.

"The problems in the Middle East have been made so much worse by the education that Saudi Arabia exported—it really is a cancer that has finally started eating at its creator. For example, I was living in a small village a few hours from here for a while and I traveled around the area getting to know the locals better. The village that was near a primary road had a glistening new school building paid for by the Saudis, full of nine-year-old female students who had even covered their hands with gloves! Nine-year-olds! I asked one of the girls why she dressed like that and she told me it was because she would go to hell if she didn't.

"Two hours away, though, removed from the main road, was another village of the same tribe—the same tribe, Francisco—where adult women had their faces uncovered. Of course, there was no glistening school building to brainwash them into believing that they were going to hell for showing their faces!"

An education officer supported the NGO worker's point. "You should know that most parents don't want to send their children to these schools, but it's the only option for many communities. In my experience, virtually all parents, when given a choice between the Wahhabi system of education and a regular curriculum, choose the more well-rounded education. They don't want their children brainwashed anymore, but if you want to get any education at all there are very few options available."

Clearly, we as Americans have an ideological advantage over Wahhabis in our values of choice and the freedom of the individual. We are also the most powerful nation in the world. If Wahhabis had been so successful at exporting their ideology, couldn't we do the same? Couldn't we also export our values of tolerance? If the Saudis could do it fifty years ago, why couldn't we do it better today? My experiences in Dadaab and Peshawar kept coming up: how the kids had been taught a moderate version of Islam in school; how their religious classes had focused on the positive characteristics of the religion and its values of tolerance and compassion; how difficult it had been for al-Shabaab to recruit Somalis who had been through the well-rounded Kenyan curriculum; how the Bajauris in the Jalozai displaced persons camp had finally acquiesced to allowing their daughters to receive a basic education.

Yes, educating populations at risk of radicalization is a difficult endeavor, and it may take one or two generations to counteract the extremist ideology that has a head start on us—but imagine the rewards! Imagine a Middle East, an Afghanistan or a Pakistan, where people didn't hate the values we espoused, where acceptance and tolerance—ideals intrinsic to Islam—became the norm, instead of a corrupted version of *jihad* that has become a battle cry to eradicate non-believers.

The conversation had become too serious for a *qat* chew, and a friend of ours was soon entertaining us with stories of illicit threesomes in Yemeni basements—apparently part of a thriving but small underground party scene that I never experienced.

* * *

After a fitful and uncomfortable night due to the amount of caffeine in my body from that night's *qat* chew, I woke up at dawn to pack and head out to the airport. Expecting even more problems there given both my Pakistani visa stamp and the fact that I was traveling to the heart of the insurgency, I arrived three hours ahead of departure time. The security guards were friendly and lax about identification (my student ID sufficed), and before I knew it I was sitting at the gate with two and a half hours to spare before my flight to Aden.

Aden, for which the Gulf of Aden is named, is considered one of the oldest settled regions in the world. Myth has it that Cain and Abel are buried somewhere in the city. The city has come in and out of favor over thousands of years, has historically had one of the most important ports in the region, and has been ruled by the British, the Portuguese, the Ottomans, and the Zaidi Imams of Yemen, among others. In early 1839 the British East India Company landed there accompanied by a fleet from the Royal Marines and took over the city, which it ruled until 1937 as part of British India. After a local insurrection, led by the communist National Liberation Front, the British were finally forced to pull out in November 1967. Aden became the capital of the new People's Republic of South Yemen, renamed the People's Democratic Republic of Yemen in 1970 after a more radical Marxist sect of the National Liberation Front took over the government. Southern Yemen soon tied itself more closely with the Soviet Union, which resulted in the Soviet Navy gaining access to its port. Although unification of Southern and Northern Yemen had been discussed since 1972, it finally happened in May 1990 to form what is today the Republic of Yemen.

Upon hearing of my imminent trip to Aden, my friends in Sana'a had commented only, "Don't believe the bullshit about it being a liberal bastion in Yemen: The women are just as covered as in Sana'a," and, "They idealize their history, living in the past, always saying how much better things were before 1994—but I can't imagine things were that much different." I would find that Sana'a-ese disdain for Aden was matched by Adenese disgust at Sana'a, a much uglier and poorer city, according to them. Nothing matched their disdain for President Saleh, however, who poured resources into Sana'a and ignored Aden, almost as though it were the ugly stepchild you hoped to ignore in your new marriage.

Many Southern Yemenis argue that Ali Salim al-Beidh, the then-President of Southern Yemen, was coerced by President Saleh to unify against his will, and dissatisfaction among Southerners remained very high after unification. They believed that Northern Yemen had not fulfilled many of its promises of resource sharing and true equality between the two regions, and officially declared their independence from the North a mere four years later, in May 1994. President Saleh soon invaded and defeated the southern secessionist movement, led by al-Beidh, who fled to Oman. Since then, dissatisfaction among southerners has remained quite high, with most people unhappy about the government's distribution policies and generally angry with their unequal treatment. In particular, most of the oil in Yemen, however little is left, is located in southern Yemen but has been used primarily to fund the Northern elite since unification.

The current Southern Secessionist Movement really garnered steam in 2007, and although al-Beidh has officially declared himself its leader (from his exile in Germany), the real power lies in Tariq al-Fadhli. Al-Fadhli was a *mujahideen* during the war against the Soviet Union in Afghanistan and is generally considered to have had ties to Osama bin Laden. Up until early 2009 he was part of President Saleh's government, but defected after dissatisfaction with the regime's attitudes toward the South and openly called for secession in April of that year. In October 2009 the government accused him of trying to assassinate the Vice President's brother, who was also the head of Yemen's powerful Political Security Organization in southern Yemen. As the movement's popularity has grown, Saleh's government has taken ever more repressive measures against it, including press censorship (seven newspapers were closed in May 2009), increasing troop presence in the South, and detaining many of the movement's supporters. As expected, these moves have made the movement that much more popular among the people. To make matters worse, President Saleh was forced to deploy troops and tanks to the South in mid-2010, further exacerbating the unrest.

President Saleh came to power in 1978 and was technically serving out his "last" presidential term in 2010. In order to bolster his international reputation, he had enacted a set of democratic reforms that required him to leave office no later than September 2013. Prior to the protests of 2011, most people thought he would change the constitution again, or try and install his son Ahmad as President of Yemen. In spite of the government's inability to maintain peace with the Houthis and the southerners, the United States and Saudi Arabia continued to strongly support Saleh's regime, out of fear that without him Yemen would become totally chaotic and allow even greater swaths of ungoverned space for al-Qaeda in the Arabian Peninsula to train and launch attacks.

* * *

The gate agent announced that they were ready to board the aircraft, and I was soon seated for the short flight. The only remarkable aspect of the flight was the presence of a couple dozen flies inside the cabin—imagine their surprise at boarding the plane in cool Sana'a and getting off in stifling hot Aden.

The airport in Aden was cleaner and newer than the one in Sana'a (both had been bombed during the civil war), and reminded me of a tropical destination's main terminal, with that humid and salty air that characterized so many arrivals at a beach resort. (The sea, I would later realize while writing on a small table next to it, smelled like my summers in Maine—a happy memory so far from home that endeared me to the city that much more.) The airport had been built with marble floors and a large sign that boasted "Aden International Airport," but was nevertheless blessed with only two conveyor belts for luggage.

Outside, I walked over to the taxi stand, which sported vehicles far more run down than their counterparts in

Sana'a, and asked the driver to take me to the Hotel Mercure. The ride was short and filled with the cab driver's friendly attempts to test my Arabic vocab and learn more about me and my stay. We briefly passed by the famous port, now decrepit. The ocean here was characterized by powerful, regular waves ideal for body-surfing, although I couldn't see anyone bathing in the water. The city seemed much more spread out, modern, with taller buildings and new construction sprouting up along the highway, and yet emptier and less lively than Sana'a.

I arrived at my hotel, checked in, and dropped off my bags in a comfortable air-conditioned room with a large bed and a television. The windows overlooked the ocean and had a small balcony that was too narrow to stand in but provided a railing to hold on to while examining the expanse. There was no beach, only a rock and cement platform with a menacing sign that read "The Hotel Beach is not suitable for Swimming. Swimming is Completely Prohibited at All Times." I wondered why. Underwater mines from the civil war? Sharks? Was the current simply too strong?

I called my contact at the UNHCR, a woman who had just arrived in Aden a week ago. After a few tries she finally picked up her cell phone, only to tell me that she was at the Sana'a International Airport. "I just lost my son. I'm leaving to my country. Go to the office and see if anyone can help you."

I felt a pang of guilt for my own mother, who was so worried about me that she had already shed ten pounds off her minute frame. In a macabre twist, it would be this woman's office that I would end up using during my visit at the UNHCR headquarters—a room plastered with pictures of who I presumed to be her son, making this stranger's tragedy all the more palpable.

I asked the concierge for a taxi to take me to the UNHCR headquarters. As usual, the UNHCR offices were heavily guarded by a private security company, had been ensconced inside thick concrete walls, and owned the comically identical fleet of white Toyota 4Runners. The local staff and head of office, as had been my experience since I began this trip, were friendly and extremely helpful in providing me with access and transportation to the camp. They took advantage of the presence of al-Kharaz's school principal and vice-principal in Aden and fit me into their schedules at the local Save the Children offices. Both men spoke English relatively well, and I was surprised to find that prior to the civil war in Somalia, English had been the formal language of instruction.

Although the population of al-Kharaz is estimated at two hundred thousand, only about twelve thousand people reside full-time in the camp. Unlike Kenya, Yemen does not have an encampment policy in place and refugees typically live all over the country in the major cities. No one really knows how many Somali refugees there are in Yemen, and I've heard and seen written estimates as low as three hundred thousand and as high as a million. Most of the refugees are concentrated in the south, where they face less discrimination because of closer geographical and cultural ties, and in Sana'a, where the girls usually end up working as maids. The al-Kharaz camp is best understood as an entry point for these refugees, who regroup there and then travel somewhere else. A large number, in fact, end up living in Saudi Arabia.

The voyage from Bosaso, a port city in Somalia located within the autonomous Puntland region, to Yemen is even more perilous than I had initially imagined. It takes approximately three days to cross the Gulf of Aden by boat; more than 50 percent of those who attempt the trip do not survive. Imagine how awful the situation in Somalia must be if so many people are willing to take a less than fifty-fifty chance of survival to get out of there. Once on the overloaded boats, many women and young girls are raped, and most boat crews throw all passengers overboard a few miles from shore because they are afraid of being caught by the Yemeni coastguard. The notorious human dumping areas along the coast have become breeding grounds for sharks, where everything you learned on the Discovery Channel about sharks not liking human flesh is sadly untrue. Thus, even if you know how to swim, which most people don't, you may still be eaten alive.

As the principal and vice-principal railed on about the evils of al-Shabaab, which had most recently banned Somalis from playing soccer and watching the World Cup (arguably the least popular decisions in the organization's short history), I asked them outright about recruitment. I explained to them the situation with al-Shabaab in Kenya, and prodded them to try and understand how many Somalis were recruited back from Kharaz. "There is no al-Shabaab presence in the camp," they both immediately concluded. I pressed them harder for information. "No, you do not understand. Kenya and Somalia have a very porous border, which al-Shabaab can cross at will. They do not have that with Yemen. Also, it is easier for us to hide among the Kenyan border because we are all black," he added, pointing at his skin. "Here, it is not so easy to hide the fact that we are black!" he chuckled. It seemed I had come to the wrong place to study terrorist recruitment.

I asked the men about the existing educational infrastructure in Somalia, only to have my suspicions confirmed. There was no public education system anymore in Somalia, only privately run institutions, many of them religious. Worse, the UN had given up on the situation getting better. The principal told me that in 2006 his school had been forced to stop teaching the Somali/UNESCO curriculum and teach instead the Yemeni curriculum, as it became clear that these refugees were never going back home.

* * *

I went back to headquarters after this meeting and the UN staff informed me I would be leaving for Kharaz the next day. I took a taxi back to the hotel to re-pack my duffel and finalize my plane ticket back to Sana'a and, finally, back to Boston. On the way back I was surprised to see so many prominent photos of President Saleh, who was extremely disliked in the south and whose grins seemed to mock the population, "You may hate me and the way I treat you, but there isn't anything you can do about it," he seemed to be saying. I laughed as we passed by internet cafes titled "300" and "Lord of the Net," with a stretched picture of Elijah Wood as Frodo on its tarp. Even here, in the heart of a country dominated by tribal structures, a flourishing al-Qaeda presence, and a strong disregard for the United States and its foreign policy, we had still succeeded in exporting our entertainment and, by default, our culture. While channel-surfing in the hotel I had stumbled upon a World Wrestling Federation channel dubbed in Arabic! It seemed silly for the State Department to focus its energy and limited political capital abroad on technology as a means to export American culture—people locally were already taking care of that.

One of the current foci of the State Department's counter-radicalization policies has been the utilization of technology to promote American values, an attitude exemplified by the work of Jared Cohen, a former member of the Policy Planning Office, on "connection technologies." As he stated in a 2008 speech on countering extremism, "Every single young person in the Middle East is reachable by one of three technologies: satellite TV, mobile phones, and the Internet. If they are not, they have deliberately shielded themselves." Other than this blanket statement being untrue, especially within refugee camps, it represents the erroneous focus of the Department of State on utilizing technology to reach those populations that are most at risk of being radicalized. This is in spite of the government's understanding that those most likely to be recruited by al-Qaeda and other terrorist organizations live within ungoverned spaces, precisely the environment surrounding most refugee camps.

The biggest problem with focusing on technology to get across the "American" message, if there is one coherent message, is that we are competing with dozens of other messages out there and a bureaucratic governmental organization is unable to understand what context will resonate with the target population. Today there are over four thousand jihadist websites, versus a dozen a few years ago, which spread militant ideology, post training manuals, and allow potential terrorists to meet online. The difficulty of our message resonating with the target population is most apparent when we realize that one of the most successful television shows on Lebanese television is a Mexican soap opera that takes place in Mexico during the Spanish colonial era, dubbed in Arabic. No bureaucrat could, or should be expected to, predict that. Against this changing landscape and the multitude of options today's youth can access over television and the internet, a focus on technology seems overly broad and naive. On the other hand, ignoring the education of refugees and internally displaced persons, an easily identified group of children with sub-par education and little opportunity, makes it even likelier that they will join a militant or terrorist organization.

American culture already does an excellent job of reaching the most remote places around the globe, in large part due to the sheer volume of television shows produced in the United States and other strong commercialization networks. A better use of government resources, and a more direct way of addressing our national security needs, would be to increase our involvement in refugee and internally displaced person education abroad, with a special focus on those camps that serve as recruiting platforms for terrorist networks.

* * *

I woke up at dawn again to board the UN convoy from Aden to al-Kharaz camp, this time composed of a single 4Runner with four passengers, plus the driver. Once on the road we saw hundreds of trailers parked on both sides of the highway, all of which had been there for over twenty-four hours while their drivers waited for more diesel to arrive at the nearest gas station. Sitting snugly next to a UN health consultant, who was going to spend two months in al-Kharaz doing a survey, I drifted in and out of consciousness, only to wake up wholly embarrassed that I had drooled all over myself and probably kept everyone awake with my intermittent snores.

The road had been paved ten years ago and was in relatively good shape, flanked at times by open, murderous desert peppered with sickly brown shrubs and at other times by the beautiful blue coast that Yemen enjoys, to our left, and the forbidding granite mountains to our right. At times you could see a small family of what I presumed were Somalis sitting or lying in the sand, their sad little tarps made of used Western clothing and providing little relief from the 100-plus degree temperatures. Rather than feel pity or sadness for these children, I felt fear—fear that they would starve or dehydrate to death; fear that there was no protection from a racist and corrupt police presence; fear that they had accepted their death sentences and were prepared to die. How could they possibly survive out here? Damned by a country they couldn't return to and damned by a country ill prepared to receive them.

As we got closer to the camp, the parallels between al-Kharaz and Dadaab became clearer—the heat, the sand and dust, the lack of vegetation. It was almost as though the glorious Yemeni coast was not within walking distance, as though the camp again were landlocked. We passed a military checkpoint far more menacingly equipped than the Kenyan one, and saw one or two olive green military jeeps with mounted machine guns and soldiers in helmets. Thirty minutes after passing the checkpoint we arrived at the UN base, where the rooms and general infrastructure made Dadaab look like a country club by comparison. There were two showers and two toilets for twenty beds, and it was clear that the rooms were not meant for longer-term stays. My own had the pungent stench of old sweat emanating from the two mattresses, which dissuaded me from lying on the bed for too long. In spite of having been here for over a decade, the camp structure gave off a feeling of temporality, as the concrete structures felt less permanent than expected.

As I waited for the staff to replace the bed sheets, the woman who had accompanied me from Aden voiced her concern over the insects in the camp. I happily, and in my most battle-hardened tone, brushed aside her worries with stories of red cobras and camel spiders in Kenya—neither of which I had personally experienced. "Yes, those monsters terrorized us at night," I added with bravado. In spite of my new Boy Scout pride at having been in the African bush, the truth was that the trip was getting harder for me. I was afraid that I was getting burned out, and that I would either do something stupid and reckless or else stop paying attention and insult my hosts and, by extension, the very people I had come here to help. Three months of travel was finally starting to wear me down, making it harder to focus, more difficult to fall asleep on thin mattresses in hot rooms, and more overwhelming to wake up in the mornings to face the misery of people living without a home.

I felt petulant and disgusted with myself for this attitude—I, of course, had a home to go back to, and my own experiences were a cocoon of luxury in comparison to those of any refugee around the world. I was ashamed of my weakness, the effect of living in a safe and loving environment all of my life, and felt pathetic to be feeling this way. To make matters worse, the staff at Kharaz encouraged me to go home earlier than planned because classes had ended a week before my arrival, a byproduct of the long and complicated Yemeni visa application process, and I could wrap up meetings with teachers, education officers, and students in just a few days. Most teachers and older students had already left to the big cities to find odd jobs during the summer holidays.

The UN offices were located in a small, usually air-conditioned trailer, where I met Pablo, an affable Ecuadorian protection security officer. The mandate for a PSO is inordinately broad, and they are responsible for security, engagement with the refugee and the local populations, food distribution, coordinating different

NGO programs, and any crises that arise. He had been sentenced to al-Kharaz for two years and was very much looking forward to his last six months here, after which he was taking four months off to marry his Colombian fiancée—who also worked for UNHCR. Given her masters in Latin American studies however, she had not been offered any jobs in the Middle East and was not allowed to live with Pablo in al-Kharaz because of the security situation. He heartily endorsed the idea that if I had a few days left over I should go visit Syria, a "beautiful place with beautiful women." I politely told him that I had little interest or time at the moment, but would be sure to visit another time.

I was introduced to Hadil, a young and cheerful fellow from Aden who had studied in Pune, India, and who became my first Southern Yemeni friend. He was employed by CARE International as an education officer in the camp. We happily compared notes on Indian girls, and he was mesmerized by the fact that I had dated one for three whole years in spite of our cultural differences. I asked him what the difference between Sana'a and Aden was, and he passionately responded, "We are better educated, more civilized, and, most important, friendlier!" He would later prove his point by inviting me to his friend's wedding, an offer I immediately accepted, far less shy in a foreign country about accepting strangers' invitations than I would have been at home. On our way to meet some of the primary school teachers, he complained about the violent nature of Somalis. "They stone our headquarters if we are one day late with their food rations. There is a lot of anger between them and against the host community also, and it is very common to see violence inside the camp."

In al-Kharaz there was only one primary school with 67 teachers, about 40 of whom were Yemeni, to host over 3,400 children. Ever since the curriculum had switched from the Somali one to the Yemeni one, most students had been largely unable to communicate with their Yemeni teachers and the drop-out rates had skyrocketed. "Not much point going to school if you can't understand the instructor," I thought. Al-Kharaz also has the problem of idle youth, but because Yemen does not have an encampment policy, most young men go to Saudi Arabia to work in construction and most women become maids in the large cities. I asked Hadil if any of the idle youth returned to fight in Somalia, and he chuckled at my naiveté.

"It's too hard to go back, and, frankly, it's the last thing they want to do."

What about al-Qaeda?

This he considered for a moment. "They don't recruit here," he said gingerly, "because the army presence is very high and it is too dangerous. However, the army did find some Somalis fighting in the North, with the Houthis, a few months ago. But we don't know if they were from the camp.

"Once the fighting ended in February 2010, though [after the Saleh government signed a truce with the Houthi rebels], the army killed most of the Somalis. I don't know if any more will go fight with them. The army was very, very angry," he added ominously.

I later met with the community elders and sheikhs to get a better understanding of the situation in the camp. As the elders spoke neither English nor Arabic, the conversation took much longer than I had antici- pated, as we had to use two translators (English to Arabic to Somali, and back). They expressed a com- mon concern about the estrangement between the local community and the refugees. The Yemeni locals hated the Somali refugees because they were invading their land, a claim the Somalis replied to by saying that prior to their arrival nothing had been there (true) and that the Yemenis only had jobs because of the refugee presence, given the influx of non-governmental orga- nizations into the area.

"Recently a Somali female student slapped one of the Yemeni teachers," explained an elder. The Yemeni vil- lager was accustomed to seeing women meek and fully covered, so this slap from a woman without a veil didn't sit well with him. "She was angry at him because he had kicked her brother out of class for being late. There was such a commotion in the camp after he insulted her after the slap that parents refused to send their children, any children, to the primary school for a whole month unless all Yemeni teachers were fired."

"What happened then?" I asked.

"Well, actually we started fighting with each other, instead of against the Yemenis, gave up our demands that they all be fired, and everyone returned to school. The problem is that since the schools switched to the Yemeni curriculum, most students have problems understanding the teachers and the instructors are very dismissive to- ward the students. But when we used to have the Somali curriculum, our students couldn't attend high school or university because their primary school education wasn't recognized by the Yemeni government."

"What we are really worried about," added the eldest sheikh, "is that after this year Save the Children and the UNHCR will no longer be in charge of education."

I asked my translator to repeat the sentence, making sure he had understood it. "I don't understand. What do you mean exactly?" I asked.

"The UNHCR will continue to fund the education, but now it will be run entirely by the Yemeni Ministry of Education."

I was aghast. This was the worst idea I'd heard of, handing over the responsibility to educate these children to a government that institutionally discriminated against Somalis and was incapable of teaching its own students, much less refugee children who didn't speak Arabic.

"So we are afraid," he continued, "that we are going to get even fewer teachers, and no more supplies or uniforms. We think that the Yemeni government is going to reallocate the funds the UN gives them to Yemeni public schools and pocket the rest."

That was precisely what was going to happen, I thought. It was natural that this would occur, and not exclusively because of the kleptocratic nature of the Yemeni bureaucracy. From the officials' perspective, why spend money on a refugee population you didn't care about when your own schools are in such dire need?

"We also think that our community may refuse to send their children to school once the Yemeni government runs it."

The fact was, the elders were probably right: Once education was under the aegis of the Yemeni government, quality and supplies would decrease even further, making it even less likely that students would attend school and perform well. It seemed everything I had learned about the treatment of refugees from my friends in Sana'a was false. In spite of the refugees' ability to work in the private sector and attend some Yemeni schools, the government had an institutional disregard for the well-being of this population, coupled with an unhealthy dose of cultural disdain.

As though to drive home the simmering anger of the population, a demonstration was staged outside the UN compound that day. I could hear the angry shouts of the mob and the unsettling clangs of the rocks being hurled against the metal gate.

* * *

I met with the head of the Yemeni-run public high school the next day. The meeting was depressing in how perfunctory it had become, with a jaded acceptance on my part that the school had no electricity or running water. The principal openly admitted that, unlike the primary school, there were not enough textbooks for all the students, as the Yemeni government only sent enough books to cover the Yemeni student population, ignoring the existence of Somali students. Unsurprisingly, although the average drop-out rate was only 50 percent, it had soared to 80 to 90 percent among Somalis. The school had no desks, and the principal complained that most teachers, frankly speaking, were not qualified to be high school teachers, as most had barely passed high school themselves. Finally, I raised the issue of a lack of communication between Somali students and Yemeni teachers, the language barrier, which he quickly dismissed as the students lying to cover up their sub-par performance. It was clear that the onus was on the student to learn, rather than on the teacher to teach.

A student council member I had met the day before had agreed to organize a focus group of boys and girls in secondary school with whom I could speak. I thanked the headmaster for his time and walked back toward the primary school lot to meet the students. I arrived a few minutes later and was warmly greeted by the student council president. Then I entered a boisterous room in the primary school with overcrowded desks and about fifty boys and ten girls. Superficially, they looked and seemed the same as the hundreds of other students I had met on this journey. The anger, predilection toward violence, and extraordinary sense of injustice that I would find here was impossible to notice with a cursory glance or a quick conversation, and only arose into the second hour of our meeting—once the students realized I really did care what they had to say.

By now I had learned that, rather than asking the students questions up front, allowing them to probe me first usually led to a more open conversation. We spent the first hour in friendly banter, as I answered where I was from, what I was doing here, and how the Somalis in Kenya lived. Throughout this journey I had encountered a strong desire by refugee populations to find out how other refugees around the world lived; they were thirsty to know whether they were better or worse off. When we finally got to the questions I wanted to ask them, we spent most of our time trying to get them to understand what the word "admire" meant. Once this obstacle was surpassed, their answers were: Allah, their teachers, and the usual list of family members. It was only when I asked them what they wanted to be when they grew up that things got interesting.

The most articulate and most outspoken student wanted to become an *imam*. So did ten other boys nearby, also some of the most outspoken. Unlike previous reasons I had heard, though, usually having to do with education and bridging religious gaps, their purpose was to spread the message of Islam and convert non-Muslims to their religion. I seemed to be a prime candidate for these students, although even in Sana'a I had been stopped by one or two strangers who had asked me whether I was Muslim.

"Are you a Muslim?" demanded to know the future *imam*.

"No, I'm a Catholic," I replied. Blank stares from the audience. "Christian," I added. Now they nodded.

"And do you read the Quran?"

I mentioned to him that I had in fact taken a class on religion, so I had studied the Quran along with the Bible and the Torah.

"Good! So then recite us a line!" he commanded.

I chuckled. The only line I knew was the *shahada*, the line that non-believers can recite to convert to Islam, and I definitely wasn't saying that out loud. "I didn't memorize the Quran," I tried to explain. "We studied it to understand and compare it, not for repetition."

"And will you convert to Islam?" continued the student.

I gave him my canned explanation that my religion was part of my culture, my relationship with my parents, and that I didn't think conversion was going to happen.

"Well, how many times a day do you pray?" another future *imam* asked. "Five? Three?"

I sheepishly lied and said I prayed once a day, certainly more true in Yemen than back in Boston. The group laughed dismissively at my religion—surely it couldn't be that important to me if I only prayed once a day!

I switched topics, asking other students what they wanted to be when they grew up. Professor. Soccer star. Engineer. Reporter.

"I want to join al-Qaeda."

My head spun around to the other side of the room, where I zeroed in on one of the students who wanted to become an *imam*. There was nervous laughter in the room, but not as it had been in Dadaab—the boy was serious about his answer. I assured him that it was perfectly okay for him to say this, and that I wouldn't tell anyone outside this room. (I had asked the teachers to leave when I got to the classroom.) "Why?" I asked him.

"Because they are winning in Somalia. Because I want peace, I want to go back home, and you have to choose a side."

So desperate was this young man for peace that he had come to associate al-Qaeda, and by default al-Shabaab, with it. A few other boys nodded their heads, agreeing with their peer. Another boy raised his hand and happily explained he wanted to be a wrestler. Others soon joined in. "Like John Cena!" someone shouted. These children were truly amazing, one second supporting an organization that brought death and destruction around the world, that espoused the ultimate goal of killing four million Americans, and yet the next embracing American pop culture so openly.

As we wrapped up our meeting I explained to them that the Yemeni government was going to take over primary school education at the start of the school year. The environment in the room was immediately poisoned, the children outraged at the idea, yelling and standing up from their desks with a sense of hopelessness and frustration. "Then it will be as bad as secondary school!" they shouted. I asked them to sit down, calm down a little, and explain to me what this meant.

"We have to pay for everything in secondary school. During our examinations we have to pay the Yemeni teachers to let us sit for the examination, otherwise they mark you as absent or cheating."

"The Somalis have to pay 1000 riyals [$4] a semester to attend. The Yemenis don't have to pay anything. They also make us pay for the free government textbooks, and they force us to give them back at the end of the year so they can re-sell them!"

"They only beat the Somalis in school, almost always with a stick, not the Yemenis. And if you couldn't come to class for a few days because you were sick or had to take care of your family, they charge you 3000 riyals [$12] or kick you out."

"If we get in a fight with the Yemeni students, we have to pay the teachers so we won't get arrested. The Yemenis don't."

They were furious, shouting louder and louder, feeding off one another's anger. The bile and injustice they had kept deep inside was boiling to the surface and overflowing in a torrent of pure hatred toward the establishment that took advantage of them in such a cruel way. I would later confirm everything they had told me with UN workers back at the camp, who assured me that it was the truth and that the students weren't exaggerating.

"We are supposed to have six periods a day, forty minutes each, but we usually only have two or three because the teachers are too lazy to show up."

"When a Somali does very well on an examination, they switch his results with a Yemeni who did worse. This is for the national exams! [The test that decides who gets to go onto university, a more important version of our SATs.] Only sometimes they let us pay them so that this doesn't happen and we get credit for our results."

"We have no future!" cried out one of the students desperately, his eyes filled with tears at the prospect of a life without hope. "We will refuse to attend primary school then. We will bring guns. We will protest until the education goes back to Save the Children!" he yelled, eliciting rancorous cheers of approval.

"Do you think it will help? If we protest?" asked one of his friends. I was torn inside, weighing the pros and cons of each action. I took a deep breath. "Yes, I think it may make a difference if you protest." There would be repercussions to this encouragement I knew, repercussions that would become all the more tangible later that day.

* * *

As I arrived back at the compound in time for lunch, still livid at the exploitation of Somali students, I saw that the security personnel and representatives from all the other NGOs were visibly agitated. They informed me that approximately fifteen men, either Yemenis or Somalis and armed with AK-47s, were outside the compound. The men either had a problem with the UN, or with another tribe, or were fighting over a girl—we weren't yet sure what was at issue. Although that day's protest was for different reasons, it was clear to me that the students' threat of bringing guns to school and violently protesting was more than just talk.

The UN security officer had asked for us to be evacuated, but headquarters in Aden rejected the idea, asking us instead to stay inside the compound and "keep a low profile." Only key activities like distributing food, operating the health clinic, and processing new arrivals were to be continued outside the compound while the threat was still active.

New arrivals.

In the midst of the commotion I thought back to the visit I had made to the New Arrival Center the day before, the first time I had seen a refugee population before it had settled down. I was surprised, and frankly embarrassed after having been in Dadaab, to learn only then that Somalia had changed its language from the Arabic script to the Latin alphabet in 1972. I was informed of this change as a result of Hadil's insistence that I read out loud some malaria signs, mostly to amuse him with my Somali pronunciation. The New Arrival Center was a cordoned off part of the camp where staff received all new refugees, helped them fill out the forms that would give them access to basic services and allow them to become registered, and sheltered them and fed them hot food for five days. The hot food was mostly porridge and the shelters consisted of canvas tents erected over thin mattresses laid on the ground, a safe place for these desperate people that would easily reach temperatures in excess of 110 degrees in the summer. These refugees were the worst off, some with blistered and bandaged feet that still oozed blood from their long journey, most with sunken eyes that looked at you with hunger and anxiety, peering out cautiously from the relative safety of a temporary home.

It was misery in its barest form to see these women and their children—there were few young men—but at least they were safe. Once again, I couldn't begin to imagine what the journey must have been like, how difficult their situation was at home to force them to flee and embark on what amounted to a crossing of death for so many. Walking back from the center to the UN compound, I saw the familiar sight of refugees waiting outside the main gates, desperately passing notes to strangers going inside in the hope that these strangers could somehow expedite their way out of here. Most of the crumpled notes had names written on them, or the word "help." Kharaz seemed worse than the other camps in all aspects—thinner animals, more violence, sicker people, and dirtier children. It was surprising that a camp of three hundred thousand people with a strict encampment policy could provide a better home than one with a paltry thirteen thousand inhabitants.

"Well, it looks like you're going to have to spend the weekend here," Pablo mentioned, shocking me back to the present and the angry protesters outside. The political security officer continued, "We are recommending that no vehicles leave the compound."

I had finished my research that day, there were no more schools to see, no more students to meet who hadn't already departed, no teachers to interview, or even any other NGO workers. The idea of a listless, hot, and uncomfortable weekend cooped up inside my smelly room loomed before me. I stammered back, "But... I thought I was leaving with the CARE convoy?"

"We have advised them not to leave, but it's really up to them if they want to drive out. I wouldn't recommend you go with them if they do leave, though. It could be dangerous."

I pondered his statement for a moment...

To hell with dangerous! At least getting kidnapped by a Yemeni tribe would be far more interesting than lying in bed pretending to read my latest, and most boring, book of the trip (the author and title of which I will, out of sportsmanship, not reveal). Plus, that American girl in Sana'a had intimated that the Yemeni tribes generally treated foreigners well! I walked outside of the trailer to look for the CARE driver. "Are you leaving?" I pleaded.

"Yes." He glanced over at the UN trailer I had just exited. "They only have problems with the UN, never with CARE."

I clambered into the pick-up truck before he could change his mind, waved happily at Pablo, and saw him kindly mouth the words "Dios te bendiga," which literally means "God bless you" but is meant to convey "may God take care of you."

The driver hopped inside the truck along with two female Yemeni CARE workers who lived in Aden, and we drove out from the main gate. We followed a Yemeni army pick-up truck, the bed of which was loaded with ten military personnel holding sub-machine guns. They raced out of the compound with us in tow, our car groaning to keep up with them over the sandy hills and unpaved gravel roads that led to the main highway. More than once we hit our heads on the car roof on an especially violent bump.

Twenty minutes later, we reached the paved road toward Aden, stopped our cars, and got out to thank our military convoy profusely by shaking their hands and emptying our cooler of cold Fantas, which they happily received. They even posed for pictures waving their guns around and smiling. We were officially on our way back!

A few miles in we encountered an amateur roadblock of large stones blocking access to the two-lane highway, brilliantly positioned between the two army checkpoints so that no help would come to our aid in case of trouble.

Uh oh.

Maybe the tribes had decided to stop NGO vehicles on the road back, rather than continue harassing the compound. Given that I was the only non-Yemeni in the car, I was probably the only one who would be kidnapped, a thought that was far less exciting than it had been a moment ago when I was happy to risk it to get out of Kharaz.

A woman with a crooked walking stick approached us from the driver's side. She looked very old, her face almost black from the sun, with deep wrinkles and dyed pale orange hair. As she neared the vehicle on her unsteady feet, she began screaming profanities at us in Arabic, banging her cane on the hood of the car. It was clear we weren't in danger, but something was very wrong. As she got closer to the window, leaning in to the driver, her eyes welled up and the woman started sobbing, screaming and waving her cane in desperation. The tears gushed down her cheeks, rivulets inside the deep wrinkles, and all our driver could say was, *"Asif jiddan, asif jiddan,"* (I'm very sorry). After five minutes of this back and forth, everyone reached for their wallets, and I was happy to contribute 1000 riyals to the 2000 riyal ($9) total that we gave her—a huge sum for a typical beggar.

The women in the vehicle would later tell me that the old woman and her son lived in the desolate shacks that we sometimes passed by on the sides of the highway, an oppressing and lonely existence characterized by thirst and famine. A pickup truck like ours had run over her son and apparently taken him to the hospital in Aden. The woman was desperate for news of her only son and was determined to stop every car on the road until someone brought her good news or gave her a ride into Aden.

The rest of the ride was remarkable only for the stunning beauty of the Yemeni coast, a bejeweled tricolor sea that extended as far as the eye could see, turning into increasingly darker shades of blue. It was truly breathtaking, easily a tropical paradise if only someone promised foreigners a degree of security. The waves were tall and powerful, perfect for surfing, and yet the entire expanse was devoid of any human form. As we entered the town of Little Aden, just outside the main city, I saw hundreds of pink flamingoes grazing in the shallow seabed. I'd never seen more than two flamingos at the same time, and it was inspiring to see them take flight, a mirage of hundreds of fluttering pink wings gliding over the sunset.

We encountered a few more roadblocks on the way home: camels and goats that had little regard for oncoming traffic and happily stopped in the middle of the highway. Walid, our driver, tortured us with a tape of old Arab music with the traditional wailing, and even after we had convinced him to try the radio, we did two full scans without finding a single station. It's not that I don't enjoy Arab music, but I didn't understand why so many drivers (even in Egypt) insisted on playing old songs. A quick search on YouTube will lead you to some great Arabic pop with singers who make Britney Spears look tame. Walid smiled at the lack of available radio stations and with glee reinserted his tape, Round 3. He then regaled us with stories of Aden, going so far as to tell me that Tony Blair was born there. (False, he was born in Edinburgh.)

Once we got close to Aden we stopped at a *souk* so he could buy some *qat* for the afternoon chew. He generously offered some to me, and I happily declined. He also brought me a bottle of water, which I graciously accepted until I realized that the plastic seal on the cap was clearly broken. The bottle had previously been opened. I had found my first refilled water bottle of the trip! This was a common practice I'd been warned about, in which vendors pick up empty water bottles and refill them with tap water, selling them as brand new bottles of filtered water. I'd been on the look-out for the practice, but now was not the time to inform Walid of that. It would be incredibly rude for me to point out the problem, or refuse to drink the water—both acts would hurt his feelings unnecessarily. I took a big gulp, thanked him, and finished it off. A painful stomachache returned with a vengeance within the hour.

* * *

Back in my hotel in Aden I cranked up the A/C and lay down on the bed to relax for a few hours. I was attending my first Yemeni wedding that night thanks to Hadil's invitation, and was stoked at the thought of a fun party. As I was channel surfing, I finally came to the most famous Yemeni channel of all. Let me preface this description by saying that it is impossible to access porn sites in Yemen, as the government bans them for being "un-Islamic." However, every time there is a big protest against the Saleh government, the Ministry of Information lifts the ban on porn sites for a few hours, which usually results in a few hundred men rushing home to enjoy these precious hours of internet freedom instead of protesting. Thus, the most famous Yemeni channel, on 24 hours a day, 365 days a year, was a channel that showed seven to ten fully clothed women dancing with one another in a circle. They weren't particularly beautiful, or particularly thin, but after two weeks of seeing women in abayas, I had to agree that the cameraman's close-ups of their large buttocks in the midst of dance moves, some of which would have put Shakira to shame, was better than porn.

The Yemeni wedding I attended was in the nearby Aden Mall, on the top floor, which is reserved almost exclusively for these occasions. The room was large, accommodating about four hundred barefoot men sitting on divans on the floor, with comfortable cushions and low tables that held bottles of water, strawberry Fanta (a disgusting drink that makes Robitussin taste like champagne and that even the Yemenis admitted they could only drink while chewing *qat*), and lots and lots of *qat*. There was no food, as the groom had invited a close set of friends to lunch earlier, obviously no alcohol... and definitely no women. In all honesty, it was the worst wedding I've ever been to. Apparently the four hundred men, boys, and some children among them, would hang out here from 4 until 11 PM, chewing *qat*, smoking, and talking.

But wait! There was a traditional guitar player and a man on the *darbuka* (a small drum you play with the tips of your fingers). The music wasn't bad—it was actually a bit catchy—and even the singing was pretty good. Inspired by my new favorite television channel, I got my hopes up that maybe there would be a performance of women dancing for us soon. Oh man, how wrong was I. In the most homoerotic display of affection I have ever witnessed, groups of men got up to dance with one another. As couples. Not touching, but circling each other and taking turns following. Sometimes one guy would lead, as the "male" in the dance, and then they would switch roles. I politely declined the outstretched hand of a random gentleman who came to proposition me, and asked Hadil about Yemeni weddings in general.

There were no speeches. Instead, people would typically go up to speak to the groom, who was sitting and chewing *qat* on a raised dais with his family members, once when they arrived and once to say goodbye. Each time was marked by one kiss to the right cheek and multiple kisses to the left cheek, each additional kiss emphasized with a pump of the hand. Ninety percent of the guests were related, and each wore a Pakistani-like long shirt tucked into a skirt wrapped around his waist. I noticed that the guests weren't carrying the traditional *jambiya* knives I had seen men wear in Sana'a, and Hadil explained to me that they typically weren't worn in Aden. "Although the part of the family that's from Yafaa, they sometimes still wear them," he said as he pointed out one or two guys. "They used to be Jehuddin! Jewish, you know? In Yafaa. They have a city like that in Israel as well. Haifa! But the guys here converted one thousand years ago."

He explained to me the economics of the wedding: Sometimes the groom would pay for lunch beforehand, depending on how rich his family was and how many guests he invited. Lunch for two hundred people would cost a minimum of 660,000 riyals, or about $3000. The groom would always pay for the place where they would meet afterward to chew *qat*, the drinks, and the entertainment, but people would almost always bring their own *qat*. "It is much too expensive to buy the *qat* for everyone. It would cost more than five million! It is silly, and usually only the wealthiest families do it to show off."

There would be breaks for prayer during the wedding, and then the dancing and chewing would resume. After three hours of speaking with some Gulf workers about the benefits of using Rogaine and their wish to grow fat and bald once they were married, I'd had enough. I took advantage of the prayer break, thanked the family for their hospitality, and merrily went back to the hotel to watch the dancing-women channel. Puberty in this country must be a nightmare.

* * *

I woke up to the news that al-Qaeda had made coordinated attacks on the regional intelligence headquarters in the neighboring Abyan province, less than twenty miles away. Little did I know that in a few days I would be asked by the scary Political Security Organization if I had anything to do with them. This was only the most recent of attacks, as three weeks ago there had been another attack on Yemeni intelligence headquarters.

The night before, on the way back from the wedding, I had experienced my first dust storm. The storm was characterized by strong winds that could easily sway a 200lb male (me, in this case) side to side, and so much dust in the air that visibility was curtailed to ten feet away from my nose. The dust coated my face, stuck to my clothes, and finagled its way into my nose, ears, and mouth. Only the truly foolish would dare to open his eyes beyond a squint. As it was, my eyes were tearing for hours afterward.

A dust storm could paralyze the entire city for hours, but the next morning there was no trace of yesterday's natural havoc, and I embarked on a sightseeing tour of this former capital. Against my better judgment, as it usually turns out to be more expensive, I hired a taxi driver for a few hours to drive me to the main sites. Aadil was tall, with a paunch, graying stubble, and brown teeth—stained like those of so many Yemeni men from years of chewing *qat*. He used to live in Dubai, where the money was better but life was worse, he told me. He had married a Filipino woman who, although she preferred Dubai, was just as happy in Yemen because her husband was here, Aadil assured me. Unlike most Yemeni men I had met, Aadil only had two children—an eleven-year--old boy and a sixteen-year-old girl—which he thought was a large enough family to support.

As we drove off toward the famous Seera Castle I realized that Aadil, like almost all taxi drivers I had met in Aden, put on his seatbelt, a rare occurrence in my travels. On the way he pointed out the Jewish and British cemeteries, which I would later be heartbroken to visit, a few small but pretty churches, and the castle, situated atop a rocky hilltop in the distance. The castle had been the last stand before the British East India Company captured the port of Aden as a coaling station for ships en route to

India. I expressed my sorrow to Aadil for this colonial past, but he quickly dismissed it, saying, "We need the British to come back, my friend. Our country is a mess." I was pretty sure this was *not* an opinion echoed by the majority of Yemenis, especially since up until 1937 Britain had ruled Yemen as part of British India, not even bothering to consider the area a separate colony.

As we got nearer the base of the castle ("1600 steps to the top!" Aadil had gleefully informed me), he pointed out the Aden fish market to our right. If the mark of the Tsukiji Fish Market, the world's most famous fish market in Tokyo, is that it is so clean you can't smell any fish, then I think it's fair to say that the Aden fish market was its exact opposite. The intermingled stench of fresh and rotting fish inundated the car, the vendors black with dirt and grime, all excitedly motioning to their wares in the 103° degree weather.

"Shark kidney!" Aadil suddenly exclaimed. "You eat before marry, like Viagra!" I'd found in my travels that Yemenis loved to compare natural products to Viagra, and were constantly alluding to fucking like bulls, tigers, and other wild animals that might sound fierce but usually came in under thirty seconds and didn't really look like they were enjoying themselves. The same was true for *qat*, which my more serious Yemeni friends had explained causes temporary impotence, although many taxi drivers had happily clenched their fists and tensed their forearm, no doubt to impress upon me the size and power of their erection when they were chewing *qat*, which they also mentioned was, "like Viagra!" On that note, Yemenis are purportedly one of the highest users of Viagra and fake Viagra in the world, and have created two domestic brands that promised the same results. I hope that at least one of these multiple remedies is working for these guys.

By the time we reached the entrance to the castle we were informed that, like most tourist attractions in Aden, it was closed between the hours of 12 and 3 PM. After some haggling between Aadil and the gatekeeper, which resulted in a payment of 200 riyals (less than $1), the gatekeeper gave Aadil the keys to the padlock. He was still going on his break and asked Aadil to leave the keys with the owner of the small convenience store in front of the steps.

As Aadil drove off to park his taxi, I heard a seductive female voice call out from behind me, in English, "What is your name?"

I turned around and found myself looking at a woman, hiding most of her face behind two drapes, on the second floor of the run-down building at the foot of the hill. She was smiling down at me, teasing me with the movement of the curtains. Maybe it was because I hadn't seen a female face in a while, or the heat beating down on me, but she was majestic to look at. Her eyes glimmered green in the reflection of the light, her smile wide and dainty at the same time, her hair long and lustrous. She was magnificent.

"Francisco," I called back. "What is your name?" I asked, grinning, and probably drooling, like the idiot I become in front of beautiful women.

"Fatima!" With that, she shut the drapes once more, holed up in her meager prison. I turned away, elated, and began the climb.

I will spare you the details of the wheezing, sweat stains, cursing, frequent stops, and multiple prayers that I invoked to get to the top. Needless to say, 1600 steps in 103 degree weather sucks. I was exhausted by the time I reached the top, my thighs shaking uncontrollably from the exercise and my shirt soaked through. The castle, although not particularly large or ornate, was impressive enough for the simple fact that it had been built all the way up here, and I had a newfound respect for the men who had lugged up the hundreds of thousands of rocks it had taken to build it—surely these were real men, homoerotic weddings or not.

The view from the top was expansive, and showcased Aden in its entirety. There was the minuscule and unhappily shuttered water park with a Ferris wheel by the sea; the multicolored rickety fishing boats, with single engines, that looked so picturesque from up here; the vibrantly green field in the soccer stadium next to a government building, so crisp and new that it seemed an affront to a city where potable water was not plentiful; a pretty mosque with only two minarets; dozens of white buildings with six, eight, even ten stories, giving the city as a whole a more modern feel than Sana'a; and finally, but most important, the sea. It was endless and imposing, glistening in the sunlight, providing Aden with access to some of the world's most important maritime trade routes, an opportunity that had been wasted. The strong breeze made the heat more bearable and, like all high points with a view of the endless ocean stretching out before you, the effect was both calming and invigorating. The ruins of the castle walls, which lay in a state of disrepair, were defaced by foreign names like Johan and Sebastian, and by what I supposed was more local graffiti that read "Fuck Bush," "Bush go to Hell," and, referring to the former Prime Minister of Israel, "Sharon Terrorist."

The way down was speedy and relatively effortless, and on our ride to the al-Aidroos mosque Aadil tried to sell me on the now-familiar idea that people in Aden were better than people in Sana'a. "More laughing, more friendlier," he, like virtually everyone else I had spoken to in Aden, assured me. So far, everyone had been as friendly and wonderful to me here as they had been in Sana'a, so I wasn't able to see a difference. The short drive was embellished by the tunes of Gloria Gaynor's "I Will Survive" and Bryan Adams' "Everything I Do," the lyrics to which Aadil enthusiastically butchered. I would later find out the songs were not playing on the radio, but in fact were part of his favorite mixed tape.

The al-Aidroos mosque is the oldest mosque in Aden, built in the fourteenth century, and is dedicated to Abdullah al-Aidroos, the patron saint of Yemen. A famous but nondescript wooden door separates the mosque from the family tomb; I was informed it was actually made in India. As I entered the foyer of the tomb, I was surprised to see to my right slabs of concrete, which were new tombs sticking out of the floor, some with peeling paint and none with an inscription, next to some empty buckets and a couple of brooms. These unmarked and simple graves included (next to the trashcans and dirty sink) the daughters of the Sultan of Lajah, and the former overseers of the tomb. Unlike in Europe, however, the overseer was the cleaner, watchman, and "fresh flowers guy"—in essence, a very poor person who had dedicated his life to protecting the cadavers of important people. These caretakers are then given the honor of being entombed next to the dead they spent their lives protecting.

Through another set of doors I entered the main mausoleum, where there stood about a dozen wooden caskets, five feet tall, with the remains of the family. The caskets were covered in garish satin and velvet sheets of dull reds and greens. The ceiling was intricately painted and included a detailed skylight that illuminated the caskets. Surrounding the coffins were young male students sitting cross-legged and meditating. "Like Buddhists!" I whispered to Aadil. From his reaction I saw this was not a favorable comparison, and he quickly corrected me. "No, like Muslims!" he hissed.

On our way to our final visit, to the famous Tawila Water Tanks, we passed through the Indian quarter. "They came here with the British, and then they just stayed here. Now they are Yemenis," Aadil told me. Indeed, they looked Indian, darker than the Yemenis, but were all chewing *qat*.

* * *

The famous Tawila water tank was unmemorable; it had the look of a Roman aqueduct, but its contents were green from disuse and smelled to high heaven. The most interesting part of this visit was the wonderfully British inscription on a plaque near the green water. It read:

> THESE TANKS: Regarding the original construc-
> tion of which nothing is accurately known were
> accidently discovered by Lieutenant (now Sir Lam-
> bert) Playfair when Assistant Resident at Aden in
> the year 1854. They were then completely hidden
> by rubbish and debris from the hills, but were
> opened out and repaired by the British Govern-
> ment. The lower circular tank (called Playfair
> Tank) was cleared out subsequently. The aggre-
> gate capacity of all the tanks exceeds twenty mil-
> lion imperial gallons – 20th February 1899.

In fact, to this day no one is quite sure when or who built
the tanks, with some theories ascribing the construction
to the pre-Islamic Arabic Kingdom of Himyar sometime
between 115 BC to 525 AD. We know for sure that by the
seventh century AD they were already in existence. The
tanks had been in and out of disrepair, and had been
renovated extensively during the British rule as a way to
capture rainfall from the mountains and fulfill the city's
water needs. The Adenese are inordinately proud of
them, and claimed that they still somewhat functioned.

Aadil had finally gone home, and as I climbed into a
new taxi I realized how consistent the fares were. The
drivers almost always quoted me the same price, as
though I had taken a metered cab. It was so nice not to
have to haggle over the price of a ride. This driver was
friendly and overjoyed at my basic Arabic. After he got
my now perfunctory agreement about how much nicer
Aden was than Sana'a, I asked him about the Hamas
symbol hanging from his rearview mirror. He said that

he was very proud of the organization and that it was helping the Palestinian people. We talked a bit about tourism in Aden, and he lamented that the only tourists who visited nowadays were German. "Not good people," he grimaced. "Very cheap, bargain too much, never laugh. We pray we get other nationality soon, *inshallah*." He told me that before Yemeni unification there were a lot of Cuban tourists (South Yemen was Communist prior to unification), and then he did the most remarkable thing: He started singing "Guantanamera," arguably the most famous Cuban song ever written, in perfect Spanish lyrics with a heavy Arabic accent. He swayed side to side as he sang, imitating a salsa move.

What an amazing country. Where else would you expect your Arabic-speaking taxi driver to sing to you in Spanish while showing off his salsa moves?

* * *

The next day I steeled myself to visit the Jewish and British cemeteries and the military museum, capping off the tourist sites in the city. The Jewish cemetery is right in the middle of the commercial district near Ma'ala Plaza, "protected" by a brick and cement wall that has crumbled in many places, exposing a few hundred tombs. The first thing I noticed as I clambered down a small hill to reach the tombs was the amount of garbage and rubble strewn about. As I walked deeper into the cemetery, the full extent of the damage done to these Yemeni Jews became apparent. The entire cemetery was desecrated, no tomb intact. Tombs had been dug up in a venomous search for Jewish cadavers; other tombs bore the clear signs of a sledgehammer pounding them right through the middle, breaking through the granite in a violent and horrific way. Hundreds of tombstones, inscribed mostly in Hebrew but a few in English, lay strewn and shattered across the field. Nothing had been spared. No respect had been accorded to the dead, any expected decency abandoned by the thought that these were Jewish bodies. It was terrible to behold, the loss of so many loved ones, the destruction of so many final resting places. I could not help but imagine the pain relatives must have felt at the thought of their mother, father, husband, wife, daughter, or son being so carelessly tossed aside.

On the other hand, the British cemetery, where former torturers and conquerors of this proud nation were interred, was intact. Protected by a metal gate with real spikes and barbed wire at the top, the tombs were orderly and clean, devoid of trash or rubble. Crosses jutted out in a greater number and in a more conspicuous manner than the Stars of David ever had. Why had there been such a violent response against the Jews, most of whom had flourished in and loved Yemen? Why respect the graves of former officers and civil servants who oppressed you, while punishing the dead who had lived and loved among you? I asked my Yemeni friends, taxi drivers, and local staff, all of whom either feigned ignorance of the desecration or dismissed the cemetery entirely because it was *Jehuddi*. The only difference I discovered was that the British government had paid to have its cemetery protected and restored somewhat. Given that Yemen did not recognize Israel (an Israeli stamp on your passport will result in your being denied entry into the country, as is stated openly on the Yemen Embassy website), such funding was not an option for Israel.

The military museum I visited afterward was a joke, with cabinets filled with a few old rifles and pictures of dead leaders. An entire room was filled with hundreds of pictures of Saleh meeting with various foreign dignitaries, giving speeches at the UN, and signing treaties. Most of the pictures were twenty years old. In one particular photograph, one of the few in which Saleh is not sitting, he is standing next to a much taller Fidel Castro, looking up at him. The picture reminded me of the look an admiring boy would give his father, and I was surprised it had made it into the display case. Only about 50 percent of the Arabic explanations had an English translation, which were all riddled with gross misspellings and were, in many cases, unintelligible.

I left the museum and headed over to my favorite restaurant, Reem Tourist Restaurant, the best and most famous restaurant in Aden, where I was always invariably the only tourist. Because of its people, the safety I felt walking on its streets, and the food, I had come to like Yemen immensely, which I imagine has tinged my narrative in a more positive view. As I walked over to the restaurant, however, I was reminded of a fact that had been lost among the food, the funny stories, and the refugees: Yemen was, in fact, very poor. Desperately so. The misery was best exemplified by people lying facedown on the bare sidewalk, spitting out *qat* juice; hungry girls sitting on their fathers' laps, voraciously sharing an egg omelet as their only meal of the day; old, gaunt, toothless faces; and finally and most heartbreaking of all, scores of starving children, their bare feet riddled with pustules and sores, selling flower-bud necklaces for a living.

* * *

You arrive at Reem Restaurant to a loud sign that proudly proclaims its name and its website (www.reemrestaurants.com), two shawarma guys outside cooking lamb and chicken, both mixed with Yemeni coleslaw, and a furious amount of activity as twenty waiters dance around three hundred customers. Inside the place is chaotic, boisterous from the conversations between the different patrons and the waiters screaming at one another and at the chefs, and everyone is coated in a thin layer of sweat, as the air-conditioner fails to cool the room. I looked around and was yet again surprised not to see a single woman in the restaurant, not even in a *niqab*. I guess it was just something I was never going to get used to.

Otherwise, it is a wonderfully democratic restaurant, where chic Yemenis in tight Euro-trash clothing and designer sunglasses sit next to old men in skirts and turbans. There is no such thing as "your table," as all tables, both large and small, are communal. And they mean communal. If a four top is seating only three people in the middle of their meal, the staff will gladly sit down a single next to them to start his dinner. There is no such thing as "your waiter," and you yell at the nearest man in a white shirt and black pants to get his attention. There is no cutlery, only bread, and the menu is a testament to the efficiency and ability of the restaurant to produce about a hundred different dishes. At lunch the staff give out free bowls of their spicy chicken broth, a byproduct of the stock that is produced when they boil their famous chicken legs on rice. What would be a waste in any other restaurant, here they serve as an extraordinary *amuse bouche*. They serve flaky and moist kebabs with soggy French fries, tandoori chicken, fried chicken, all varieties of rice and eggs you can think of, chopped liver (including shark liver), hummus, moutabel (a Yemeni version of baba ganoush), and a wide range of fresh fruit juices.

* * *

That afternoon I finally went swimming in the Gulf of Aden. The beach was deserted except for a few hotel guests at the Sheraton, and the large elephant-shaped rock was illuminated by the hazy red sun as it set on the horizon. The *muezzin* began his prayer call and I turned to see the mosque, high atop a rocky hill, from which the call was emanating. The few fishing boats left were slowly motoring back to the harbor. As the call ended and the sun finally set, I swam back to shore. It was time to go home.

* * *

At this point I should admit that I did something very silly while I was in Aden. Heartbroken at the destruction of the Jewish cemetery, I picked up two of the most complete tombstones and paid the homeless man who lived there, in a makeshift plastic tent, 1000 riyals ($4). He was so grateful that he even helped me carry the tombstones and load them into the back of my taxi. I wrapped the tablets in bubble wrap and towels and bought a separate duffel bag to carry them with me on the plane. Better at the Harvard Semitic Museum than lying on the ground waiting for another bout of anger from the locals, I thought. I didn't think I was doing anything wrong, and I couldn't imagine that anyone would care. Both of these predictions would prove horribly incorrect and land me in heap of trouble. As I left the Aden airport, the customs agent who x-rayed the bag asked me what was in it. I offhandedly replied, "Tablets. No problem," smiled at him, and went to my gate. No problem here. Arriving at the airport in Sana'a, however, would be a different matter.

Airport security personnel again x-rayed my duffel bags when I arrived in Sana'a. (What airport x-rays bags when you get *off* the domestic flight?) They then stopped me and asked me to empty the bag's contents. As they began to roughly handle the tablets I became afraid they might break and intervened, asked for a knife and carefully cut away the tape while keeping the towel and bubble wrap together. When they saw the tablets and the Hebrew letters, they were furious. They told me that these tablets were extremely old (not technically true, as they were only 100 to 150 years old) and accused me of trying to smuggle out antiquities. This was an extremely serious charge, and a few months ago three

Frenchmen had been caught and put in jail for that very same reason. I immediately protested, telling them that the tablets weren't that old. Still furious, they called in the representative for the Ministry of Culture, an expert who could tell me how old they were.

You can imagine the quality of the archeological expert who is forced to work at the airport on a Sunday night at midnight. He didn't speak Hebrew or English. He heed and hawed about the tablets, and professed that they indeed were very old. This statement only fueled the anger of the four security agents who had gathered around me now. The expert started writing out an official report, and the agents photocopied my passport and asked me where I had gotten the tablets.

I foolishly told them truth. I explained to them that I had picked up the tablets from the Jewish cemetery that was virtually destroyed and full of trash, and that the caretaker had helped me load them into the back of the taxi. The agents looked confused, either because they didn't believe me or because they didn't expect me to be so open. They asked me if I had paid the caretaker and I told them I had given him 1000 riyals. The low sum didn't sit well with them, and it became obvious that they were confiscating the tablets. As they started to pile the tombstones on top of each other, scraping the inscriptions and further damaging them, I loudly intervened and began to re-wrap them protectively, giving the agents my duffel bag to decrease the likelihood that they would be broken.

An hour had passed and they had already grilled me about the trip to Aden. (I said I was working with the

UNHCR and researching refugee education.) At this point they asked for my trusty Canon, and the head of the feared Political Security Office at the airport began to look through the 500-plus pictures. I saw him take out his cellphone and take a picture of a picture I had taken. I walked over to see a close-up of a cracked Star of David.

Uh oh.

He turned to look at me, the anger in his eyes visible and frightening, and started screaming at me, rotating through other pictures of Jewish symbology. I couldn't understand him and I kept asking for a *mutarjim*, a translator, which only seemed to anger him more as I had been speaking basic Arabic before his outburst.

One finally arrived, and quickly asked me, "Do you think you are important with the Jews?" This was obviously not going well. "Are you Israeli? Have you been to Israel?" He was suggesting I was an Israeli spy, and I broke out in a cold sweat as I clenched my fists to stop them from trembling too noticeably.

"No, no, of course not! I'm Catholic, I'm Catholic!" I protested.

I had called Fadhl, my Yemeni friend with powerful connections, but now it was clear that even with his help they weren't letting me go anytime soon. They left me next to the sole x-ray machine in the airport, unsupervised, and moved into the notorious little room to discuss my fate. I was waiting in a foreign airport, in a country with a scary intelligence service and loose rule of law, after midnight, and I couldn't communicate with the man who could have me tortured, which meant

I had no idea how deep in shit I was. As it got closer to 1 AM, I became more and more paranoid, more and more worried. What if they didn't believe me and thought I was spying for Israel? What if they knew I had been asking the refugees about al-Qaeda? I was becoming more anxious by the minute, frantically chewing at my nails and imagining that some very ugly people were going to take me away to a dark room where no one could hear me scream.

The only thing distracting me from these James Bond-like images of torture was my front-row seat to the Yemeni customs checkers for Federal Express packages arriving in Sana'a. The check consisted of two guys slashing open all of the boxes, retaping them badly after rummaging through their contents, and taking special joy in launching heavy boxes marked "fragile" across the floor. I felt bad for the people who had, no doubt, paid exorbitant fees to have their packages packed and shipped, only to have them be sorely mishandled by two guys who could clearly not wait to go home. Even the envelopes didn't survive this treatment, the customs checkers crumpling and bending important documents as though they were Kleenexes to be discarded.

By now I had been waiting for over an hour since they had moved into the little room to deliberate. What if I ran? They had given me back my passport, but had a photocopy of it and would immediately arrest me if I set foot in the airport again. I could take a bus to the Saudi Arabian border instead! I had a friend who could get me a visa and get me into the country. I could fly out of Riyadh in no time. As I was half-seriously considering this hare-brained plan, they called me into the little room. There were two men sitting down, and they motioned me toward the one available chair that had four men looming over it.

I sat.

"Why were you in Pakistan?" they began. Of course they had seen the Pakistani visa.

As I was about to explain why I had gone to Islamabad, I made a mistake and blurted out, "Well, I was in Peshawar for two weeks studying refugee education."

Shit. I'd mentioned Peshawar.

They looked at each other ominously, shocked by my answer and murmuring rapidly in unintelligible Arabic. I was tired and stressed out, and the truth was starting to come out. I wondered how much longer I could keep up any façade before breaking down. I explained to them that I was researching refugee education and that that's why I had gone to al-Kharaz and to Peshawar.

"But you have a tourist visa! Not research!"

Shit. Shit. Shit.

"Yes, yes, but I'm doing both! Spending some time sightseeing with Fadhl and some time researching!"

They started grilling me about my friendship with Fadhl, why I wasn't staying with him, how we became friends, and so on. This went on for a good hour, with them asking me more circular and more repetitive questions, trying to catch me in lies and inconsistencies. They became progressively angrier and the head agent more and more aggressive. "Why didn't he go with you to Kharaz?" he demanded.

Finally, I saw an opening, a light at the end of the tunnel. I had to go on the offensive I knew, as otherwise I was going to be interviewed into submission and end up in that frightening dark and soundproof room.

I laughed. Loudly.

"Have you ever *been* to Kharaz?" I responded. "It's a hot and horrible place. Why would Fadhl want to go with me?" I laughed again.

This response caught them off guard, and they switched topics. They asked me if I had been to Abyan province (where the most recent al-Qaeda attacks had occurred), and continued to ask me the same questions over and over again with different wording, hoping that I would change my answers and they could catch me lying. We went over Pakistan, Kenya, the twenty hours I had spent in Cairo on a layover, how I was paying for university, and more. But I was on a roll now, and I was bent on going down fighting.

I was making jokes. I was laughing. I was comfortably leaning back in the wooden chair now. I lightly touched the head guy's knee for added effect on a certain point. After two hours, and after they had warmed to my newfound charisma, the interview ended. And I was free to go.

Almost.

They held me up for an additional fifteen minutes while they made and received a few final phone calls, most likely to make sure someone could follow me once I left the airport. Probably for the rest of my time here. I jumped into the first cab I saw outside of the airport and constantly looked back at the long empty road. No one was following us, and the roads were entirely deserted at this hour. After entertaining this fiction for a few minutes, we stopped at the first roadblock, where the four military guys hovered near my window and made fun of me as the foreigner who had just come back from Aden. No wonder. Who needs to be followed when you've got manned checkpoints that could look out for me? The same thing happened at the next checkpoint, half a mile down the road. And the next. And the next. They would always hover, point, and laugh at me before letting us pass. I always assumed that there was an intelligence officer following me here and in Pakistan, but it was outright scary when the attention was so overt.

The streets of Sana'a were mostly empty and the few passengers unlucky enough to be driving at this hour were stopped, forced to get out of their vehicles, and interrogated at every checkpoint. Their cars were searched. Obviously the most recent al-Qaeda attacks had impacted the government more than usual, and Sana'a was on its way to becoming more like an Islamabad or a Peshawar. In total we passed eight checkpoints before reaching Old Sana'a, each manned by a group of Yemenis in camouflage fatigues and green berets, holding AK-47s.

Once in the Old City we drove past the once-bustling souk, now quiet and deserted at 3 AM. Every stall's wares were covered only with a blue plastic tarp, virtually free for anyone who wanted to steal them. And yet, no one did. I was again surprised at the contradictions so rife in Yemen. The taxi dropped me off at the famous Burj al-Salaam Hotel and I walked down the pitch-dark alleys, empty but for a few dozen scared mutts that trembled and scurried away as I passed them on my way home. No doubt severely abused by the local population, they had come to expect violence from humans, which is most likely why I had never seen dogs during the busy day.

I spent the next day pathetically holed up in my room, still shaken from the interrogation of the night before, reading J.R.R. Tolkien's *The Silmarillion* and venturing out only to eat half a roasted chicken with rice. At night Dan and I went back to the Souk al-Samak, the fish market, for dinner. We picked out some fresh shrimp, squid, and a trout. I felt now that I should apologize to the Aden fish market for assuming that the stench and dirt were indicators of the quality of the catch. The Sana'a fish market was dirtier, smellier, and inland, and yet the catch was exquisite, unbelievably fresh. I imagine Aden's fish market was even better, and I had missed out. Never judge a market by its smell.

* * *

The next day, my last day in Yemen, I realized that my camera was missing. I had last flipped through the pictures after the airport interrogation, looking at pictures of my front door to remember how to get home that night. I was certain I had placed the camera on the small desk in my room, next to my passport and a few hundred dollars in cash. The passport, the wallet, and the cash were intact. We searched the entire house to no avail. Only three people had been inside it over the past twenty-four hours, all roommates and above suspicion. I felt paranoid, scared. I also felt a deep loss, my eyes

welling up as I fought back tears of fear, anger, and disappointment. Five hundred and fifty-three pictures of
Yemen, of the wonderful food, of my friends, of the boys
who wanted to become mullahs, of the other refugees
who wanted to join al-Qaeda, of the Jewish cemetery
and the sights in Aden—all gone. I was convinced the
security service had taken the camera, but was afraid
to voice my fears because I didn't want to seem to be
losing my mind.

I finally asked my Yemeni friends that night at dinner,
voicing my concern that someone had broken in specifically for the camera. This supposition was surprisingly
received by nods of agreement and stories of break-ins
into some of their houses in which only laptops or files
had been taken. There was no mark of a forced entry
in any of the cases. Dan refused to accept that someone
had violated the sanctity of our home that way, and insisted I had left the camera in the cab. If this were the
case, I would have a very high probability of recovering
it, as I'd heard countless stories of Yemeni cab drivers
returning forgotten wallets, cell phones, and purses.

I called the cab company I had taken that night and
offered a reward of $250 for the memory card alone.
This was an incredible amount for a Yemeni cab driver,
almost a fourth of the Yemeni GDP per capita. As I had
expected, though, no one claimed the reward, in spite
of the significant efforts by the dispatcher to contact my
cab driver from that night. But why hadn't the security service just confiscated the camera at the airport?
Because I would have raised a huge stink and probably
used my friends' influence to make sure that didn't hap-

pen, I realized. It would have been a huge headache for them. Simply taking it was much easier, and it sent a very clear message. But what for? To study the images that they had already seen at the airport? Perhaps. Or perhaps because they didn't want the world to see the images of destruction of the Jewish cemetery, which even my anti-Israeli Yemeni friends agreed was very *haram* (effectively, prohibited by Islam).

"So is there a chance of getting it back? Can I pay someone off?" I asked the group at dinner.

They all looked at me as though I had actually lost my mind, even though an earlier conversation had focused on how to bribe a zoo official to buy the zoo's cockatoo. "No, man. You don't fuck with the PSO. If they've got it, you're certainly not going to see it again."

It was the overtness with which I felt I was being watched that finally got to me. The PSO had become far more intrusive than the Pakistani ISI's invisible followers and phone calls to my Pakistani associates. These were my last four hours in Yemen before my 3:30 AM flight, and I was ready to leave.

* * *

At midnight I walked the empty, dark, but familiar alleys of Old Sana'a, the frightened strays, all limping or scarred, shaking with fear as I got near them. I threw my duffel into the backseat of a taxi, and said a quiet goodbye to the city I had come to love and fear. I was finally going home.

Conclusion: Winning the Hearts and Minds

Cambridge, MA

"We can't kill our way to victory."
— Admiral Mike Mullen, Chairman of the
Joint Chiefs of Staff

"We can't COIN everywhere."
— John Brennan, President Obama's Chief
Counterterrorism Advisor (Obama's Wars)

My flights back to Amman and then to Boston were uneventful, and I held my breath as I handed over my passport and customs sheet to the immigration officer at Logan Airport. He glanced back and forth between the customs form and my lobster-print shirt, raising an eyebrow as he read the line that asks travelers to state what countries they visited prior to arrival. He finally looked up, more confused than concerned, and asked, "So... what exactly were you doing in Pakistan and Yemen?"

"Studying refugee camps, sir," I replied, and I handed him a letter from the university that outlined my research and its funding.

He quickly looked at the letter, sighed, and then smiled one of those warm American smiles that only barrel-chested guys with beards can give you. "Well, I guess if you wanna study refugee camps, you gotta go to these shitty countries. Welcome home, son!"

I took back my documents, beaming with joy at not having been put in the little room for a few hours. I was finally home.

* * *

A couple days later, newly shaved and showered, I found myself eating a grilled cheese and bacon sandwich in my father's house in Maine, trying to make sense of the past few months. I felt that I had learned so much from my experiences, not just about Yemen, Pakistan, and Somalia, but about the relationship between extremism and crisis populations, namely refugees and internally displaced persons. Sadly, since I had gotten back home the situation in all three countries had deteriorated dramatically, with al-Qaeda and al-Shabaab almost taking over all of Mogadishu; al-Qaeda in the Arabian Peninsula (AQAP) ratcheting up its attacks on Yemeni government offices and officials; and Pakistan experiencing one of the worst natural disasters in its short history.

A few weeks after I had left Peshawar, in July 2010, heavy monsoon rains in multiple provinces overflowed the Indus River basin and left almost a fifth of the country underwater. Ban Ki-moon, the UN Secretary General, said the floods were the worst catastrophe he had ever seen; the Pakistani Prime Minister stated it was the worst natural disaster in Pakistan's history; and the UN reported that the number of people suffering in Pakistan exceeded those affected by the 2004 Indian Ocean tsunami, the 2005 Kashmir earthquake, and the 2010 Haiti earthquake combined. Close to fourteen million people had been affected and the disaster created over seven million displaced persons, one and a half million of whom still remain in camps.

The Pakistani government had been overwhelmed and unable to provide relief to hundreds of thousands, if not millions, of people, which led to a series of serious consequences, among them: a tripling of food prices in Peshawar, forcing many to go hungry; an increase in anti-government sentiment around the country; a cessation of military incursions into North Waziristan while the army focused on relief efforts, which allowed al-Qaeda and the Taliban a safe-haven from which they could continue to plan and execute attacks against the United States and our troops in Afghanistan; and, most alarmingly, a dramatic increase in the humanitarian services provided by extremist Islamic organizations like Jamaat-ud-Dawa.

Although reports vary as to how significant a problem terrorist recruiting has become in the camps, no one seriously argues that it is less of a problem today than it was before the disaster. Longer term IDP populations are especially at risk, in provinces like Sindh for example, as sometimes the only aid and education available is being distributed by extremist organizations with the ultimate goal of recruiting and converting more Pakistanis to their intolerant way of thinking. Pakistan, already a country where extremism has flourished in the border regions, is at a higher risk today than ever before that this threat will spread to populations that were previously more tolerant and supportive of the government. If we hope that one day Pakistan will become a society that rejects extremism and forgoes its support for terrorist organizations that seek to destroy our way of life, we should take advantage of the existing situation to address some of our national security interests and begin to change the population's outlook.

Unfortunately, even the death of Osama bin Laden, a great victory for both the United States and Pakistan, has been met with anti-American protests and general disapproval. In a 2011 Pew poll after the successful American raid on bin Laden's compound, over 70 percent of Pakistanis said they considered the United States more an enemy of Pakistan than a partner and 55 percent believed that it was a "bad thing that Bin Laden is dead." Since the attacks of September 11, 2001, the United States has donated over $20 billion to Pakistan in both military and economic aid, and yet our relationship in 2011 was at its lowest point in eight years. It is commonplace to hear our politicians call for a disengagement from Pakistan and an exclusive focus on counterterrorism instead, but counterterrorism without a commensurate counter-radicalization strategy will not succeed. We ignore this increased radicalization in Pakistan at our own peril. Pakistan remains the most dangerous country in the world, given a nuclear arsenal that is likely to overtake France's in the near future and an increasing number of successful terrorist attacks against military installations.

Most alarming, since the US raid that killed Bin Laden, many Pakistanis have begun to view the Army's senior leadership unfavorably, while continuing to hate and distrust their civilian government. This shift can only lead the Pakistani people to sympathize even more with non-state actors and extremist ideologies, which provide an attractive competing narrative. By disengaging from Pakistan now, we are likely to face a problem of horrific proportions ten years from now: an economically broken Pakistan that hates us, trusts extremist groups more than its government, and maintains a dreadful nuclear arsenal protected by military officers who are partial to an extremist narrative. These events—the floods, the reaction to Osama Bin Laden's death, and the continued domestic support for terrorist organizations— only highlight the reality that the problem of extremism isn't going away anytime soon and in fact seems to be strengthening around the world. The question then is: What can we do to fight this trend? How can we make the United States safer? How can we begin to win hearts and minds?

The Power of a Well-Rounded Education

Throughout my interviews with hundreds of children and dozens of teachers and NGO workers, one consistent message emerged in all three countries: *Obtaining a well-rounded education, even for those students that were poor, makes extremism and recruitment far less likely.* From Dadaab to Kharaz to Peshawar, those students who were granted access to a well-rounded education, one that doesn't necessarily exclude Quranic memorization or classes on Islam but most certainly includes classes on literacy, math, science, history, geography, and even foreign languages, were more tolerant and less extremist than their uneducated counterparts. Every school principal I interviewed throughout my journey agreed that poverty was secondary to education, and that even very poor students were unlikely to join the Taliban or al-Shabaab if they had been through a real school program.

What this means for American engagement abroad is that more of our focus should be on promoting and providing a well-rounded education to populations that are at risk of becoming radicalized or currently support extremist organizations. John Brennan, President Obama's Chief Counterterrorism Advisor, and Admiral Mike Mullen, the former Chairman of the Joint Chiefs of Staff, both agree that the war we are fighting against al-Qaeda will not be won on the battlefield, but instead depends on our ability to reduce the attraction of extremist ideologies and thereby the space in which terrorist organizations are allowed to operate. Our success, and our desire to make America safer, depends on our ability to win more hearts and minds than the enemy. We do not have the military or economic resources to undertake counter-insurgency campaigns everywhere that al-Qaeda finds support, but we also cannot ignore the growing threat that extremist ideologies pose to our national security. The CIA already considers al-Qaeda in the Arabian Peninsula more dangerous than the core al-Qaeda leadership in the Pakistan/Afghanistan border, but this notorious designation could very well apply to al-Shabaab in the future, or even al-Qaeda affiliates in northwest Africa.

By increasing our aid to educational programs for populations that are at risk of being radicalized, or already support extremist organizations, we can reduce the support and space for al-Qaeda to operate in, directly addressing our fears of ungoverned spaces. The problem isn't that these spaces are ungoverned—large parts of the world are—but that they are susceptible to an extremist ideology. Our programs could counter this susceptibility and make these environments more hostile to extremist ideologies. For example, now that the Bajauri displaced persons in Peshawar have seen the benefits of educating their daughters, they are much less likely to accept the Taliban ideology once they return home, which would doom their daughters to a life of ignorance and confinement. Since they are less likely today to accept the Taliban's ideology than before their daughters received education, they are also less likely to allow the Taliban to repopulate and operate in their communities. Although the Taliban has the ability to coerce this population into submission, force alone is not sufficient to control a population, as we ourselves have seen in Iraq and Afghanistan. Funding this type of educational programs, which are a fraction of the cost of a counter-insurgency campaign, can also be a sustainable strategy across administrations, without worrying about bankrupting the country or having to set timelines. This part of our strategy should prioritize our resources based on which areas are most at risk of becoming radicalized and supporting terrorist organizations, rather than which areas are most in need of educational programs, as security priorities should supersede humanitarian concerns.

I realize that it is impossible to completely eradicate extremism or convince all individuals to embrace more tolerant ideals. As critics of my conclusions may argue, many of the most senior commanders in al-Qaeda and other terrorist organizations are educated and come from middle-class backgrounds. Although this is true, most individuals who join movements like al-Shabaab and the Taliban, which require some significant manpower, are not educated. Similar to a technology acceptance model, as one family demonstrates to the community the benefits of receiving a well-rounded education, other families are likely to follow their lead, which in time leads to the majority of the population accepting a more complete curriculum and learning from one another, leveraging those students who are already educated. Most important, as more children and families are reached through these educational programs, we are reducing the space in which extremist organizations are able to operate as these groups increasingly reject their values and their presence in their communities and make it far more difficult for them to plan and execute attacks against the United States.

I am by no means advocating that America's counterterrorism efforts should focus exclusively on combating ideological extremism through educational initiatives, nor do I believe that the United States should base its national security on humanitarian concerns. However, too much emphasis today is being placed on the military aspect of our counterterrorism strategy and too little, outside of Afghanistan, on the long-term goal to reduce a population's propensity for extremism. Counterterrorism is a tactic—not a strategy—that is meant to yield short-term security gains. However, in many cases the United States has started to rely almost exclusively on counterterrorism without providing a successful competing narrative against extremism at the same time. As Joe Nye, the professor at Harvard University who coined the term "soft power," states, ""In the fight against terrorism, for example, it is essential to have a narrative that appeals to the mainstream and prevents its recruitment by radicals."

Under the Obama Administration drone strikes against Pakistan and Yemen have increased dramatically, and at times have been very successful, but the Administration has not followed up these short-term security gains with counter-radicalization programs or an engagement of the communities being targeted. If we continue this strategy, we will end up with a Yemeni and Pakistani population that associates the United States exclusively with death from above, which naturally predisposes the community to, in the best case, fear us, and in the worst case, hate us. In Somalia, for example, our exclusive focus on counterterrorism (by supporting the Alliance for the Reconstruction of Peace and Counterterrorism and the Ethiopian invasion) led to short-term tactical gains against the Islamist presence, but over the long term led to the creation of al-Shabaab and a community that supports it. Counterterrorism alone has already proven insufficient in Yemen, for example. Even though a drone strike successfully targeted the leader of al-Qaeda Yemen in 2002, and the Yemeni government arrested his successor in 2003, al-Qaeda in the Arabian Peninsula is a greater threat today than ever before. In spite of being able to target the organization's leadership successfully, we have failed to reduce this Yemeni community's support for terrorist organizations and prevent radicalization. Our tactics in Yemen have bolstered AQAP's anti-American message, helped them recruit new volunteers, and made the local population far more receptive to their narrative. In many instances the drone strike campaign in Pakistan has radicalized communities even further, as the United States has not made an effort to reach out to those communities being targeted, making them more likely to shelter extremists and target our troops in Afghanistan. If we continue to focus exclusively on counterterrorism without a broader strategy for counter-radicalization, we are sowing the seeds of virulent anti-Americanism and an increase in extremist regimes in the future.

Yemen is a perfect example of the wide-ranging power that targeted educational initiatives can have, in this case for the worse. A few decades ago, Yemen was a relatively tolerant society where most women did not wear the full *niqab* and Western tourists in Aden wearing skirts were not terribly uncommon. Starting in the 1970s, however, Saudi Arabia began funneling hundreds of millions of dollars through charitable organizations and through Emam University to set up schools and mosques that espoused their Wahhabi interpretation of Islam, a much stricter and less tolerant interpretation that went against most Yemeni ideals of tolerance and hospitality. Today, Yemen has become significantly more conservative than before, and the rural populations that have been influenced by these Wahhabi institutions much more extremist and intolerant. In less than forty years Saudi Arabian charities were able to have a dramatic, and very negative, effect on the Yemeni population's propensity to shelter and join extremist organizations. As Robert Worth pointed out in his *New York Times* article, this is precisely the strategy that AQAP employs today in southern Yemen, providing teachers and basic services to a population that the government has largely failed. For every sixteen teachers that AQAP provides to a community, those mentioned in the article, they can comfortably indoctrinate eight hundred children, making it more likely that these children will grow up to hate the United States, and provide space for AQAP to train and launch attacks against the US and our allies.

AQAP understands the importance of education as a means to garner popular support, and will continue to exploit these children in the future. These are precisely the type of programs that we need to counter with new educational initiatives, rather than rely on our military power to defeat AQAP's soft-power campaigns. As the Saudi Arabian example notes, the biggest drawback to this strategy is that it may take many generations before whole communities reject extremism and reduce the space in which terrorist organizations can operate. Nonetheless, it is clear now that this battle for the hearts and minds is a long-term one, and that had we begun this type of program in Afghanistan after the fall of the Soviet Union, it would have been far more difficult for the Taliban and al-Qaeda to take over the country, which in turn would have made our presence there today less likely.

Crises as Opportunities
The natural disasters and violence that force rural populations to evacuate their homes and live together in camps are first and foremost humanitarian crises. But they are also opportunities. In many cases these

populations have historically been too dispersed to be targeted successfully by humanitarian organizations, or have been largely ignored by their governments because of their location outside of the principal urban centers. This institutional discrimination, which affects their access to basic services and education, typically creates a population that is uneducated, has developed a strong dislike for the central government (if one exists), and is more vulnerable to the rise of extremist groups and their ideologies. During crises, however, these same individuals are forced to live together in cramped quarters for months or even years, which provides the United States with an opportunity to influence large swaths of people who were previously unreachable. The 2010 floods in Pakistan, for example, created hundreds of thousands of refugees from the Sindh and Khyber-Pakhtunkhwa provinces. Educational programs in these camps could take advantage of these groups' temporary proximity to each other to espouse values of tolerance and influence them in a positive way.

The Winning the Minds Foundation
The Winning the Minds (WtM) Foundation is an organization I founded a few months after coming back home, and one I think will make a major difference in the lives of so many of the amazing children I met as well as address some of our most important national security concerns. I began the program in the Jalozai camp of Peshawar, Pakistan, and expect to expand it to the camps in Dadaab, Kenya and Kharaz, Yemen. The foundation gives four- to six-year scholarships to male

and female refugees and IDPs who live in the camps, have graduated from secondary school, and have been accepted into a local accredited university. Eligible students are asked to take an exam and are chosen based on their results in this common examination, an examination already in existence for the German-funded DAFI Scholarship Program.

The WtM Scholarship pays for tuition, school supplies, clothes, transportation, and the cost of living. In exchange for becoming a Winning the Minds Scholar, recipients agree to undergo a teacher training course, once a month and for two weeks before each summer, and then go back during their summer holidays to become teachers in their camps. They will initially teach math, science, literacy, and English, a curriculum that will expand as we have more and more volunteers. After graduation, recipients are expected to return to their camps for a minimum one-year commitment and become full-time teachers. In order to make this one year commitment more attractive, the Scholar's monthly stipend increases, as the foundation is no longer paying for tuition and can redistribute this extra cash to the Scholar. At the same time, the Scholar will be put in touch with a local mentor, typically a high ranking government official or successful businessman, who will be able to advise him or her as they begin their careers.

The idea for the foundation was born during my conversations with the idle youth in Dadaab, as so many of them who had graduated from secondary school couldn't afford to go to a Kenyan college. In turn, this reduced the incentive that younger children had to graduate, with them instead opting to drop out early and either languish in the camps or seek menial jobs. With WtM, as more and more graduating students receive the opportunity to attend a local university, they encourage and inspire younger refugees to study harder and graduate, thus increasing the percentage of the refugee and displaced person population that is educated. In turn, when scholarship recipients return to their camps over the summers and post-graduation to teach, young students receive higher quality instruction from a university student, as opposed to someone who has barely graduated from secondary school. This creates a virtuous cycle in which students are inspired by the success of the older students and are able to learn more from a better educated and better trained teacher.

Finally, by providing scholarships and mentoring opportunities for refugees, WtM makes it more likely that they will succeed in society, breaking the desperate cycle of poverty and misery in which many are forced to live. Funding scholarships for potential doctors is a particular favorite of mine, as they are able to teach students and increase the availability of health services in the camp at the same time.

Programs like the Winning the Minds Foundation are a more effective way to increase the quality of education in refugee and displaced persons camps because they focus on the one variable that matters most: the quality of teachers. Throughout my travels students made it clear that the quality of the teacher made the biggest difference in their ability to learn, and was far more important than more books, desks, or even blackboards. All of the remarkable Afghan women I met in Peshawar, who were valiantly struggling every day against all odds to become certified teachers, had one thing in common: They had all been fortunate enough to have one or two excellent teachers in their lives. Good teachers, they told me, can keep your attention even when you're under a tree in the hot sun and the dust is blowing in your face, even when you can only afford one textbook for every seven children, even when the desks are overflowing and falling apart.

The question that NGOs have always struggled with is how to motivate better teachers to come to these difficult areas like Dadaab, fifty miles away from the raging civil war in Somalia. Virtually all refugees who were lucky enough to receive a scholarship to go study in the nearest city, or abroad, never returned to the camp and worked hard to bring their family with them in a few years. Although this is perfectly understandable behavior, the Winning the Minds Foundation still allows recipients to strive for a better life, but also requires them to give back to their communities for a short amount of time.

What is most exciting about this foundation is that it takes advantage of force multipliers, leveraging our investment far more than if it were just a traditional scholarship program. For example, every Bajauri displaced person who receives a scholarship to study at the University of Peshawar will go back to the Jalozai camp and teach between fifty and one hundred students. These students in turn are far less likely to become radicalized or join a terrorist organization. So, every scholarship not only benefits the individual recipient, but makes it less likely that one hundred other refugees will become radicalized. In Dadaab for, example, by focusing on the 2.5 percent of the refugee population that graduates from secondary school and providing them with scholarships, we are able to positively influence the rest of the student population and make it less likely that they will join or shelter al-Shabaab.

It is programs like these that I believe should be the future of American public diplomacy efforts, as they fulfill a basic humanitarian need while also addressing our national security concerns. Programs like the Winning the Minds Foundation are a cheaper, less risky, and at times more effective tool for increasing American influence and promoting values of tolerance abroad. Although there will always be individuals who seek to harm us and destroy our way of life, these programs reduce the space in which these actors are able to operate and plan attacks against the United States and our allies.

The Current U.S. Strategy vis-à-vis C-RICS
C-RICS stands for "Counter-radicalization in Crisis Situations," a concept that seeks to incorporate the two previous points of education as an effective weapon against extremism and the fact that formerly spread-out populations are temporarily in geographical proximity. The United States has historically approached crisis situations and displaced populations as a humanitarian concern, and even today relies almost exclusively on funding the UN and large non-governmental organizations to provide services in these areas, without directing and prioritizing how this aid should be spent. I believe that our main focus in crisis situations in which the displaced

population is at risk of terrorist recruitment, or has historically supported extremist ideologies, should instead be counter-radicalization.

The majority of American aid to refugee and displaced persons camps today is funneled through the State Department's Bureau of Population, Migration and Refugees (BPRM), which in 2011 was budgeted approximately $1.8 billion to aid refugees and IDPs around the world. Of this $1.8 billion, less than 0.2 percent was spent directly on educational programs in the camps. It should be noted that the State Department does not directly provide physical assistance or infrastructure to any refugee organization, but relies exclusively on funding inter-governmental organizations (IGOs like the United Nations) and non-governmental organizations (NGOs like Save the Children) to provide services.

Within the BPRM, funding for educational programs is channeled in two ways: multilaterally through the Office of the United Nations High Commissioner for Refugees (UNHCR) and bilaterally through a number of non-governmental organizations. The BPRM donates approximately 38 percent of its budget to the UNHCR, a little over $687 million in fiscal year 2011, which represents close to 37 percent of UNHCR's total budget. This contribution makes the United States the largest contributor by far to the plight of refugees around the world. In addition, the third largest donation is to the United Nations Relief and Works Agency (UNRWA), an organization that deals exclusively with the plight of Palestinian refugees, and to whom the BPRM donates 15 percent of its budget, or about $250 million; in this case, the United States represents close to a quarter of the entire operating budget for UNRWA .

In addition to being the largest aid recipient, UNHCR serves as the key vessel through which the BPRM funds educational programs in refugee camps. Nonetheless, a separate allocation is not made through UNHCR directly to education, but is instead expected to be part of the overall budget—which gives UNHCR complete freedom as to how much of this budget to allocate to education and what type of education is being undertaken in the camps. This lack of supervision is a problem for two reasons: a) American interests and UN interests are not necessarily aligned in this case, as the UN is not particularly incentivized to focus on counter-radicalization in refugee and displaced persons camps; and b) It is much easier to measure and provide basic services to a refugee population (shelters built, meals given out, and so on) than to create a robust educational program. Thus, organizations are motivated to focus on the services for which success is more easily and quantifiably defined, rather than expend their limited energy and resources on a difficult endeavor the success of which is many years down the line and is difficult to monitor. In its 2008 budget, UNHCR stated that it expected to spend approximately $80.1 million in education projects, or less than 8 percent of its total expected budget.

Of fifty-seven non-governmental organizations that received funding directly from the BPRM, only ten had an educational component to their services, and received less than 20 percent of the total budget allocated to NGOs.

The BPRM does not actively seek programs that will increase access and quality of education to refugee children through these grants. Instead, the State Department requests proposals based on country or region and does not typically provide detailed guidelines of the issues it hopes the NGO will address in the refugee camps. For example, past queries stated that the BPRM was looking, "for NGO Program Benefiting Refugees in Ethiopia and Kenya," and that "Proposals may focus on protection, health (including support for disabled persons), water, sanitation, shelter, community services, psychosocial support, prevention of and response to gender-based violence, and livelihoods development (including education) and training." Of the thirteen funding opportunity announcements in 2009 and early 2010, none focused exclusively on education. Moreover, the ones that did mention education did so as part of a broader set of interests that typically included food and shelter, two priorities that are easier to accomplish.

There is currently no person in charge of overseeing refugee educational programs at the Department of State, in spite of the BPRM employing one-hundred and twenty people. General education programs are coordinated by the Bureau of Educational and Cultural Affairs, which does not oversee refugee education and engages primarily in cultural and academic exchanges. Given this organizational structure, I imagine it is difficult to pay much attention to the bilateral educational allocations that make up less than .02 percent of the overall budget, and that most educational charities are not rigorously analyzed to determine whether they provide robust education programs that are in line with our national security concerns.

The State Department should create a position that oversees efforts for counter-radicalization in crisis situations, primarily in refugee and IDP camps. More aid should be apportioned to educational initiatives that provide at-risk populations with a well-rounded education and address our national security concerns. If we continue to outsource our humanitarian aid to third parties without increasing our engagement or oversight, we will continue to repeat the mistakes of the past, in which aid is apportioned primarily on humanitarian concerns and almost exclusively used to fulfill basic services. This cycle leads to a lack of funding for educational programs in crisis situations, which creates a population that is fed and sheltered but is largely uneducated and poses a greater risk of radicalizing or adopting an extremist ideology.

The State Department should also retool its current refugee resettlement policy to give some preference to those refugees who speak English or have achieved a higher degree of education than others. Although this doesn't seem humanitarian in nature, the lives of refugees once they have arrived in the United States are extremely difficult if they are unable to communicate or contribute to society in a meaningful way. In addition, our welfare programs are not designed to support refugees for years or decades on end, which in many cases is a real and unavoidable need as newcomers have to adjust to a new life outside a camp, learn a new language, and train themselves to have marketable skills—all barriers that are extremely difficult to overcome. By reserving a percentage of asylum slots for those refugees who already speak English and have a higher level of education, we make it easier for them to succeed in their new home and reduce their financial dependency on government programs and charitable organizations. Most of the camps that I visited already had programs that taught refugees English as a second language, and it would be relatively easy to use TOEFL scores as a helpful input in ranking. The interviews that already take place for all refugees who will be resettled in the United States could be used to ascertain a higher degree of education. However, this prioritization should only apply to those refugees who are living inside a refugee camp, as that way our resettlement program would continue to benefit those who need it most.

Finally, the State Department should also increase its funding for accelerated literacy and education programs for refugees who have arrived in the camps at an age where they are too old to join primary school and who have been unable to attend a school before. These types of young men made some of the most accessible recruits for al-Shabaab in the Dadaab camp, and integrating them into the existing educational infrastructure would reduce the probability that they will end up joining a terrorist organization.

Problems with the Current U.S. Strategy vis-à-vis Yemen
Our strategy in Yemen has historically ignored our need to win hearts and minds, and has instead focused almost exclusively on increased counterterrorism cooperation

and military funding. Our former strategy sought to strengthen a central government that had historically been too weak to impose its will across the country as a whole, focusing instead on targeting the Houthi rebels and the southern secessionist movement. Increasing Saleh's military strength only encouraged him to clamp down harder on any dissent inside Yemen, and he stopped compromising with more moderate tribes who had legitimate concerns that deserved to be addressed. In turn, this only increased the likelihood that more moderate tribes became more anti-government and sought to challenge the existing regime, at times with the help of AQAP. The harder that Saleh clamped down on disenfranchised southerners and Houthis, the more likely they became to join forces with terrorist organizations to achieve their goals.

In the case of the southern secessionists, in February 2010 Turki al-Fadhl videotaped himself raising an American flag in his compound in the Abyan province and playing the Star-Spangled Banner, while his followers stood at attention looking at the flag. This was broadly interpreted as a sign of al-Fadhl's desire to increase cooperation with the United States and proof that he was not anti-American. However, the US ignored this overture for better relations out of fear of destabilizing the lukewarm counterterrorism cooperation with Saleh's government, further alienating a powerful and potential ally. In April and July 2011, the leaders of the popular Youth Movement reached out to the United States, asking for similar support that the youth movement in Egypt had received. Once again we succumbed to Saudi Arabia's wishes, rather than pursuing a long-term strategy that would protect our national interests. Since Saudi Arabia and the GCC refused to legitimize the Youth Movement and are terrified of a democratic Yemen, we in turn did not push for democratization. As these two movements are attacked by Saleh's forces on one end and by General Ahmar's forces on the other, both who were trained and funded by the United States, AQAP's violent rhetoric and anti-Americanism have become more compelling to Yemenis.

As mentioned before, even after the advent of the Arab Spring in 2011, the United States continued to ignore the root causes for extremism in Yemen, helping AQAP increase its popular support and become an even greater threat to our national security. The current turmoil in Yemen should be seen as a golden opportunity for the US to reset its relationship with the Yemeni people, in the hopes that they will eventually become our allies. By developing a strong relationship with the Youth Movement, the southern secessionists and the Houthis, the United States would gain the ability to shape the country's future in a way that would most benefit us. Instead of engaging with these powerful and potentially moderate allies, as of mid-2011 the United States was once again allowing its foreign policy to be driven exclusively by counterterrorism concerns. It was tacitly backing General Ahmar, an Islamist detested by the Houthis, as the future head of the military and security services, and supporting Hamid al-Ahmar (no relation), a man reviled by the Youth Movement as a corrupt autocrat, and his likely bid for the presidency. Our backing of General

Ahmar was driven by the fantasy that his rise to power would lead to a continuation of the counterterrorism cooperation we received from President Saleh, which was lukewarm at its best. It is clear that the institutions we have traditionally relied on for counterterrorism co-operation in Yemen are no longer reliable, in large part because of the ongoing chaos and the likely increase in extremist leaders post-Saleh in these very institutions. Thus, going forward US strategy in Yemen must rely more heavily on counter-radicalization techniques over counterterrorism in order to successfully address our national security interests there.

By supporting the Youth Movement, the United States would be able to burnish its image in Yemen significantly, support a foil against the Islamists, and, if the Youth Movement is successful in its vision, revolutionize our strategic relationship with Yemen long term. Without our support, the Youth Movement is likely to fail in its quest to democratize Yemen, blame the United States for failing to live up to its rhetoric, and become more likely to join and support AQAP against a new regime that will likely ignore its demands.

We should take advantage of the fact that Yemenis are not virulently anti-American—yet. An exclusive focus on military aid, while ignoring our ability to publicly (unlike in Pakistan) fund humanitarian projects and extend educational programs to the extremist areas in the South, is unlikely to make America safer. Unfortunately, one of the main obstacles to increasing humanitarian aid to Yemen is the endemic corruption and lack of accountability of the government. Taxpayers and foreign governments are rightly concerned that the aid they donate reach its designated recipients instead of lining the pockets of corrupt officials. Rather than continue to depend on Saudi Arabia to provide humanitarian aid, the United States should take advantage of this neutral or even positive view of Americans to increase basic services and education in the provinces of Abyan, Shabwah, al-Bayda, and Lahij. Tribal structures are typically well defined, and given the ongoing turmoil, Saleh's government is no longer able to prohibit us from negotiating directly with tribal leaders or supporting Western non-governmental organizations. The US could negotiate directly with friendly tribes in these provinces to provide basic services and pay for teachers, which would contain the AQAP threat while at the same time showing the tangible benefits to the local population of eschewing an AQAP presence. Although we have historically been prohibited from this role by the Saleh government, the current turmoil and weakness of the central government provide a historical opportunity for the United States to engage more directly with the Yemeni population. Providing funding for well-rounded education programs in the southern provinces, where AQAP is located, is a more effective tool against radicalization than the $1.2 billion increase in military aid to President Saleh's government that was previously recommended by CENTCOM (Central Command, one of the Unified Combatant Commands of the US military, responsible for the Middle East). Many Yemenis I have spoken to most recently have welcomed the idea of greater US participation in the provision of basic services, and firmly believe that it would generate significant goodwill toward the United States.

The expectation of continued counterterrorism cooperation with a new Yemeni government is premised on the ability of the new government to continue to cajole unfriendly tribes to divulge information about AQAP. Any new government will be less able to control the tribes, and any security apparatus under General Ahmar is even less likely to target Islamists. As such, our direct outreach to the tribes is essential for us to continue to gain intelligence on AQAP and isolate Islamists more successfully in Yemen; in effect, utilizing the same strategy Saleh used, except without his interference. Our approach to counterterrorism in Yemen needs to become more fragmented to make up for the collapse of the central government. As tribal leaders gain more prominence as they become able to provide more basic services, they are more likely to cooperate with the United States to target AQAP than before. In addition, there is a strategy that could help over one million Yemenis and their families climb out of abject poverty while at the same time making sure that all of the money ended up in the individuals' hands, bypassing the corrupt bureaucracy. Ironically, it involves Saudi Arabia.

Almost twenty years ago, during the Gulf War, Yemen decided to abstain from condemning Saddam Hussein's invasion of Kuwait in the United Nations, an act that was largely viewed as a sign of diplomatic support. Saudi Arabia, which at the time was terrified that it too would be annexed by Saddam's army, was so angry at Yemen that it expelled over one million Yemeni guest workers. To this day, Saudi Arabia has not legally reopened its border to allow Yemenis to apply for guest worker visas. In a country where close to 90 percent of the private sector positions are made up of foreigners, oil-rich Saudi Arabia, as Yemen's neighbor, represents the best opportunity for Yemen to put to work a percentage of its unemployed work force, especially since 80 percent of the Yemeni population is under twenty-five years of age. Changing this policy would also help Saudi Arabia, which would prefer Yemeni workers because they speak Arabic, are Muslim, and, although still different culturally, are more similar to the Saudis than the Indian or Filipinos that are currently employed.

The economic benefits to Yemen of this change in strategy would be tremendous, and have a very real impact on the wellbeing of individuals. For example, if we assume that Saudi Arabia would hire 150,000 Yemeni construction workers over the next five years, and each construction worker is paid $400 a month, this would create over 720 million dollars in additional income per year. If Yemen eventually reached its former dominance as the main provider of cheap labor to Saudi Arabia, one million workers could provide close to 5 billion dollars in additional spending power. In a country where you can have an excellent and filling meal at a restaurant for less than $1, this is a big difference in individuals' purchasing power. In today's terms, we are talking about an increase of up to 20 percent of GDP.

U.S. Aid and Public Diplomacy Projects

In Yemen, perhaps because of the general lack of anti-Americanism, multiple taxi drivers happily pointed out the benefits of the paved road funded by "the Americans." The positive publicity the road generated was a force multiplier of sorts, as people in Hodeida and Aden also heard about the road and its positive connotations. I am not arguing that a road is a more important, or even a more helpful, project for the Yemeni population than a rural hospital or an agricultural training center outside of Sana'a. I am arguing, however, that large scale, visible infrastructure projects serve US interests more effectively than smaller projects, and help burnish America's image abroad.

In Pakistan, the biggest infrastructure problem is the government's inability to meet domestic electricity demand. It is an issue that affects the entire population and forces the government to rely on paper copies of all documents and close its offices early to save energy. Rather than spend $1.5 billion a year on small-scale agricultural and civil society projects in Pakistan, the United States should focus its resources on providing electricity in both urban and rural areas across Pakistan. Focusing on small-scale projects in Pakistan forces us to funnel the aid through non-governmental organizations and other local intermediaries, which in turn leads to a less effective utilization of our funds to bolster our image there, as most NGOs are loathe to admit they accept American funds. However, by engaging in large-scale infrastructure projects that are very visible and have the potential to benefit hundreds of thousands of lives, the United States could use its aid more effectively to promote a more positive view of American engagement abroad. The positive publicity that would be generated from these projects, even if they directly benefit fewer people than the sum of smaller projects, is a better utilization of US funds to counter anti-Americanism. In addition, by focusing on large-scale, costly projects, the United States makes it less likely that the existing institutions will be overwhelmed by a significant influx of new American aid.

The Need for Diplomacy

The horrific events of September 11, 2001, and the subsequent War on Terror, have rightly dominated our foreign policy over the past decade. We have now been involved in the longest running war in American history, have learned to take off our shoes and belts without complaint before flying, and have increased our counter-terrorism cooperation exponentially with both friends and enemies—all in the hope that a new 9/11 will never happen; or worse, that a nuclear 9/11 will never happen. But in spite of the sacrifices of so many valiant Americans and their families and a defense budget that has virtually doubled in the past ten years, we have made little progress on the front that matters most: reducing the space for organizations like al-Qaeda to train and plot new attacks against us.

Al-Qaeda today has more branches and is more active than it was ten years ago, and even though the core leadership has been diminished, more than enough young terrorist leaders will emerge to take their places. From their links with al-Shabaab to their franchise in northwest Africa (al-Qaeda in the Islamic Maghreb), extremism has flourished in certain areas, filling al-Qaeda's coffers and making it easier for the organization to recruit. This success is due in large part to our inability to counter its extremist message and our failure at reducing the ideological space in which it is able to operate. Too much of our emphasis over this past decade has been on military solutions, which, although a necessary part of a successful counterterrorism strategy, are not enough on their own to successfully defeat the al-Qaeda ideology.

In both Yemen and Pakistan, from which the most recent terrorist attacks have emerged, we have spent the vast majority of our resources and effort on military cooperation. Worse, as Leon Panetta, the former Director of the CIA and current Secretary of Defense, has pointed out, the Times Square bomber (trained in Pakistan) and the Christmas Day bomber (trained in Yemen) both failed because of their own technical difficulties exploding their respective devices—not because of any intelligence or military success on our part. If we continue to ignore the underlying causes that create space in these communities to train future bombers, we will eventually run out of luck and experience another catastrophic terrorist attack on our soil.

In order to defeat al-Qaeda and other extremist organizations, we need to undercut their ideological support by educating the communities that today shelter and support them. We must reform our attitude toward diplomatic and soft-power efforts, and begin to resource engagement strategies that do not have a military component. We need to realize that these types of programs, focused on winning the hearts and minds of reconcilable al-Qaeda supporters, are the only long term solution to the War on Terror. This is not a novel concept, as both former Secretary of Defense Robert Gates and Secretary of State Hillary Clinton have agreed that going forward we need a bigger emphasis on our civilian and diplomatic strategies.

What is novel, however, is the idea that our diplomatic efforts should focus on winning over the hearts and minds of the communities that support extremism through education, rather than focusing our humanitarian efforts primarily on economic development as a means to counter al-Qaeda's message. As Secretary Clinton stated in an article in *Foreign Affairs* in November 2010, the main humanitarian efforts of the Quadrennial Diplomacy and Development Review (QDDR) will be a global health initiative and a Feed the Future program. Although both are laudable goals, they focus too narrowly on the humanitarian factor, rather than addressing the underlying reasons for radicalization. Our limited resources and finite tax dollars should be spent first on humanitarian programs that fight extremism, rather than on broad un-targeted programs that seek to only improve a person's quality of life. Counter-radicalization is the most important form of public diplomacy and it should take priority over other programs.

In fact, in Secretary Clinton's entire article there is not one mention of education and its ability to reduce the space for extremism to flourish, or even education at all. The article continues to disseminate the idea that poverty is a better predictor of extremism and terrorist sympathies than a lack of education, an argument that my travels and interviews consistently debunked.

Funding educational programs for at-risk communities to reduce their support for extremism is a more effective, and less costly, strategy for counterterrorism than one focused exclusively on a military component. It is also more effective, as a method of counter-radicalization, than focusing on economic development. Most important, providing these communities with a well-rounded education will reduce their support for terrorist organizations, which could provide a long-term solution to our national security problems.

It is clear that terrorism isn't going away or becoming any less of a problem, at least during my lifetime, but we need to create a more proactive strategy, rather than continue to be reactive and add military resources wherever the most recent terrorist attack came from. It is my belief that with a well-resourced and coordinated strategy that promotes access to a well-rounded education for those populations that are most at risk of radicalization, we can make a significant difference in these communities while at the same time making America safer. With this new focus, the hope is that one day al-Qaeda will be a distant memory, doomed to the dustbin of history.

Already, my decision to study terrorist recruitment and embark on this trip has changed my life. Most important, I have learned that access to a well rounded education is the most powerful weapon we have against terrorism. The Winning the Minds Foundation is a small but important step, not just in improving the lives of so many children desperate for the opportunity for a better life, but also to support counter-radicalization in these communities. If you are interested in becoming more involved with the foundation, or would like to donate, please contact contact@winningtheminds.org or visit www.winningtheminds.org.

Afterword

"At the one-year anniversary of bin Laden's demise, the tone is that it is all over, and that's all bullshit. Sanctuary for al-Qaeda minded elements is probably greater today than it has ever been."

— Veteran Intelligence Official (quoted anonymously in Newsweek on May 21, 2012)

"Education is the only way of counterbalancing extremism in Somalia."

— Abdi Farah Said Juxa, Minister of Education in Puntland

The death of Osama bin Laden was a great accomplishment for the United States, bringing to justice an evil coward responsible for the deaths of thousands of innocent civilians. Unfortunately, the successful raid complicated the U.S.-Pakistan relationship in more ways than we anticipated. The raid on Pakistani territory, within striking distance of a renowned military academy, combined with the death of twenty-four Pakistani soldiers by NATO forces in November 2011 and our continuing campaign of drone strikes on Pakistani soil have fueled anti-Americanism to new heights. Most alarmingly, it has become almost impossible for Western NGOs to carry out their activities there without engendering grave suspicion, aggression and cumbersome oversight – all due to the fact that bin Laden's compound was found in part using a fake polio drive that went door to door. To top things off, in April 2012 the U.S. State Department unveiled a $10 million bounty on Hafiz Mohammad Saeed's head, adding his picture to their "Rewards for Justice" website. His photograph was placed right below that of Ayman al-Zawahiri's (who commands a $25 million bounty) and next to Mullah Omar's somewhat dashing visage. Saeed, as you know, is the founder of the terrorist organization accused of the 2008 Mumbai bombings, Lashkar-e-Taiba, and of its popular philanthropic arm, Jamaat-ud-Dawa, which though widely reputed to be a cover for Lashkar, is well liked by the thousands of Pakistanis it benefits.

In and of itself, the bounty is no more than the most recent blunder by the Administration in dealing with Pakistan; however, it does help highlight our strategic failures there. For example, though the bounty drew praise from a number of Indian officials, few believe it will have any effect on the Pakistani government's reticence to take action against Saeed or his organization. In spite of outstanding U.N. sanctions and an Interpol warrant against him, Saeed openly lives in Lahore and moves freely around Pakistan. Over the past few months he has led rallies around Pakistan and, within hours of receiving news of the bounty against him, shrugged it off in a telephone interview with al-Jazeera, stating, "We're not hiding in caves for rewards to be set on finding us. We are addressing hundreds of thousands of people daily in Pakistan." The bounty will not have any effect on Saeed's ability to move around Pakistan or address his supporters. If anything, the bounty makes it more difficult for the Pakistani government to place him under arrest without looking as if they are kowtowing to American pressure. Most importantly, as of this writing Pakistan had still not re-opened NATO's crucial supply lines, closed after the deaths of its 24 soldiers. Placing the bounty on Saeed's head has made this reopening even less likely, as Saeed brilliantly connected the $10 million reward to his opposition to the NATO supply lines, instead of the Mumbai attacks. This argument makes it even more difficult for the Pakistani government to take any action against Saeed without alienating large swaths of the population who are against reopening those supply lines.

Some policy analysts argue that the announcement of the bounty had little to do with the U.S. relationship with Pakistan, and should instead be seen in the framework of the U.S.-India relationship. This is certainly possible, especially since the bounty was announced by Under Secretary of State Wendy Sherman while she was visiting India. However, if this was the primary purpose for announcing the bounty, it seems the U.S. has received very little credit for it, as critics in India point out that the Indian government requested this type of pressure years ago, and now it seems like too little too late. From a Pakistani perspective though, having the Under Secretary of State announce a bounty for a popular Pakistani leader while she was visiting India projects the image of a tight-knit alliance, one which is likely to further inflame anti-Americanism in Pakistan and the view that the U.S. is willing to subsume Pakistani interests in favor of India's requests. This can only make it more difficult for the Pakistani government and Pakistani military to openly cooperate with the U.S.

Not only is the U.S.-Pakistan relationship at its nadir, but the U.S. has broadly lost its ability to engage in a positive manner with elements of Pakistani civil society.

Critics may argue that we don't need to bother with engagement, or counter-radicalization programs for that matter, that our drone strike capabilities have become so advanced that we need not worry about more and more communities supporting extremist groups. To those who take comfort in this argument though, be wary of underestimating the potential for extremist organizations to adapt to these new technologies. In mid-April 2012, the Taliban staged a significant coordinated offensive in Kabul and three other provinces for eighteen hours, killing eleven members of the Afghan security forces and at least four civilians. Military commanders were surprised that their drone surveillance programs and cell phone tapping failed to pick up on any of the planning for this large scale attack, which presumably took place over two months. President Karzai's office stated, "The fact terrorists were able to enter Kabul and other provinces was an intelligence failure for us and especially for NATO." More alarmingly, as Joe Nye reported in his book, "The Future of Power," "in 2009 the American military discovered that insurgents were hacking into the downlinks of data from Predator unmanned aircraft using software that cost less than $30." The technology that is available to us today will be available to our enemies, big and small, tomorrow, likely at a fraction of the price we paid to develop it – such is the curse of Moore's Law and the reason why engagement with these communities is paramount to our national security.

In Somalia, the mandate of the Transitional Federal Government (TFG) is set to expire in August 2012. Since my visit to Dadaab, al-Shabaab has been expelled from

Mogadishu by AMISOM forces and on March 30, 2012, Paddy Akundi, the spokesman for the African Union Mission in Somalia (AMISOM), proudly claimed that, "The TFG and AMISOM forces were successful in seizing the entirety of the Dayniile (part of Mogadishu)." Although this claim has been disputed by al-Shabaab and even by one of AMISOM's Burundian commanders, it is clear that the Kenyan military operation "Linda Nchi," which began in mid-October, along with a new incursion by the Ethiopian military in November, is successfully displacing al-Shabaab from its former strongholds. Recent advances are looking favorable enough that David Cameron called the most recent Somalia conference in London a "turning point" and Hillary Clinton threatened sanctions, including travel bans and asset freezes against anyone who sought "to undermine Somalia's peace and security or to delay or even prevent the political transition." With this in mind, it seems Somalis should be heartened that their plight could soon end. Sadly, the situation is far from improving and it's clear that the international community has learned very little from its failings in the Horn of Africa over the past 20 years.

The current situation resonates deeply with those who cheered on the Ethiopian Army's quick defeat of the Islamic Courts Union in 2006, thinking they were ousting an extremist government linked to al-Qaeda. If only policy makers had known that the Ethiopian Army would be unable to hold the territory against al-Shabaab's guerrilla tactics, leaving Somalia in the hands of a group that in February 2012 officially became an al-Qaeda franchise, they would have felt differently. Today's military operations, performed jointly by the Kenyan Army, Ethiopian Army and AMISOM forces, will prove no different than the failures of the past 20 years and will likely galvanize the population against the international community. There are a series of clear, targeted lessons from Ethiopia's invasion of 2006 and al-Shabaab's short history that policy makers are ignoring at their own peril.

First, they should understand that Al-Shabaab is most dangerous as a guerilla organization. Though al-Shabaab may control less territory than before, it would be a mistake to think it will be any less effective at the guerrilla tactics and suicide bombings it has perfected over the past few years. In March 2012, for example, al-Shabaab ambushed an Ethiopian Army base in central Somalia, claiming to kill as many as 73 Ethiopian soldiers. These attacks will become more regular and devastating as the Kenyan and Ethiopian armies take over more of Somalia, thereby increasing al-Shabaab's target base. By controlling less territory, al-Shabaab has been liberated from the more difficult task of holding and administering areas, and can now focus on the easier task of targeted assaults.

Members of the intelligence community have consistently rejected the notion that al-Shabaab's official designation as an al-Qaeda affiliate has changed the underlying environment, claiming that they have been working together for years. However, these intelligence analysts should not underestimate the effects of al-Shabaab's official designation as an al-Qaeda franchise. Although al-Shabaab pledged allegiance to al-Qaeda as early as September 2009, Zawahiri's comments welcoming al-

Shabaab into the al-Qaeda network are likely to increase its ability to raise funds. While I was in Dadaab, it was clear that with additional funding al-Shabaab could recruit three or four more times the number of refugees it was bringing back to Somalia. But if al-Shabaab gains increased access to the al-Qaeda patronage network, what does al-Qaeda gain? Recruits with American passports.

Al-Shabaab has always posed a serious concern to the American intelligence community because of the large number of Somali-Americans who have joined the organization. As J.M. Berger pointed out in February 2012, their recruits include both first and second generation immigrants and radicalized Muslim converts. Al-Qaeda, and especially al-Qaeda in the Arabian Peninsula (AQAP), is likely to receive an influx of American volunteers from al-Shabaab's existing ranks. As of May 2012, Yemeni authorities had killed or arrested over a dozen Somalis who had been found fighting alongside Ansar al-Sharia, AQAP's offshoot in southern Yemen. More importantly, many of these recruits joined al-Shabaab after the 2006 Ethiopian incursion, motivated by reports of systematic human rights abuses by Ethiopians against Somali women and children. There is no reason to believe that the Ethiopian Army will behave any differently this time around. It is important to remember that Somalia is a predominantly Muslim country and that Ethiopians are mostly Christian, which feeds into al-Shabaab's and al-Qaeda's narrative of Christian invaders raping and killing a Muslim population.

Those who continue to be optimistic about the ongoing military campaign are likely to point out that the Ethiopian Army has promised to leave Somalia by mid-2012. What they fail to address is who exactly the Ethiopian Army will transfer territory to. Even if the Kenyan, Ethiopian and AMISOM forces are able to oust al-Shabaab fighters from their strongholds, there is no Somali army that can hold these gains. The TFG is seen as so inefficient by the international community that its mandate will not be renewed after its August expiry, and thus far the only idea for a federal institution to replace it is a vaguely defined "caretaker authority." This means that foreign forces will have to keep a significant presence in Somalia in the medium to long-term future if they plan to keep al-Shabaab from regaining lost territory. More importantly, Somali scholars widely agree that the TFG Army has never been more than a disaggregated group of clan militias with little officer training; after the end of the TFG's mandate, they will return to their pre-2004 roles and continue to fight each other.

There are those who believe that the current conditions are ripe for another internationally sanctioned peace conference on Somalia. Optimists even point out that the Transitional Federal Parliament (TFP), part of the current mandate, would be an excellent starting point for peace negotiations and will be different than the last fourteen that failed. The problem with this framework, other than the foreseen difficulty of negotiating among 550 representatives, is that many Somali intellectuals and Islamic leaders reject the current clan-based formula on which representation in Parliament is based. Even worse, minority clans are only considered half a clan in Parliament, which makes them even less likely to participate in a peace process and more likely to take up arms to advance their claims.

Most recently, on May 7, 2012, one-hundred and twenty-five Somali "elders" met in Mogadishu to help choose 825 members for the constituent assembly that is meant to draft Somalia's newest constitution. As a useful comparison, Egypt's Constitutional Assembly has only 100 members, all of who were elected and who get to meet regularly, when they choose to, in the security of a country that has not been at war with itself for the past twenty-one years. In spite of these enhancements, they have been unable to reach any agreement with each other. If the Egyptians, with all of their relative advantages, are unable to draft a constitution, what hope does Somalia have, given that its assembly's membership is eight times larger and has little to no popular legitimacy? Once again, the United States has failed to learn from the history of the last fourteen failed peace conferences on Somalia. The common characteristic of these past failures has been the imposition of culturally Western modes of conflict resolution which do not apply to the local conflict and are not successful at integrating the different factions.

Rather than view the existing social structures based on lineage and clanism as hindrances to establishing peace in Somalia, Somalis should be allowed to utilize these existing mechanisms to help solve their conflict – which is precisely what these structures were initially created to do. Although some experts fear that allowing Somalis to undertake their own peace negotiations within a more traditional context will lead to a partition of Somalia along clan lines, these fears seem largely overblown, as the Somali academic Afyare Elmi states, "The second strategy in dealing with identity conflict would involve partitioning Somalia along clan lines. This strategy was unanimously rejected by all (Somali) interviewees. Such complete rejection is obvious as clan identity is based on 'segmentary lineage', which is very fluid. If Somalia were to be divided along clan and sub-clan lines, there would be hundreds of governments within this small and poor country."

Ioan M. Lewis, the noted British anthropologist who is considered an expert on Somali culture, highlights an interesting contrast between the peace conferences in southern Somalia and Somaliland, "Over the period 1990 to 2005, high-profile peacemaking initiatives in southern Somalia, involving costs running into millions of dollars, produced few positive results. In Somaliland, in contrast, between 1991 and 1993 the local clan elders organized a series of remarkably successful peace conferences, using traditional procedures, to secure a level of interclan understanding that surpasses anything yet achieved in the south. Except for a little assistance with logistics and conference food costs, foreign intervention was extremely limited. Our conclusions suggest that the slow, local, traditionally based Somali process is the most effective process of peacemaking."

The failure of the international community to mediate a successful peace process in Somalia can be attributed to outsiders' inability to include all of the relevant actors in the ongoing peace negotiations, as the international community is unable to correctly identify the leaders of the community, and the general lack of legitimacy which the internationally backed governments have suffered from inside Somalia (a designation which applies both to the current TFG and to the earlier Transitional National Government). "Generally, Somalis expressed disappointment about the role of international organizations. In most places, members of the councils reported that international organizations and external non-governmental organizations did not recognize them as representatives of the local communities."

The international community's inability to identify the key actors has led in some cases to exclude "good" actors, those who had not resorted to violence, and has in many cases led to the U.S. allying itself with unpopular partners who terrorize the population. The Somali academic Afyare Elmi talks about the fluid nature of clan identity, and states that even for Somalis it is sometimes, "...very difficult to determine who is to be included and who is to be excluded in both peacemaking and peace-building activities. Several warlords of sub-sub-clans such as the Daud and Sa'ad sub-clans, which belong to Hawiye, have participated in peace conferences, while bigger clans who were not armed were excluded. For example, the then leader of the Banadiri group, Mohamed Rajis, was not allowed to participate in the Djibouti conference as his clan was unarmed. He reportedly said, 'We were excluded because of the "crime" that we did not kill.'"

The fluid nature of clan identity, our inability to include all relevant stakeholders and at times our empowerment of the wrong group best exemplify our inability to correctly "choose sides" or "pick a winner." This is due in large part to a lack of credible and complete intelligence of the situation on the ground, as well as our inability to discern between genuine and tainted intelligence that is colored by the biases of some of our partners in the region.

Our inability to correctly identify community leaders and create truly inclusive peace processes is further complicated by the fact that, "Traditionally in Somali pastoral society governance is decentralized and based on consensus... these clan councils have not been permanent institutions, but ad hoc gatherings formed in response to particular needs and, depending on the issue at hand, might last for days or weeks. When a conflict arises a special committee, called a Guurti, may be formed to facilitate this resolution. In this acephalous society any adult male can be considered an elder (oday) with an equal right to speak in a council." This emphasis on conflict resolution techniques that rely on consensus, and which allow any adult male to serve as a community leader, serves to illustrate why minority groups have been so successful over the past twenty years as "spoilers" of the peace process, and why it is necessary (and virtually impossible, as foreigners) for internationally mediated conferences to be fully inclusive of every stakeholder group in order for any peace agreement to have local legitimacy. This also helps to explain why Somaliland has been effective at creating a lasting peace, as its peace negotiations were considered to be inclusive and were based on local existing social structures.

The Somali experience of "nomadic-pasturalism", whereby a majority of the population formerly depended on migrating through different territories in order for their livestock to graze, has fostered the creation of social institutions and collective action mechanisms that rely primarily on "kinship". Although these mechanisms are part of the reason why it has been so difficult to create a centralized state with representative elections, these same barriers to centralization also provide Somalis with the necessary tools, through these existing social structures, to create a durable peace of their own – as long as they are given the space and security in which to conduct these grass-roots level negotiations. For example, the formation of local councils and sharia courts (which in some cases were led not only by religious scholars, but also incorporated businessmen and community elders) after the departure of UNOSOM (the United Nations Operation in Somalia) illustrates the ability of the Somali people to create viable institutions of governance and engage in peace-building measures without the overt influence of the international community. Although multiple Somalis interviewed at the time were grateful for the U.N.'s and other NGOs' support by providing food to the participants and encouraging them to dialogue, this hands off approach allowed the participants to structure these peacemaking efforts in a way that achieved legitimacy in their communities, addressed their concerns, and were inclusive in nature.

This outcome encourages the idea that what Somalis need most is not for the international community to "choose sides" in the conflict, but rather for the international community to help them create space in which they can dialogue. This space, as had happened before, is likely to result in a sustainable agreement that could stabilize southern Somalia (or certain parts of it). In the Somaliland case, "This comprehensive peace movement was first initiated at the local level by traditional political leaders, using conventional methods of arbitration between neighboring and intermarrying clans. Starting at the grassroots level, this movement progressed to district and regional levels. It reached its height at the Borama conference (known as guurti), where 150 delegates, consisting of clan councilors representing all the groups in Somaliland, managed to agree on separate regional and national peace charters. Here, for the first time in the post independence period, the elders extended their peace-making functions by acting as an institutional framework for the formation of an executive interim national government."

It is also important for these meeting grounds to be inside Somalia and near the leaders' communities because, "[Allowing delegates to meet daily with their constituencies is a] simple but critical provision [that] was pivotal in legitimizing the [Jubbaland peace accord] proceedings in the eyes of the community, enabling local people to play the nightly role of 'ratifier' to the negotiating teams." This strategy, the most likely to bring peace to Somalia, has not been fostered by the international community and also sharply contrasts with al-Shabaab's actions, since they prefer to ally themselves with one or two sub-clans in the area, provide a modicum of protection to them, and allow them to exploit other minorities and less well-armed groups.

Finally, it is important to note that, "Observers contend that without a negotiated settlement with groups still outside the TFG, it will be difficult to maintain peace and stability in Somalia." This is the infamous "spoiler problem in peace processes ", a problem that the international community has been unable to avoid in its failed attempts at peace negotiations in Somalia. A Somali-led approach to peace is less likely to encounter this problem, as the community is acutely aware of who the leaders who need to be included in the process are, much more so than outsiders looking in (this also solves the problem of increased violence by warlords prior to a peace conference to appear more relevant to outside actors and win a seat at the negotiating table). It also makes it more difficult for warlords and community leaders who were at the conference to renege on their earlier promises, as the Somali concept of consensus forces them to publicly recognize the legitimacy of the peace agreement and their proximity to the communities they are representing means that they have also bought into the result.

Al-Shabaab's pernicious influence has not been constrained to Somalia, as other extremist groups in Africa have also identified access to education as the greatest threat to their existence and have begun to target students and teachers. In Nigeria, for example, Boko Haram has developed into a potent al-Qaeda franchise, killing over one thousand people in multiple attacks. Tellingly, its name means, "Western education is a sin." The fact that the most powerful al-Qaeda franchise in west Africa has chosen to target "Western" education in its very name is a powerful reminder that access to a well-rounded education is the most effective tool against extremism. Boko Haram's leaders are well aware that the more educated their neighboring communities become the less likely they are to be able to recruit from them or find shelter within them. Its very existence is evidence that the recommendations in this book are the most effective way to fight extremism.

Last, as I wrote in my May 2, 2012 article, "Where Democracy is America's Second Choice," first published on the Foreign Policy website, nowhere have the changes been more dramatic, or heartbreaking, than in Yemen. The Arab Spring brought to this magical country the hope of real positive change for the twenty-four million Yemenis who had lived under President Saleh's corrupt, sclerotic, and crushing regime, only too happy to clamp down on dissent by wielding death and torture. The appearance of tens of thousands of demonstrators in Change Square, the creation of the celebrated Youth Movement, and the surprising resignation of President Saleh in November 2011 ushered in a new era of hope and dreams of democracy. In spite of these momentous changes, U.S. strategy there has remained single-mindedly focused on eradicating AQAP. Democracy promotion, and the hopes of millions of Yemenis who supported the revolution, do not appear to be among the Obama Administration's concerns in the country. Nowhere was this more clear than in a March 2012 press conference in Sana'a, where Jeffrey Feltman, the Assistant Secretary of State for Near Eastern Affairs, reinforced U.S. support for the existing transition plan, which doesn't call for elections until February 2014 and which has widely left President Saleh's patronage network intact. (His son, Ahmed Ali

Abdullah Saleh, still controls the Republican Guard and Special Forces – a fact that inspires considerable disquiet among members of the pro-democracy opposition.)

Since the beginning of the demonstrations against President Saleh's regime, the U.S. has signally failed to support the pro-democracy youth movement, a group that consists largely of the young and dissatisfied men that AQAP recruits so assiduously. The youth movement, with its calls for democracy and broader representation, is the best hope for a more tolerant and stable Yemen. In April 2011, the youth movement openly petitioned the U.S. for support, only to be ignored as the U.S. instead supported the Gulf Cooperation Council's (GCC) negotiations with the old regime, squashing any hopes of an authentic democratic revolution and antagonizing Washington's most likely local allies. A few months later, Tawakkol Karman, one of the leaders of the group and the 2011 Nobel Peace Prize laureate, published an op-ed in the New York Times asking for the U.S. to support the youth movement even while explicitly approving America's "right to attack terrorist sanctuaries." Just imagine a Yemen in which a democratically elected government openly aids American counterterrorism operations with popular support – a far cry from the current situation. Sadly, after being ignored by Washington and subverted by U.S. support for former regime figures, the youth movement no longer asks for American help. As Khaled al-Anesi, a leader of the youth movement, stated in late February 2012, "This revolution has been stabbed in the back."

Instead of advocating a better strategy, U.S. Ambassador Gerald Feierstein has continued to emphasize the need for a vague "national dialogue" while casting aspersions on demonstrators who are literally dying to try and make Yemen a democratic country instead of accepting the ancien regime. "We've also been clear in saying we don't believe that the demonstrations are the place where Yemen's problems will be solved," he stated at one point in March 2012. "We think that the problems have to be resolved through this process of dialogue and negotiations." This is empty rhetoric at its best. The lack of U.S. support means that these young men and women, who effectively ousted Saleh and continue to call for democratic institutions, have broadly failed to have a voice in the formation of Yemen's new government or have their legitimate concerns be taken seriously.

As a result, Yemen's pro-democracy activists largely blame the U.S. for failing to live up to its rhetoric – a disillusionment that potentially makes them vulnerable to recruitment by other well-organized forces that are against the existing regime, namely extremist groups like AQAP and separatist movements. From their perspective, the only real changes in Yemen -- the establishment of a semi-autonomous region by the Houthis and the propagation of sharia law in various cities in southern Yemen by Ansar al-Sharia -- have come through violence. The U.S., meanwhile, has consistently conveyed the message that it is more interested in propping up the Yemeni government than promoting Yemeni democracy. Feierstein criticized a pro-democracy march from Taiz to Sana'a as "provocative" during a Christmas Eve 2011 press conference. Soon afterwards 13 Yemeni demonstrators were killed by government security forces – so it's hard to

fault many for assuming that the ambassador was pre-
emptively giving a pass to Saleh's government to target
civilians. Some Yemenis were so angry at his remarks
that they built an anti-Feierstein Facebook page and
demanded his expulsion from the country. (Feierstein
never disavowed his statement and the U.S. Embassy in
Sana'a did not respond to requests for comment.)

By failing to stand by the democratic values that we
espouse, the Administration has abandoned Yemen's most
courageous and most vulnerable population: women.
Without the vibrant and brave support of women across
the country, thousands of whom joined the demonstrators
in major cities, President Saleh would likely still be in
power. In a country that has seen the continued erosion
of individual female liberties over the past few decades,
the Arab Spring in Yemen provided women with a voice
and platform to demand their rights as equal human
beings. Instead of embracing these amazing individuals,
the best examples of real change in the Middle East, the
U.S. has chosen to ignore them, abrogating its responsibility to provide help to those who need it most and
condemning them to a life of repression under AQAP in
the South or Saudi-funded salafis in the North.

In contrast, by supporting the youth movement, the
U.S. would be more likely to engender goodwill in the
electorate, ultimately making it easier for a broad-based,
democratically elected government to openly target foreign AQAP members in Yemen. Rather than keeping
mum about the well publicized drone program, which
has allowed the jihadis in Yemen to manipulate the conversation and report higher levels of civilian casualties

(reminiscent of the Pakistani Taliban's successful strategy to demonize the U.S.), Washington could openly negotiate the parameters of U.S. military action on Yemeni soil. There is, of course, some risk in a policy that depends on Yemenis rejecting foreign fighters in their communities, but it is one that would cement a long-term partnership between the two countries.

A true democratic transition, messy and likely to leave even more of a power vacuum, could indeed complicate the CIA's relationship with Yemeni intelligence, a partner it relies on for information to combat AQAP strongholds. On April 26, 2012, two days after Robert Mueller, the Director of the FBI, visited Sana'a, President Obama approved the CIA's request for expanded drone strike capabilities in Yemen. This new authority allows the CIA to target individuals even without knowing their identities, effectively permitting it to kill people based on suspicious behavior. This most recent expansion of CIA capabilities compromises its role even further. How will U.S. analysts be able to tell the difference between Yemeni tribes that are plotting against the central government and AQAP members that are stockpiling weapons? How is the U.S. able to protect itself from taking sides in a civil war when it depends on a self-interested central government for targeting intelligence? It seems the U.S. has not learned anything from its most recent debacle, when U.S.-trained Republican Guards were complicit in targeting civilians in Taiz. (John Brennan, the architect of U.S. counterterrorism policy and the former CIA station chief in Riyadh, has acknowledged as much, stating that the political turmoil in Yemen had caused U.S.-trained units "to be focused on their positioning for internal political purposes as opposed to doing all they can against AQAP.")

The Obama Administration has dramatically ramped up drone strikes in Yemen, with some success at killing suspected terrorists. Unfortunately, the administration has not followed up these short-term security gains with counter-radicalization programs or an engagement of the communities being targeted. Counterterrorism is a tactic -- not a strategy -- that is meant to yield short-term security gains. In Yemen, however, the U.S. relies almost exclusively on counterterrorism without providing a successful competing narrative against extremism at the same time. If the U.S. continues with this strategy, it will end up with a Yemeni population that associates it exclusively with death from above, an outcome that makes support for AQAP and violence more likely.

It is clear, more today than ever before, that counterterrorism victories alone will not solve America's problems with Yemen. Even though a drone strike successfully targeted the leader of al-Qaeda Yemen in 2002, and the Yemeni government arrested his successor in 2003, al-Qaeda in the Arabian Peninsula is a greater threat today than ever before. Targeting the group's leadership has clearly failed to reduce Yemeni support for terrorist organizations and prevent radicalization. It is time for the U.S. to stop undermining democratic values and long-term stability in Yemen in exchange for short term counterterrorism gains and a half-hearted continuation of the status quo. If Washington continues on this path, it will end up at best with another Somalia; at worse, another Afghanistan.